Cognitive Computing Models in Communication Systems

Scrivener Publishing
100 Cummings Center, Suite 541J
Beverly, MA 01915-6106

Concise Introductions to AI and Data Science

Series Editor: Dr. Prasenjit Chatterjee, MCKV Institute of Engineering, West Bengal, India,
Dr. Loveleen Gaur, Amity International Business School (AIBS), India,
Dr. Morteza Yazdani, ESIC Business & Marketing School, Madrid, Spain

Scope: Reflecting the interdisciplinary and thematic nature of the series, Concise Introductions to (AI) and Data Science presents cutting-edge research and practical applications in the area of Artificial Intelligence and data science. The series aims to share new approaches and innovative perspectives in AI and data analysis from diverse engineering domains to find pragmatic and futuristic solutions for society at large. It publishes peer-reviewed and authoritative scholarly works on theoretical foundations, algorithms, models, applications and case studies on specific issues. The monographs and edited volumes will be no more than 75,000 words.

Submission to the series:
Please send proposals to one of the 3 editors:
dr.prasenjitchatterjee6@gmail.com
gaurloveleen@yahoo.com
morteza_yazdani21@yahoo.com

Publishers at Scrivener
Martin Scrivener (martin@scrivenerpublishing.com)
Phillip Carmical (pcarmical@scrivenerpublishing.com)

Cognitive Computing Models in Communication Systems

Budati Anil Kumar

*ECE Department, Gokaraju Rangaraju Institute of
Engineering & Technology, Hyderabad, India*

S. B. Goyal

Faculty of Information Technology, City University, Malaysia

and

Sardar M.N. Islam

The American University of Ras Al Khaimah (AURAK), United Arab Emirates

Scrivener
Publishing

WILEY

This edition first published 2022 by John Wiley & Sons, Inc., 111 River Street, Hoboken, NJ 07030, USA and Scrivener Publishing LLC, 100 Cummings Center, Suite 541J, Beverly, MA 01915, USA
© 2022 Scrivener Publishing LLC
For more information about Scrivener publications please visit www.scrivenerpublishing.com.

Wiley Global Headquarters
111 River Street, Hoboken, NJ 07030, USA

For details of our global editorial offices, customer services, and more information about Wiley products visit us at www.wiley.com.

Limit of Liability/Disclaimer of Warranty
While the publisher and authors have used their best efforts in preparing this work, they make no representations or warranties with respect to the accuracy or completeness of the contents of this work and specifically disclaim all warranties, including without limitation any implied warranties of merchantability or fitness for a particular purpose. No warranty may be created or extended by sales representatives, written sales materials, or promotional statements for this work. The fact that an organization, website, or product is referred to in this work as a citation and/or potential source of further information does not mean that the publisher and authors endorse the information or services the organization, website, or product may provide or recommendations it may make. This work is sold with the understanding that the publisher is not engaged in rendering professional services. The advice and strategies contained herein may not be suitable for your situation. You should consult with a specialist where appropriate. Neither the publisher nor authors shall be liable for any loss of profit or any other commercial damages, including but not limited to special, incidental, consequential, or other damages. Further, readers should be aware that websites listed in this work may have changed or disappeared between when this work was written and when it is read.

Library of Congress Cataloging-in-Publication Data

ISBN 978-1-119-86507-0

Cover image: Pixabay.Com
Cover design by Russell Richardson

Set in size of 11pt and Minion Pro by Manila Typesetting Company, Makati, Philippines

Printed in the USA

10 9 8 7 6 5 4 3 2 1

Contents

Preface

Domain-specific system architectures such as software and hardware are attracting attention for use in overcoming the stagnation of size scaling of memory and domain functions in wireless communication systems. The need for improvements in performance to lower latency, and for faster simulation and power efficiency requires dedicated software and hardware focused on accelerating key applications. This type of system is widespread, and artificial intelligence, hardware description languages, machine learning, neural networks, advanced computer algorithms, and deep learning are especially becoming mainstream in all areas. The rapid growth of applications and system software is also reflected in hardware system architectures, signal processing speeds, wired/wireless communication systems, computational algorithms, and data storage/transmission systems.

Ensuring the security and efficiency of communication system design and implementation is a top priority. Recent research has been aimed at a higher degree of autonomy of such systems in architecture/system design, implementation, and optimization, especially in areas such as advanced system architecture, digital signal processing, communication systems, and the internet. This poses new challenges for implementation and validation. Therefore, much research is being conducted in the area of embedded security and autonomous software systems of things and various aspects of communication systems and computing technologies. To this end, this book provides a comprehensive overview of current research on cognitive models in communication systems and computing. Furthermore, it aims to fill in the gap between various communication systems and solutions by providing current models and computing technologies, their applications, the strengths and limitations of existing methods, and future directions in this area.

The main purpose of this book is to publish the latest research papers focusing on problems and challenges in the areas of data transmission technology, computer algorithms, artificial intelligence (AI)-based devices, computer technology, and their solutions to motivate researchers. Therefore, it will serve as an instant ready reference for researchers and professionals working in the area of Cognitive Models.

The Editors
July 2022

Acknowledgement

We, the editors of *Cognitive Models in Communication Systems and Computing Methods*, wish to acknowledge the hard work, commitment and dedication of the authors who have contributed their wonderful chapters to this book within the stipulated time frame.

Furthermore, we would like to convey our special gratitude to Dr. Prasenjit Chatterjee, Dean (Research and Consultancy) of MCKV Institute of Engineering, West Bengal, India, for his consistent support and guidance at each stage of the book's development.

We wish to bestow our best regards to all the reviewers for providing constructive comments to the authors to improve their chapters to meet the publisher's standard, quality and coherence. A successful book publication is the integrated result of more people than the people granted credit as editor and author and we acknowledge these unsung heroes.

Finally, we, the editors, acknowledge everyone who helped us directly and indirectly.

Budati Anil Kumar
S. B. Goyal
Sardar M.N. Islam
August 2022

1

Design of a Low-Voltage LDO of CMOS Voltage Regulator for Wireless Communications

S. Pothalaiah[1], Dayadi Lakshmaiah[2*], B. Prabakar Rao[3],
D. Nageshwar Rao[4], Mohammad Illiyas[5] and G. Chandra Sekhar[6]

[1]*Electronics and Communication Engineering Dept., Vignana Bharathi Institute of Technology, Hyderabad, India*
[2]*Electronics and Communication Engineering Dept., Sri Indu Institute of Engineering and Technology, Hyderabad, India*
[3]*Electronics and Communication Engineering Dept., JNTUH, Hyderabad, India*
[4]*Electronics and Communication Engineering Dept., TKRCET, Hyderabad, India*
[5]*Electronics and Communication Engineering Shadan College of Engineering and Technology, Hyderabad, India*
[6]*Electronics and Communication Engineering Dept., Sri Indu Institute of Engineering and Technology, Hyderabad, India*

Abstract

In this document, a low-voltage, low-dropout (LDO) voltage regulator process is proposed and executed by means of a 0.25-μm complementary metal–oxide semiconductor (CMOS). This debate of a 3- to 5-V, 50-mA small CMOS give up a single 1-pF compensating capacitor in a linear voltage regulator. Tentative outcomes prove that the highest yield load current is 50 mA and the control yield electrical energy is 2.8 V. The controller provides a total weight fleeting reaction by lower than a 5-mV overshoot in addition to the undershoot. The lively outline part is 358.28 μm × 243.30 μm. Voltage regulators are used to provide a stable power supply voltage independent of load impedance, input voltage variations, temperature, and time. LDO regulators are distinguished by their ability to maintain regulation with small differences between the supply voltage and the load voltage. LDO is used for wireless communications and satellite. In this chapter, the authors discuss how LDO works.

Corresponding author: laxmanrecw@gmail.com

Budati Anil Kumar, S. B. Goyal and Sardar M.N. Islam. Cognitive Computing Models
in Communication Systems, (1–14) © 2022 Scrivener Publishing LLC

Keywords: LDO, low-voltage regulator, CMOS, linear controller, power supply circuits, regulator

1.1   Introduction

A low-dropout (LDO) controller is a direct current linear electrical energy regulator that is able to run through extremely minute input–output discrepancies of electrical energy. Claim intended small-voltage, small fall-away regulator is rising since rising consists of convenient electronics, i.e., mobile or radio. The same manufacturing also has self-profiling relevance [1]. Lately, growing requirement meant for handy plus sequence operate yield contain required circuit toward work below short-voltage situations, and elevated current competence have as well grown essential toward capitalizing the life span of battery [1]. The regulator ought to enclose a tiny dynamic region.

Low drop-out aim has turned into additional demand owing to the rising insistence of high-performance small dropouts, of which small-voltage fast-instantaneous LDOs are particularly significant methods to pick up the traditional LDO configuration contain to be projected. However, with structural restriction, which is the major problem in concurrently achieving steadiness, more output voltage correctness plus small retort point, at a halt can't exist defeat [2]. The structural restraint of traditional small dropouts is mostly due to the connected solitary pole–zero termination scheme, into the break off capacitor through the elevated corresponding sequence confrontation necessary for obtaining small regularity pole–zero termination. The resulting sphere expansion was not satisfactorily elevated toward reaching a fine line and load system, and the loop gain bandwidth was not satisfactorily large for little reaction time in adding, essential elevated equivalent series resistance (ESR) introduces useless response. A low-voltage plan is moreover imperfect due to the voltage buffer surrounded by traditional LDOs [3]. An additional enhancement on top of the traditional structure is not easy due to the limitation of the constancy of LDO. Therefore, to accomplish fine specifications, a novel LDO among the extremely easy circuit configurations was engaged. The organization has twice over pole–zero termination schemes, along with a blueprint providing how save for present is a instant.

1.2   LDO Controller Arrangement and Diagram Drawing

The configuration of the planned LDO is displayed below (Figure 1.1). It is self-possessed into two phases: the first phase, as in a traditional LDO,

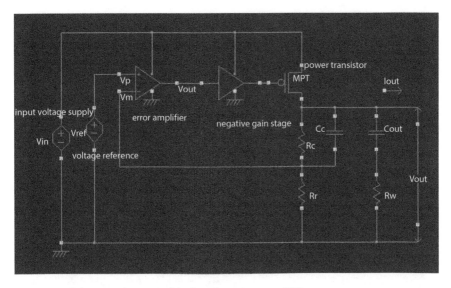

Figure 1.1 Schematic diagram of the low dropout control [2].

comprise an error electronic equipment applied to supply fault electronic equipment for voltage regulation, while the second phase is a common source amplifier that incorporates a lot of the output sway. Thanks to the cascade design, amplification depends on the harvest of electrical energy gain of the two gain phases.

The circuit in Figure 1.2 shows a liability amplifier of the discrepancy couple M2 and M3 through dynamic loads M4 and M5, whereas the second gain phase is the common source (CS) phase M6 in the bias current spring M7. The output swing of the second phase was greatly enhanced compared to the source admire into the revolving ON/OFF power transistor, and so this arrangement is appropriate for low-voltage LDOs. The current mirrors M, M7, and M8 offer current bias for the two phases.

Maximum power transfer (MPT) was planned to function within the saturation state at fall away. While the voltage gain of the MPT is less than unanimity, the gain is not tainted because of the error electronic equipment in addition to the second gain phase. A mere gain of 60 dB was achieved in the projected plan, which is adequate for high-quality line and load regulations [1]. In the design blueprint, for fine transitory reaction presentation, the transistor dimensions reached centimeters, which generates larger gate capacitors. At gate, the swing rate of MPT and freq reaction for low dropout disadvantage meant of designed LDO Vin workings as of 3–5 V, it projected LDOs control range.

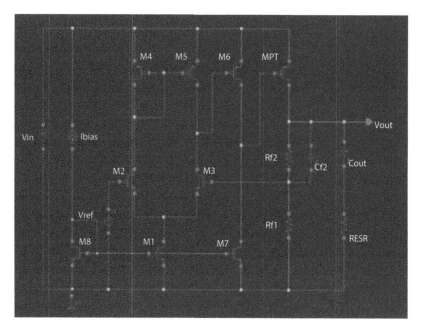

Figure 1.2 Representation of the planned low-dropout (LDO) control device [3–5].

1.2.1   Design of the LDO Regulator

Intent of small dropout is capable of subdivided keen on the drawing of power transistor (MPT) and intent of two-phase operational amplifier.

1.2.1.1   Design of the Fault Amplifier

During this part, the method was modernized to allow determination of the first-cut design of the second-phase operational amplifier. The tender estimate approached 70% of the design method. The two-phase operational amplifier was subsequently developed (Table 1.1).

BW, bandwidth; GB, gain bandwidth; ICMR, input common mode range; P_{diss}, power dissipation; C_l, load capacitor; SR, swing rate; V_{out}, output voltage; V_{dd}, drain voltage; V_{ss}, source voltage

$$C_c = 0.22 \text{XCL} = (2.2/10) * 10p = 2.2 \text{ pF} \approx 3 \text{ pF} \qquad (1.1)$$

Thereafter, the smallest value of the extremity current I_5 was determined based on the swing rate requirements.

Table 1.1 Requirements for the design of the two-phase operational amplifier [5–8].

Parameter	Symbol	Value
Operational amplifier gain	A_v	≥2,220 V/V
Gain	GB	5 MHz
BW	P_{diss}	≤1.2 mW
Power		
Indulgence	C_l	10 pF
Load		
Capacitance	SR	≥10 V/µs
Swing rate	V_{out}	±2 V
Output voltage		
Range	ICMR	−2.5 to 3.2
Input common		+2.5 V
Mode range	V_{dd}	+2.5 V
Positive	V_{ss}	
Voltage		−2.5 V

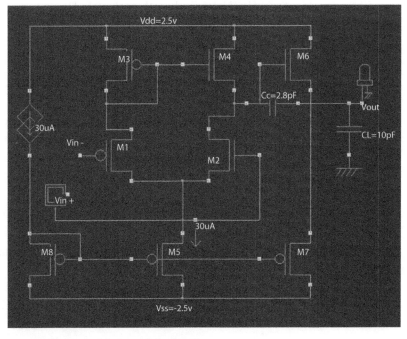

Figure 1.3 Diagram of fault amplifier [5–8].

$$I_5 = SR(C_c)$$

$$= 10 * 10^6 * 3p \tag{1.2}$$

$$= 30 \ \mu A$$

The characteristic ration of M3 is able to be resolved with the requirement meant for optimistic input common mode series.

$$S_3 = (W/L)3 = I_5/(K_{3'})[V_{dd} - V_{in(max)} - |VT_{03}|(max) + VT_{(min)}]2 = 15$$

$$S4 = S3 \tag{1.3}$$

The requirements of the transconductance i/p transistor are resolved with the idea of C_c and GB. Transconductance, g_{m1}, was computed using the following equation:

$$g_{m1} = GB * C_c = 94.24 \ \mu s \tag{1.4}$$

The feature percentage $(W/L)_1$ was directly calculated using g_{m1} as follows:

The aspect ratio $(W/L)_1$ was

$$S_1 = (W/L)_1 = S_2 = g_{m12}(K_{1'}) (I_5) = 3 \tag{1.5}$$

The required sequence is now obtained near computing the diffusion electrical energy of transistor M5. Due to the unfavorable ICMR equation, VDS_5 was computed using the following association:

$$VDS_5 = V_{in(min)} - V_{ss} - (I_5)_{1/2} - V_{t1(max)} (\beta_1) = 0.35 \ V = 350 \ mV \tag{1.6}$$

With the obtained VDS_5, $(W/L)_5$ can then be extracted using the equation below:

$$S_5 = 2I_5 K_{5'}(VDS_5)_2 = 4.5 \tag{1.7}$$

Thereafter, the first stage of the operational amplifier is done. Subsequently, the production phase is planned. Designed for a stage edge of 60, the location of the productivity extremity is understood to be toward 2.2 times the GB, after which 0 is positioned on the slightest 10 times superior than GB. The transconductance, g_{m6}, can then be resolved using the following relation:

$$g_{m6} \geq 10g_{m1} = 942.4 \ \mu s \tag{1.8}$$

Thus, used for realistic stage edge, the value of g_{m6} is about 10 times the input stage transconductance g_{m1}. Present are two likely approaches near implementation of the design of M6 (i.e., W_6/L_6 and I_6). The primary one was to attain good mirror of the first-phase current mirror loads of M3 and M4, such that $VGS_4 = VGS_6$; then:

Assume $g_{m6} = 942.4 \ \mu s$ and manipulate g_{m4}:

$$10 * 5M * 3p = 150 \ \mu s.$$

We utilized the following equation to obtain

$$S_6 = S_4 * g_{m6} g_{m4} = 94 \tag{1.9}$$

Consider g_{m6} and S_6 describing direct current I_6 with the following expression:

$$I_6 = g_{m6}2\ 2 * (K_6) (W/L)_6 = 198.14 \ \mu A \tag{1.10}$$

The mechanism dimension of M7 was determined using the equation below:

$$S_7 = (W/L)_7 = (W/L)_5 * (I_6/I_5) = 14 \tag{1.11}$$

Setting test $V_{min(out)}$ even though the W/L of M7 is great sufficient is possibly not essential. The value of $V_{min(out)}$ is

$$V_{min(out)} = VDS_{7(sat)} = \sqrt{((2 * I_6)/(K_7 * S_7))} = 0.3 \tag{1.12}$$

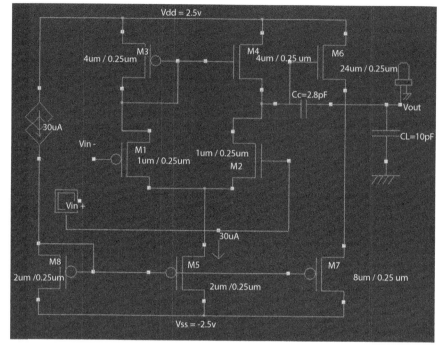

Figure 1.4 Intent of the two-stage operational amplifier.

Since are fewer variously necessary? Now the first-cut design is complete.

1.2.1.2   Design of the MPT Phase

Underneath are the steps during the MPT phase (Table 1.2).

MPTL (modular plug terminal length); *MPTW* (modular plug terminal width); *MPTM* (modular plug terminal mosfet); V_{REF}, voltage reference; C_{OUT}, output of capacitance; R_{f1}, feedback resistor 1; R_{f2}, feedback resistor 2; C_{f2}, feedback capacitor 2.

Yield correctness of the planned low saturation is elevated by considering the outcome of the equalized electrical energy, here couple of strategies needed for high-quality corresponding M2–M3 and M4–M5. The offset electrical energy due to great changes in the fault amplifier output, LDO condensed inside planned LDO owing to the near increase phase created through M6 and M7. Owing to the easy path arrangement, the harvest sound of the planned LDO was small. A fixed resistor was used for

Table 1.2 Design requirements of maximum power transfer (MPT) [1–8].

Parameter	Parameter symbol	Value
Length	MPTL	2.5 μm
Width	MPTW	0.625 μm
Reproduction feature	MPTM	3,000
Orientation output voltage	V_{REF}	0.93 V
Capacitance bias	C_{OUT}	20 μF
Bias resistance	R_{f1}	50 kΩ
Bias resistance	R_{f2}	100 kΩ
Bias capacitance	C_{f2}	01 pF

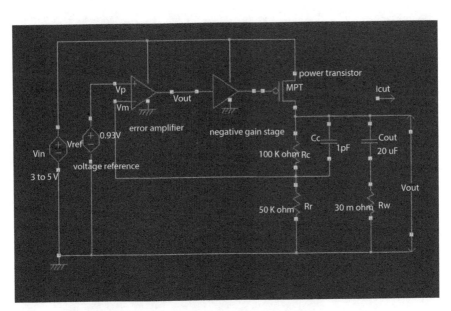

Figure 1.5 Complete blueprint of the maximum power transfer (MPT) stage [9].

constant poles and zeros; thus, no combination noise is forced on the fault amplifier. In addition, production noise of fault amplifier preserve exists minimized in great g_{m2} and g_{m3}.

The planned LDO was carried out using 0.25-μm CMOS tools. The complete chip outline is shown in Figure 1.13, with the region just

359.28 μm * 243.3 μm. The LDO able to use as 3-5V, which covers a wide variety of classic series electrical energy (Figures 1.3, 1.4, 1.5).

Figure 1.6 shows the input/output distinctiveness of the 2.8-V LDO control device. LDO o/p voltage start stabilize on 2.8V, i/p voltage is 3v. The leave low-loss voltage is 200 mV (3–2.8 V) at 50 mA.

An I/P voltage of 3 V and a partiality current of 30 μA are useful for low loss. The inactive current is practical toward 129 μA, as revealed in Figure 1.7.

Remaining toward high loop gain provides *via* plan organization and great range of the transistor, and the line and load extents are fine.

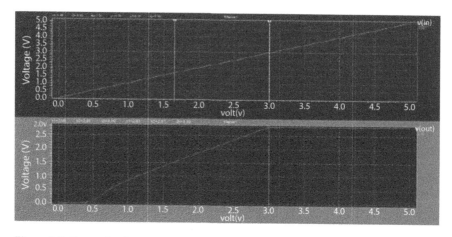

Figure 1.6 Dropout voltage.

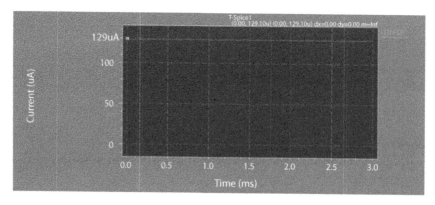

Figure 1.7 Inactive current.

The designed line and load conventions were 1.85 mV/V and 56.4 µV/mA, respectively, as displayed in Figures 1.8, 1.9, 1.10 and 1.11.

The load regulations of LDO were calculated *via* an N-channel metal–oxide semiconductor (NMOS) freight because control through the 1-ms time stage illustrated a 50-mA current when ON and a 0-mA current when OFF. V_{in} remained stable with a 5-V direct current.

The pass response was 44.5 µs. Power provide refusal was 68.3 dB, while operational by 3 V (as shown in Figure 1.12).

The gain of LDO was invariable at 55.03 dB (as shown in Figure 1.13), and the stage at 438.7 kHz was 64.1°.

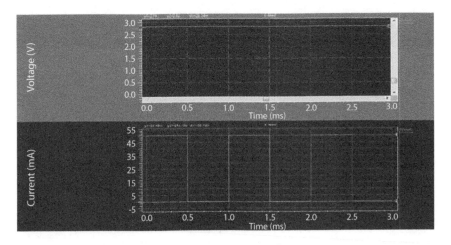

Figure 1.8 Line regulation.

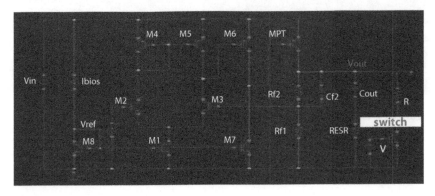

Figure 1.9 Low dropout (LDO) in the N-channel metal–oxide semiconductor (NMOS) control as load [10].

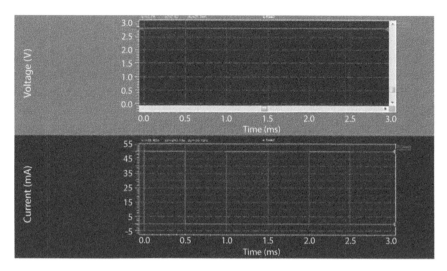

Figure 1.10 Load guideline.

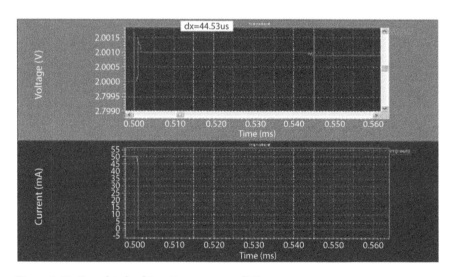

Figure 1.11 Complete load transitory response [10].

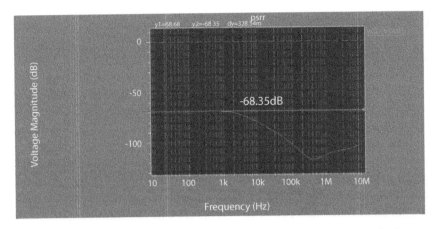

Figure 1.12 Power supply rejection ratio (PSRR) of the projected low dropout [10].

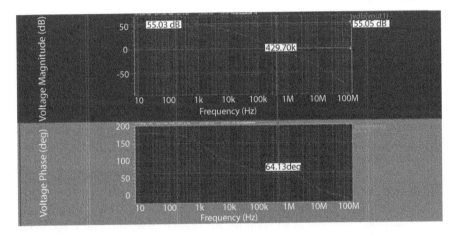

Figure 1.13 Gain and stage edge of low dropout [10].

The effectiveness of the low-voltage dropout regulator was inadequate due to the inactive current and the I/P and O/P voltage, given below:

$$\text{Effectiveness at 3-V I/P} = ((10 * V_0)/((IO + I_q) * V_i)) * 100 = 93\% \tag{1.13}$$

$$\text{Effectiveness at 5-V I/P} = 55.85\%.$$

1.3   Conclusion

A small dropout directive through a recompense capacitor was planned. The design was easy, but showed superior organization and proposed a double pole–zero termination scheme. It satisfied the majority of the characteristic conditions of a profitable LDO. Tentative fallout planned LDO have tiny overshoot and undershoot while have brilliant line and load convention. Though planned propose has drawback is deliberate freight temporary retort. Intended low voltage drop be fitting intended for powering awake small-voltage complementary metal oxide semiconductor diverse functions, that need elevated accuracy supply voltage also small recuperation speed of calculated perform. LDO is used in communication.

References

1. AI-Shoyoukh, M., A Transient-Enhanced Low-Quiescent Current Low-Dropout Regulator. *IEEE J. Solid-State Circuit*, 42–49, 8, Aug. 2007.
2. Rincon-Mora, G.A., A Low-Voltage, Low Quiescent Current, Low Drop-Out Regulator. *IEEE J. Solid-State Circuits*, 33, 36–44, Jan. 1998.
3. Leung, K.N., *A Low-Voltage CMOS Low-Dropout Regulator with Enhanced Loop Response*, IEEE, 2011.
4. Rincon-Mora, G.A., Optimized Frequency-Shaping Circuit Topologies for LDOs. *IEEE Trans. Circuits Syst. II Analog Digit. Signal Process.*, 45–51, 6, 703–708, Jun. 2008.
5. Rincon-Mora, G.A., Study and Design of Low Drop-Out Regulators, *IJER*, 2012.
6. Simpson, C., Linear Regulators: Theory of Operation and Compensation, in *Proceeding: National Semiconductor Application Note*, vol. 1148s, pp. 1–12, May 2015.
7. Simpson, C., A User's Guide to Compensating Low-Dropout Regulators, in: *National Semiconductor Power Management Applications*, pp. 1–14, 2017.
8. Kugelstadt, T., Fundamental Theory of PMOS Low-dropout Voltage Regulator, in: *Texas Instruments Application Report*, Apr. 2011.
9. Lee, B.S., Technical Review of Low Dropout Voltage. Regulator Operation and Performance, in: *Texas Instruments Application Report*, pp. 1–25, Aug. 2012.

Performance Analysis of Machine Learning and Deep Learning Algorithms for Smart Cities: The Present State and Future Directions

Pradeep Bedi[1], S. B. Goyal[2*], Sardar MN Islam[3], Jia Liu[4]
and Anil Kumar Budati[5]

[1]Galgotias University, Greater Noida, Uttar Pradesh, India
[2]Faculty of Information Technology, City University, Petaling Jaya, Malaysia
[3]ISILC & Director of Decision Sciences and Modelling Program,
Victoria University, Melbourne, Australia
[4]School of Cyberspace, Hangzhou Dianzi University, Zhejiang, China
[5]Department of ECE, GRIET, Hyderabad, Telengana, India

Abstract

To manage growing urbanization, there is the development of smart cities with an aim for environment preservation, improvement of the socio-economical standard of living of people by adopting technological advancement in information and communication technology (ICT). For design, implementation, and deployment of smart cities leads to an exploration of artificial intelligence (AI), machine learning (ML), and deep learning (DL). In this work, the application of machine learning or deep learning is explored for applications of smart cities such as smart transportation systems (STSs), smart grids (SGs), smart healthcare, etc. Major challenges that are faced while designing smart city plans are such as the plant should be energy efficient network architecture, privacy-preserving as well as data needed to be efficiently analyzed of big data. To explore more accurate and precise decision-making system ML/AI techniques have shown their proficiency in the improvement of efficiency as well as to deploy low-cost smart network architecture design and management. In this chapter, an analytical study will be presented with the application of AI, ML, and DL in different sectors/application areas of smart cities. The main aim

*Corresponding author: drsbgoyal@gmail.com, https://orcid.org/0000-0002-8411-7630

Budati Anil Kumar, S. B. Goyal and Sardar M.N. Islam. Cognitive Computing Models
in Communication Systems, (15–46) © 2022 Scrivener Publishing LLC

is to focus on and explore the efficiency level of ML/AI techniques. This chapter will also provide an in-depth analysis of innovative development, deployment, analysis, security, and management in smart cities. So, this chapter will help in the exploration of research challenges and future direction for researchers.

Keywords: Machine learning, deep learning, smart cities, smart grids, IoT

2.1   Introduction

To manage the challenges of growing urbanization, smart cities, which utilize information and communication technologies (ICT), are being developed to deploy and promote sustainable development practices. The design, implementation, and deployment of smart cities lead to an exploration of artificial intelligence (AI), machine learning (ML), and deep learning (DL). In this work, the application of machine learning and deep learning is explored for smart city applications, such as smart transportation systems (STSs), smart grids (SGs), smart healthcare, etc. Major challenges to be faced when designing smart cities include the plant's energy-efficient network architecture, the preservation of privace, and the efficient analysis of big data. To explore more accurate and precise decision-making systems, ML/AI techniques have been shown to be proficient in improving efficiency and deploying low-cost smart network architecture design and management. In this chapter, an analytical review is presented on the application of AI, ML, and DL in different sectors/application areas of smart cities. The main aim is to focus on and explore the efficiency level of ML/AI techniques. This chapter also provides an in-depth analysis of smart cities' innovative development, deployment, analysis, security, and management. Hence, this chapter will help in the exploration of research challenges and suggest future directions for researchers.

2.2   Smart City: The Concept

Advancements in automatic sensors and their reliability in terms of precision measurement have made complete city automation possible by deploying 5G-based cellular technology along with mobile crowd sensing-based equipment. The objective of city automation cannot be achieved without considering these technological innovations [1].

The smart city concept is implemented by taking into account certain data sets that are collected by making use of various sensors, and the accumulated data are transferred to the corresponding processing framework for analytical calculations and data transmission. The data processing and modification is undertaken in the application layer of the working framework. The security of architectural framework of the smart city is addressed in the security layer [2].

The smart city has a large number of applications from smart mobility applications that improve traffic efficiency and reduce CO_2 emissions, to automated streetlights, smart healthcare, etc. The working architecture of a smart city comprises the following key five layers (Figure 2.1) [3, 4]:

- Application
- Sensing
- Communication
- Data Analysis
- Security aspects

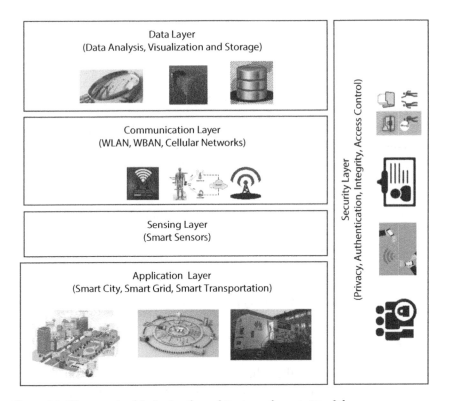

Figure 2.1 Five aspects of designing the architecture of smart cities [8].

2.3   Application Layer

The interactive layer between the smart city and the people using it, which are mostly the clients or inhabitants of the city, is the application layer. The misuse of resources can be reduced by the use of ubiquitous and continuous monitoring that enhances security and safety measures. There are several methods to enhance the interaction between data sets and their users, the most common of which is direct interaction, which involves the use of an online platform that collaborates with smartphone applications, or indirect interaction, which involves the use of actuators for environmental control. Several research studies have focused on the interactive environment between the clients and the associated data sets and concluded that interoperability is the technical challenge in the applications designed for smart city implementation. Several services face challenges, such as smart transportation, smart homes and smart healthcare hospitals, and so on that form a part of homogeneous and integrative services. The invention of the electric vehicle (EV) and its pervasiveness, which depends on the electrical utility grid, is a vast area for smart application development and improvement, which depends on the IoT platform [5–14]. The myriad applications of smart cities are as follows:

2.3.1   Smart Homes and Buildings

One of the application of smart city deployment is smart homes or buildings. Homes that have the capability to reduce human effort and provide a comfortable living environment are known as smart homes. There are two conceptual levels of smart buildings:

- Physical level: the smart building's community has the functionalities of wired and wireless networking, inclusive of the transportation system along with power grid control.
- Virtual level: the levels involve smart applications, such as information sharing between the clients, cooperation, and interactive environment applications.

2.3.1.1   Smart Surveillance

Today's growing urban culture has increased the need for surveillance and security systems. Security is an important concern nowadays; however, its importance has increased substantially with increased data transfer strategies. Modern security surveillance systems are complex in architecture. Data transfer speed, robustness, and automated analysis are other issues which are a part of security.

2.3.2 Smart Transportation and Driving

To enhance the safety, efficiency, and experience of traveling for both passengers and drivers, the smart transportation system provides vehicles with smart devices, such as sensors, which have high-speed communication, computing, and processing capabilities. To reduce additional wiring inside the vehicle, the wireless sensor network is used inside the vehicle.

2.3.3 Smart Healthcare

The grouping of sensor data is a smarter way to offer healthcare services than to utilize sensors and actuators to enhance the quality of life and to create healthier communities for feasible cities. Many medical, social, and behavioral fields can be improvised toward smart health applications. Human gait activity recognition is very important for orthopedic health monitoring of individuals, particularly the elderly, which is a typical smart health application area.

2.3.4 Smart Parking

To optimize parking space usage, improve the efficiency of parking operations and help reduce traffic congestion, smart parking systems have been introduced in urban areas. On-road sensors like magnetometers and RFID tags or light sensors and off-road sensors, like cameras, are used to identify available parking spaces in smart parking systems.

2.3.5 Smart Grid

The idea behind smart grids is to collect data in an automated fashion and analyze the behavior of electricity consumers and suppliers to improve efficiency, as well as the economical use of electricity. Smart grids are able to detect sources of power outages more quickly and at individual household levels like a nearby solar panel, making distributed energy systems possible.

2.3.6 Smart Farming

With the increase in the world's population, the demand for food is increasing. Governments are helping farmers to use advanced techniques and research to increase food production. Smart farming is one of the fastest growing fields in IoT. Sensing for soil moisture and nutrients, controlling water usage for plant growth, and determining custom fertiliser are some of the uses of IoT.

2.3.7   Sensing Layer

The application of the smart cities requires several applications involving sensors along with actuators that function as physical signal recording units for recording environmental radiation, temperature, etc. A smart city monitors the myriad physical parameters, which relies on the utmost precision, accuracy, and sensitivity of the equipment. There are constant interactions between users and their environment. There is flexibility and expandability due to addition of sensing layer. The devices used have to be monitored in relation to robustness, security concerns, nonintrusiveness, and ecological amicability. Adaptability and security concerns have to be monitored and solved efficiently to ensure the successful implementation of automated smart city projects [15].

2.3.8   Communication Layer

The data acquired from the sensing layer are preprocessed and aggregated and delivered to the other layers with the aid of the communication layer, which provides communication between devices in the field by detecting parameters with the cloud platform. This link is required to support low-latency, high-throughput, flexible, and secure communication. As a result, the developers are forced into trade-offs, to the requirements of their applications. Scant power availability mainly hampers the capabilities of communication. When we compare the proficiency and scarceness effect of the communication, it is more profound than in the data layer more energy is required as compared to sensing layer. The most economical solution is to create trade-offs among the information rate, latency, and transmission to prolong the battery lifetime of sensing devices (which host the front-end electronic communication equipment) [16].

2.3.9   Data Layer

In this layer, the collected data or sensed data from the communication layer are processed. The processing of data includes meaningful conversion, analysis, prediction, or forecasting. For this, data mining algorithms are used that require high computational resources. This high-level processing is not possible at the sensing layer with its limited capacity and energy level [17].

2.3.10 Security Layer

This layer is integrated with all the other layers to provide privacy security, which is a primary concern for every smart application. There are many techniques to cope with security issues. These security issues relate to confidentiality, access control, authentication, and integrity. There are many algorithms, such as Advanced Encryption Standard (AES), Elliptic Curve Cryptography (ECC), and blockchain cryptography, etc., that can protect data and users from security attacks [18, 19].

2.4 Issues and Challenges in Smart Cities: An Overview

The smart city architectural design incorporates smart lighting, intelligent transportation system, smart health, hospital availability, etc. The projects involve the data associated with various sensors across the city that

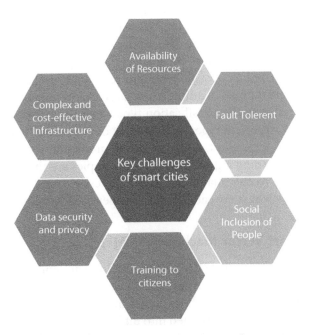

Figure 2.2 Key challenges faced when deploying a smart city plan.

involves further processing and communicating platforms. The working framework is analyzed to be operational in a low cost-efficient manner along with innovative and subtle projects. However, multiple challenges associated with such a platform have been detected (Figure 2.2). Table 2.1 overviews some of the most prevailing problems that stand in the way of smart city development [20].

2.5   Machine Learning: An Overview

Recently, for solving more complex statistical prediction problems, machine learning has been adopted by many researchers. The mechanisms include machine learning algorithms, artificial intelligence-based advanced techniques, and the basic structure are that rely on which is the factual identification procedure. The framework is expected to bring about results requiring no human intercession [21, 22].

2.5.1   Supervised Learning

To attain the learning objective in this case, the various data sets and their exact labels are utilized to function as an input parameter to machine learning algorithms and, hence, is named supervised learning. The algorithm is trained for the convergence and approximation of the key function $y = f(x)$. The function comprises x as the data input example and y as the associated label. Further output variables form the reason that supervised learning has been categorized as classification and regression models. The regression models yield outputs in uninterrupted form as in predicting tasks. The other is referred to as the classification type when the output variables are grouping and categorical type, such as color or shape, etc. However, most of the platforms these days make use of the prediction technology based on supervised learning algorithms. A few examples are the random forest method, support vector machines, linear regression models, and logistic regression types which are categorized as supervised learning [21].

2.5.2   Support Vector Machines (SVMs)

A support vector machine (SVM) is a technology designed and developed following regression and also for classification tasks. The methodology develops a hyperplane (line) whose main function is to achieve segregation and grouping of data that is trained into different classes. As the generation of the hyperplane expands the classes and the distance between them, it

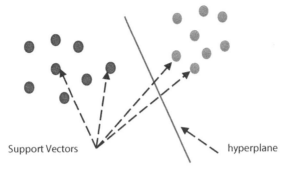

Figure 2.3 Support vector machine architecture.

becomes more likely to generalise that information in the otherwise invisible data (Figure 2.3). The SVM is the best technique for the prediction of time-series statistics (data) as it does not lead to data overflow. It comprises of best classification technique with accurate training and organizing of data sets into classes.

Various studies have concluded that the SVM technique is preferrable for data segregation and classification purposes and is less capable of making precise assumptions from the data set. The SVM technique may be a linear or nonlinear approach wherein determination of hyperplane forms the linear model approach where data are converted into line format.

2.5.3   Artificial Neural Networks

Artificial neural network-based predictive algorithms follow the concept of human brain neuron cells for learning mechanisms and training purposes. The algorithms are trained to generate certain transfer functions for attaining proper data set classification and increasing the entity number. Various functions in the combinational form are processed using ANN model architecture as a classifier, and further for diverse data sets variables, their precision is also calculated. The real-world problems form the part of multidimensional data sets, and their classification and grouping are an inexplicable part of the prediction process. The learning and training sets are analyzed from the process. The accurate testing of these records makes it easier to categorise the data sets. The neural networks are trained with similar information, and during the process, the backpropagation algorithms do the calculation for directing the neural framework (Figure 2.4).

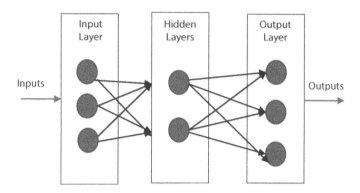

Figure 2.4 Artificial neural network architecture.

2.5.4   Random Forest

The regression and classification procedure is very easily enacted by the random forest learning mechanism (Figure 2.5). The method follows the bagging method which describes the combinational algorithm performance that produces outcomes with an improved accuracy of results.

The decision trees are acted upon by algorithms that enable the shaping of these trees and combining the principles of these decision trees to bring about the collective learning technique for enabling precise prediction. This combination of various classifiers that are weak and collectively built up robust classifiers has the effect of producing a more literal prediction and deep learning of various data sets. This learning architectural framework provides randomized input of data sets for operation derived from weak decision trees that helps in the generation of learning rules. Therefore, these rules are generated as a grouping of weak classifiers to build up a robust one.

Random forest-based predictive analysis is carried out on testing data set statistics. The output from the learning algorithm creates a yield from the analysis in the format of classes or labels. The various decision trees work in accordance to create the stronger learner, referred to as bagging. The data that are generated after the application of the algorithm have certain information already available known as Out of Bag (OOB) data. This OOB data availability stands differently for various decision trees and their distinctive training samples are the key factors for such differences. The OBB, specific to each decision tree, assists in more proficient data set evaluation, thereby improving the learning mechanism through forest predictive algorithms.

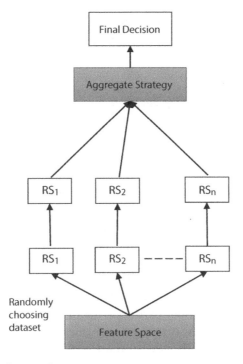

Figure 2.5 Random forest architecture.

2.5.5 Naïve Bayes

The Bayes theorem forms the basis for laying out the architectural design framework for the naïve Bayes learning technology for the classification of data sets that are unknown (Figure 2.6). This learning and prediction algorithm utilizes the previous data set structure to realize future ones. This architecture forms a probabilistic learning technique that incorporates algorithms for grasping uncertainties in an exceptionally principled approach, which is done by keeping the deciding factors of future results.

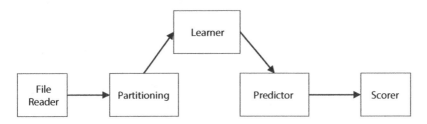

Figure 2.6 Naïve Bayes architecture.

The algorithm is strong enough against noise in input data sets, which forms the base for its capability to solve the predictive and diagnostic issues in the data sets.

2.6   Unsupervised Learning

The next learning technology, which deals with input data variables without any output label being defined, is known as the unsupervised learning technique. The training of the learning mechanism makes use of only the input statistical variables. The algorithm focuses on studying the pattern of those inputs and making further predictions. This type of learning is categorized as the clustering technique and association method to perform significant tasks. Common clustering algorithms include [22]:

- Hierarchical clustering: constructs a multilevel hierarchy of clusters by creating a cluster tree.
- K-means clustering: partitions data into k distinct clusters, depending on the distance to the centroid of a cluster.
- Gaussian mixture models: models clusters as a mixture of multivariate normal density components.
- Self-organizing maps: employs neural networks that learn the topology and distribution of the data.
- Hidden Markov models: uses observed data to recover the sequence of states.

2.7   Deep Learning: An Overview

Deep learning, a part of artificial intelligence, is derived from machine learning that is created with more layers of algorithms or networks. It is similar to machine learning but consists of a large algorithm or network. Deep learning architecture is similar to the human brain as all the nerves or neurons are connected to the brain in a complex manner and process all the complex data generated. Similar to the human brain, deep learning is designed to handle complex data with the help of large algorithms [23, 24].

There are many deep learning approaches which have been designed, some of which are discussed in the following.

2.7.1 Autoencoder

An autoencoder is designed by combining an encoder and decoder type of neural network, as shown in Figure 2.7. Raw input data are fed into encoder units where features are extracted, and these features are fed into the decoder to reconstruct the data from the extracted features. While training the deep autoencoder model, the divergence of the encoder and decoder is reduced gradually. The feature extraction by the encoder and reconstruction by the decoder is not supervised information. Different types of deep autoencoders, such as denoising autoencoders and sparse autoencoders, focus on researchers.

2.7.2 Convolution Neural Networks (CNNs)

Convolution neural networks (CNNs) are a type of deep neural network designed to interpret in a similar way to the human visual system (HVS). CNNs have made great achievements in the field of computer vision. Recently, it has been applied in other fields also. Many recent human-computer interfaces are designed using CNNs. CNNs have advantages over feed-forward networks because they are capable of finding feature localities. Thus, it is capable of extracting features and processes. CNNs can work on 2-dimensional (2D) as well as 3-dimensional (3D) data in which input data are converted into matrices (Figure 2.8).

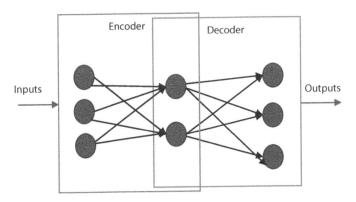

Figure 2.7 Architecture of an autoencoder.

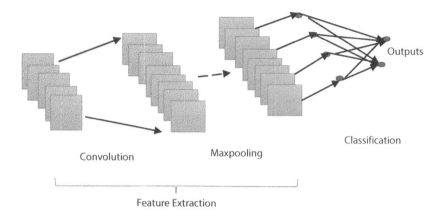

Convolution

Maxpooling

Classification

Outputs

Feature Extraction

Figure 2.8 Architecture of CNN.

2.7.3   Recurrent Neural Networks (RNNs)

Recurrent neural networks (RNNs) are a type of neural network architecture designed for sequential data and is especially used for time series predictive problems. In these networks, the output of the previous state is fed into the current state, whereas, in all traditional networks, all inputs and outputs are independent of each other. In RNNs, the hidden state remembers information about the sequence. The structure of an RNN is shown in Figure 2.9. Standard RNNs can handle only limited-length sequences. A modified version of RNNs has been proposed to solve such an issue, termed long short-term memory (LSTM), gated recurrent unit (GRU), etc.

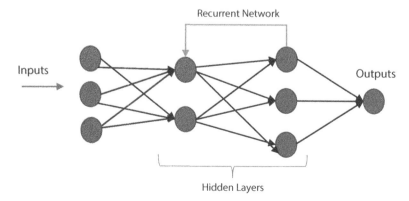

Recurrent Network

Inputs

Outputs

Hidden Layers

Figure 2.9 Architecture of RNN.

2.8   Deep Learning vs Machine Learning

Deep learning, a subset of machine learning, has several advantages over machine learning algorithms. Deep learning presents data differently to machine learning. In machine learning, structured data are always required as an input to be processed whereas in deep learning, data do not need to be structured [25]. In deep learning, artificial neural networks (ANNs) are taken as a base algorithm.

Some of the major advantages of deep learning over machine learning are discussed as follows:

- Labeled data are required by machine learning for learning as well as producing results. It is required to learn/teach the machine as to whether the output is incorrect. On the other hand, deep learning does not always need labelled data for learning as its architecture is multilayered. So, data are placed in the hierarchy and the network learns from its own mistakes. But sometimes, deep learning also gives incorrect results as the data provided may not be good enough for decision making. So, data are a deciding factor that determines the performance level of both.
- Machine learning is an evolution from artificial intelligence, whereas deep learning evolved from machine learning with deep architecture.
- Thousands of data points are used in machine learning whereas millions of data are required in deep learning.
- Machine learning output is a numerical value, whereas deep learning output can be in any form, either numerical, image, signal, etc.
- In machine learning, different algorithms such as kernel learning, ensemble learning, etc., algorithms are used to learn and predict the output. But in deep learning, the base algorithm is a neural network which is used to process data, interpret data features, and establish the relations among them to predict or generate results.
- A deep learning algorithm solves complex machine learning problems.
- Machine learning does not perform better over large and complex data whereas deep learning gives better output for large and complex data or big data.

So, in this research work, deep learning is adopted to train and learn such a large amount of data.

2.9   Smart Healthcare

2.9.1   Evolution Toward a Smart Healthcare Framework

As depicted in Figure 2.10, the following steps healthcare framework is designed including steps as:

- Data acquisition: different sensors are deployed over the patient's body to collect data and transmit it to the control unit.
- Control: the acquired data is collected and sent via the Internet for medical analysis.
- Data analysis: This step is generally performed remotely. All the collected data are stored at the cloud server where the analyst can access it, perform an assessment and send a report to the patient. The patient can also access the cloud server.

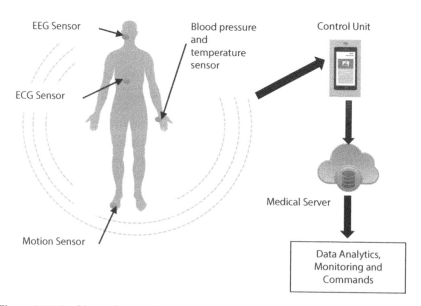

Figure 2.10 Healthcare framework.

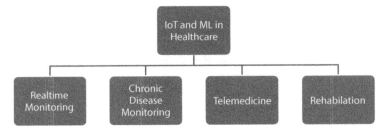

Figure 2.11 Application of IoT/ML in healthcare.

The healthcare sector is facing several issues in relation to the cost-effective real-time assessment and diagnosis of patients and in providing timely treatment (Figure 2.11). The diagnosis and assessment of disease is one of the critical concerns of a healthcare system. The healthcare system is facing several challenges during data collection, control, and decision making, despite the rapid development of technology [26]. To address these challenges associated with smart and secure diagnosis and assessment tools, machine learning or deep learning tools are used. These applications will help to establish collaborative knowledge for the discovery and predictive analysis of a patient's report, whereas many research works have collaborated on a specific domain such as heart disease diagnosis, brain tumour detection, etc. [27].

2.9.2   Application of ML/DL in Smart Healthcare

Some of the contributions of researchers to the field of smart healthcare monitoring are detailed in Table 2.1.

After analyzing the above contributions of machine learning to a smart healthcare monitoring system, the following objectives for future research have been derived while working on healthcare assessment tasks:

- To design and develop platform-independent applications.
- To improve the interoperability for data handling and maintenance.
- To handle high-dimensional data acquisition.
- To handle channel abnormalities (such as noise) on patient's real-time data (such as EEG, ECG, CT scan, etc.) for accurate analysis by doctors remotely.
- To deploy healthcare assistance at home to save the patient time and money.

Table 2.1 Machine learning application evaluation in healthcare assessment.

Ref	Application	Features	Technique	Result	Limitations
[28]	Cardiovascular diseases predictive model	Android-based application with cloud storage	SVM, KNN and the Naïve Bayes	87% Accuracy	Domain-specific model
[29]	Health Assessment	Assessment model using ML	AdaBoost	95% Accuracy	Real-time application is not supported
[30]	Heart Disease Prediction	Application of Deep learning	Ensemble Deep Learning	98.5% Accuracy	Doesn't handle missing data, data redundancy issues.
[31]	Human activity recognition	Smartphone sensor-based data collection. Application of ML to recognise human activities.	SVM, k-NN, ANN, Decision Tree	98% Accuracy	Unable to handle uncertainty
[32]	Risk assessment	Discussed objectives and application of ML and blockchain for health risk assessment.	ML and blockchain	-	-
[33]	Heart Disease Prediction	Assessment model using ML	Random forest	89% Accuracy	Cannot handle large feature sets
[34]	Secure ECG Monitoring	Biometric security	ML and biometrics for assessment	Cost-effective	Domain-specific model

- To design a secure and efficient framework to preserve the privacy of sensitive information.
- To develop an efficient, secure model for secure access to electronic health records stored on the cloud.
- To improve the quality, safety, performance, and account-ability of the entire system for development in the direction of a smart city.

2.10   Smart Transport System

2.10.1   Evolution Toward a Smart Transport System

The digital era in which we currently live is underpinned by information and communication technology (ICT) and affects every aspect of life, for example lifestyle, working style, ways of thinking, etc. Development is a continuous process, so with small incremental changes, day by day differ-ent aspects of a person's life are also gradually improving.

Nowadays, people are aware of innovative technology and how it can be used to support a person's ability to work smart; thus this era can also be called the era of smart things. This is a progressive movement from intelligent transportation systems (ITSs) to smart transport systems (STSs) [35]. ITS have become procurable due to smart city technologies [36]. The advent of ICT has revolutionized the field of transportation.

To design and implement smart transportation systems, smart sensors and communication models are deployed for a smart and automated trans-portation system. The design should improve efficiency in terms of cost, time, accuracy, safety, and security. To facilitate this, roadside infrastruc-ture should be upgraded with smart sensors and communication models. Smart sensors should also be deployed in vehicles for vehicle-to-vehicle or vehicle-to-infrastructure communication. These communication enhance-ments will provide diverse services to customers. Some major applications of the smart transportation system are illustrated in Figure 2.12.

There are several challenges associated with the deployment of smart applications in a smart transportation system, which are identified in this section and illustrated in Figure 2.13 [37]. These challenges can be resolved by integrating machine learning concepts [38–40].

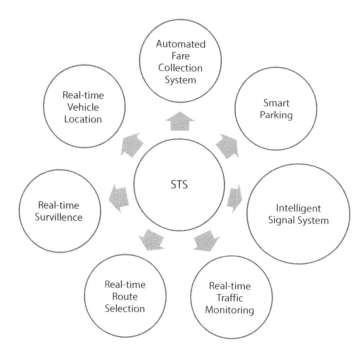

Figure 2.12 Framework of a smart transport system.

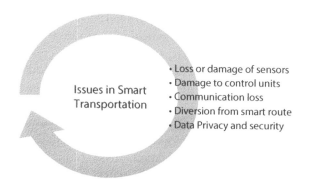

Figure 2.13 Challenges in a smart transportation system.

2.10.2   Application of ML/DL in a Smart Transportation System

Some of the contributions of researchers in the field of a smart transportation system are as follows (Table 2.2):

Table 2.2 Machine learning application evaluation in a smart transportation system.

Ref	Application	Features	Technique	Result	Limitations
[41]	Congestion Control	Vehicle speed was predicted	Long Short-Term Memory (LSTM) approach was used	84–95% Accuracy	Univariate method
[42]	Traffic Management	Analyzed the dynamic pattern of traffic	Online Incremental ML	0.07 mean absolute error (MAE)	Traffic flow was only predicted. Congestion control was not discussed.
[43]	Traffic Management	Analyzed the dynamic pattern of traffic	Deep Learning and SVM	5% error rate	Local monitoring
[44]	Traffic Management	Flow and speed analysis of traffic	Multi-layer neural network	4% error rate	Lower accuracy and high time consumption
[45]	Smart Parking	Space prediction for parking	Deep extreme learning model	60% accuracy	Low performance rate
[46]	Road safety	Accident prediction	ML approaches such as SVM, ensemble learning, deep neural network, etc.	90% precision	Trained with one data set
[47]	Vehicle monitoring	Carbon emission prediction based on traffic flow	ML and DL	90% Accuracy	Only focused on traffic features to evaluate carbon emission

After analyzing the above contributions of machine learning in smart transportation monitoring systems, the following objectives for future research were derived while working on smart transportation deployment and management [48]:

- To design and develop geographically dependent applications for decision making.
- To improve the existing infrastructure rather than creating a new one.
- To incorporate an intelligent and smart management system, which improves productivity despite limited resources.
- To deploy secure transactions and updates for smart parking or an automated fare collection system.
- To design a framework that analyses traffic flow and accident probabilities.
- Quick and smart accident detection system.
- To improve the efficiency level by integrating ML/IoT/Blockchain technologies.

2.11   Smart Grids

2.11.1   Evolution Toward Smart Grids

The modern world depends on electricity. The power grid network system is considered the backbone of a city, delivering power to make everyday operations possible [49]. Every smart city is built on two pillars: one is sustainability and the other is clean energy and smart grids can be considered as a fundamental element of the smart city. To transform a traditional grid system into a smart grid, there is a need to merge information and communication technology. The existing power grid architecture delivers the energy produced from large generation stations to the end consumer. The stages in the delivery of electric services are shown in Figure 2.14. The traditional grid system comprises the following:

Generation Station: Energy generation power plants convert different forms of energy into electricity. Fossil fuels, nuclear power, and renewable energy sources (RES) are examples of natural resources. In the last few years, RES has attracted a lot of attention because the conversion losses are minimal. The produced electricity is then transported to the consumer via the transmission and distribution network. Power plants are usually constructed near raw material sites, for example, thermal power plants are

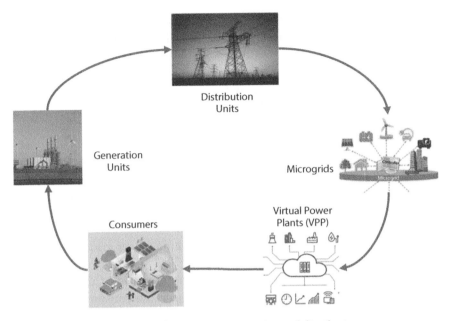

Figure 2.14 The architecture of smart power generation and distribution.

built near coal mines to decrease the transport charges of the coal so that the cost of electricity might be controlled. The transmission of energy is also a problem due to the long distances involved, which is a problem now that the smart grid brings the producer and consumer within the same vicinity, which negates the long distances of the transmission cables and transformers [50].

Transmission Network: The generated voltage from the power plant is converted to high voltage (HV) using step-up transformers due to the transmission of energy over long distances. HV transmission is preferred over low voltage transmission because in HV, the current flow is less, producing less heat and a low resistance load. For the transmission of high voltage power, three-phase alternate current (AC) signals are used as it is easy to transmit and energy demand can be easily optimized during the distribution of power at a different location.

Distribution Network: This is the power distribution unit. The electricity generated from the grid is distributed among consumers via this network at a different location. In this unit, high-voltage power is converted into medium voltage, as well as low voltage according to the demand of consumers.

Some censorious business concerns are occurring with the existing energy generation power grids. Drawbacks of the existing power grid are summarized as [51]:

- On average, approximately 60% of energy is wasted during the conversion of electricity from natural resources.
- About 10% of energy is lost in the transmission and distribution network due to the transformation between HV to MV and LV. Heat occurs with the transformers in the process of conversion.
- The existing conventional nature of the grid is more exposed to natural disasters, terrorist attacks, or even cyber-attacks.

The solution to these drawbacks of the existing power grid is as follows:

- The best way to decrease conversion losses is to use RES (solar, wind, etc.) to bring the producer and consumer into the same region.
- The key solution is to use distributed energy resources (DER) and distributed generation (DG).
- It is necessary to create a self-correcting distributed network that can handle fault tolerance in a dynamic situation with the help of machine learning or artificial intelligence.

2.11.2 Application of ML/DL in Smart Grids

Some of the contributions of researchers in the field of smart grid systems are detailed in Table 2.3.

After analyzing the abovementioned contributions of machine learning in a smart grid monitoring system, the following objectives for future research are proposed while working on smart grid assessment tasks:

- Demand and supply forecasting for short-term, medium-term, as well as long term.
- A fault-tolerant grid system that can handle a fluctuating load.
- A smart distribution system that can lead to minimum losses, as well as delay.
- The framework should be designed to handle attacks on the grid.

Table 2.3 Machine learning application evaluation in the smart grid.

Ref	Application	Features	Technique	Result	Limitations
[52]	Efficient energy utilization	Identification of dishonest entities	ML	Reduction in energy consumption	Analyzed for less time
[53]	Detection of stealthy false data injection attack	Prediction of the attack on the IEEE-14 bus system	Ensemble SVM	90% accuracy	Large training time.
[54]	Building energy model	Demand management for residential buildings		Carbon emission reduction up to 39% Heating cost reduction up to 40%	High error rate
[55]	Demand forecasting	Energy usage pattern	ARIMA	0.5% error rate	Not suitable for short-term forecasting
[56]	Profit maximization of providers	Customer behavior analysis	Fuzzy logic	Profit increment by 7%.	Focused only on customer behavior
[57]	Analysis of loss over time	Prediction of power grid health	LSTM	Average loss was less than 8%	Not applicable to dynamic abnormalities.

- An automated and intelligent grid system that can understand the customer's needs and meet their expectations.
- Automatic power shortage evaluation and meet their demand by renewable resource power generation.
- To improve quality, safety, performance, and accountability of the entire system for development in the direction of a smart city.

2.12   Challenges and Future Directions

An individual's lifestyle is enhanced with an advancement in technology and deploying this to cities to turn them into smart cities. This chapter explores different applications of smart cities, such as smart healthcare, smart transportation, smart grids, etc. In smart homes, the standard of living can be enhanced with monitoring. The arrival and departure of vehicles is traced by the smart parking system to manage parking lots in smart cities. Smart parking lots are designed by counting the cars in that area. Smart vehicular traffic management with proper inspection is very beneficial for the citizens and govt in a wide range. People can easily determine their time of arrival at the destination with the help of these data. One of the greatest anxieties experienced by people relates to their physical security in their living area. Smart technologies, like ML and DL, are designed to solve this issue. Another challenging problem is retrieving and processing data and solving the issues associated with security identification. Furthermore, several fields can be explored in future research such as smart farming, smart educational systems, smart real estate, etc. Some major challenges that are observed in this chapter while deploying smart cities are as follows:

- Energy efficiency while engaging in data collection and transmission
- Data transmission strategies
- The efficiency of central control units
- Fault tolerance
- Remote access
- Security and privacy issues

The integration of ML and DL raises the level of automation efficiency in all of the aforementioned challenges. One of the most significant flaws in machine learning models is that the model's accuracy has a significant impact on the overall system's accuracy since it is dependent on the training set. The model loses sensitivity as the update frequency decreases, but the model loses feature variables as the update frequency rises. Another significant challenge is how to update internal parameters in a faster and more accurate manner. As a result, there is still a need to improve the system's efficiency, which necessitates more study on many aspects in the future.

2.13   Conclusion

The concept of a smart city was designed to use the capability of growing information and communication technologies that can connect, enhance and protect the lives of those who live in the city. Data are collected from multiple sources to provide real-time information for better decision making and improve the overall quality of life. With the improvement in technology, cities expand. Several aspects relating to quality of life and an improvement in public services will lead to a rise in demand for smart cities. For future improvement, it is necessary to analyze the component's interactions as well as their economic usage. For machine learning or deep learning, approaches are integrated for better decision making, which results in a boom to the economy.

References

1. Mirchandani, P. and Wang, F.Y., RHODES to intelligent transportation systems, in: *IEEE Intelligent systems*, vol. 20, pp. 10–15, 2005.
2. Calabrese, F., Colonna, M., Lovisolo, P., Parata, D., Ratti, C., Real-time urban monitoring using cell phones: A case study in Rome. *IEEE Trans. Intell. Transp. Syst.*, 12, 1, 141–151, 2011.
3. Khatoun, R. and Zeadally, S., Smart cities: Concepts, architectures, research opportunities. *Commun. ACM*, 8, 46–57, 2016.
4. Bedi, P., Goyal, S.B., Kumar, J., Kumar, S., Blockchain integrated framework for resolving privacy issues in smart city. In: Chakraborty, C., Lin, J.CW., Alazab, M. (eds.), *Data-Driven Mining, Learning and Analytics for Secured Smart Cities. Advanced Sciences and Technologies for Security Applications.* Springer, Cham, 2021, https://doi.org/10.1007/978-3-030-72139-8_6
5. Habibzadeh, H., Soyata, T., Kantarci, B., Boukerche, A., Kaptan, C., Sensing, communication and security planes: A new challenge for a smart city system design, in: *Computer Networks*, vol. 144, pp. 163–200, Elsevier B.V., 2018, https://doi.org/10.1016/j.comnet.2018.08.001

6. Amin, S.M. and Wollenberg, B.F., Toward a smart grid, in: *IEEE Power and energy magazine*, vol. 3, pp. 34–41, 2005.
7. Waraich, R.A., Galus, M.D., Dobler, C., Balmer, M., Andersson, G., Axhausen, K.W., Plug-in hybrid electric vehicles and smart grids: Investigations based on a microsimulation. *Transp. Res. Part C: Emerg. Technol.*, 28, 74–86, 2013, https://doi.org/10.1016/j.trc.2012.10.011.
8. Solanas, A., Patsakis, C., Conti, M., Vlachos, I., Ramos, V., Falcone, F., Postolache, O., Perez-Martinez, P., Pietro, R., Perrea, D., Martinez-Balleste, A., Smart health: A context-aware health paradigm within smart cities. *IEEE Commun. Mag.*, 52, 8, 74–81, 2014.
9. Ceballos, G.R. and Larios, V.M., A model to promote citizen driven government in a smart city: Use case at GDL smart city. *IEEE 2nd International Smart Cities Conference: Improving the Citizens Quality of Life, ISC2 2016 - Proceedings*, 2016.
10. Hettikankanama, H.K.S.K. and Vasanthapriyan, S., Integrating Smart Transportation System for a Proposed Smart City: A Mapping Study. *Proceedings - IEEE International Research Conference on Smart Computing and Systems Engineering, SCSE 2019*, pp. 196–203, 2019.
11. Vaidya, V.D. and Vishwakarma, P., A Comparative Analysis on Smart Home System to Control, Monitor and Secure Home, based on technologies like GSM, IOT, Bluetooth and PIC Microcontroller with ZigBee Modulation. *2018 International Conference on Smart City and Emerging Technology, ICSCET 2018*, 2018.
12. Gowtham, S., Nazeer, A., Saranya, G., Survillence drones imparted with optimised cloud server techniques. *IEEE International Conference on Innovations in Green Energy and Healthcare Technologies - 2017, IGEHT 2017*, 2017.
13. Serikul, P., Nakpong, N., Nakjuatong, N., Smart Farm Monitoring via the Blynk IoT Platform : Case Study: Humidity Monitoring and Data Recording. *International Conference on ICT and Knowledge Engineering*, pp. 70–75, 2019, 2018-November.
14. Tolcha, Y.K., Nguyen, H.M., Byun, J., Kwon, K., Han, J., Yoon, W., Lee, N., Kim, H., Pham, N., Kim, D., Oliot-OpenCity: Open Standard Interoperable Smart City Platform. *2018 IEEE International Smart Cities Conference, ISC2 2018*, 2019.
15. Zhang, X., Yang, Z., Sun, W., Liu, Y., Tang, S., Xing, K., Mao, X., Incentives for mobile crowd sensing: A survey, in: *IEEE Commun. Surv. Tutor*, vol. 18, pp. 54–67, Institute of Electrical and Electronics Engineers Inc., 2016, https://doi.org/10.1109/COMST.2015.2415528
16. Palattella, M.R., Dohler, M., Grieco, A., Rizzo, G., Torsner, J., Engel, T., Ladid, L., Internet of Things in the 5G Era: Enablers, Architecture, and Business Models. *IEEE J. Sel. Areas Commun.*, 34, 3, 510–527, 2016.
17. Habibzadeh, H., Kaptan, C., Soyata, T., Kantarci, B., Boukerche, A., Smart City System Design: A Comprehensive Study of the Application and Data Planes. *ACM Comput. Surv.*, 52, 2, 1–38, 2019, https://doi.org/10.1145/3309545

18. Arias, O., Wurm, J., Hoang, K., Jin, Y., Privacy and Security in Internet of Things and Wearable Devices. *IEEE Trans. Multi-Scale Comput. Syst.*, 1, 2, 99–109, 2015.
19. Ames, S., Venkitasubramaniam, M., Page, A., Kocabas, O., Soyata, T., Secure health monitoring in the cloud using homomorphic encryption: A branching-program formulation, in: *Enabling Real-Time Mobile Cloud Computing through Emerging Technologies*, pp. 116–152, IGI Global, 2015, https://www. igi-global.com/gateway/chapter/134204
20. P. P. T. and S. K. L., Smart City Services - Challenges and Approach. *International Conference on Machine Learning, Big Data, Cloud and Parallel Computing (COMITCon)*, pp. 553–558, 2019.
21. Internet Society, "Artificial Intelligence and Machine Learning: Policy Paper", April 2017. Available from https://www.internetsociety.org/resources/doc/ 2017/artificial-intelligence-and-machine-learning-policy-paper/.
22. Ertekin, S., Bottou, L., Giles, C.L., Nonconvex Online Support Vector Machines. *IEEE Trans. Pattern Anal. Mach. Intell.*, 33, 2, 368–381, 2011.
23. Lempitsky, V., Autoencoder, in: *Computer vision*, K. Ikeuchi (Ed.), Springer, Cham, 2020.
24. Bisong, E., Recurrent Neural Networks (RNNs), in: *Building machine learning and deep learning models on google cloud platform*, 2019.
25. Paterakis, N.G., Mocanu, E., Gibescu, M., Stappers, B., Van Alst, W., Deep learning versus traditional machine learning methods for aggregated energy demand prediction. *2017 IEEE PES Innovative Smart Grid Technologies Conference Europe, ISGT-Europe 2017 - Proceedings, 2018-January*, 1–6, 2017.
26. Cook, D.J., Duncan, G., Sprint, G., Fritz, R.L., Using Smart City Technology to Make Healthcare Smarter. *Proceedings of the IEEE*, vol. 106, pp. 708–722, 2018, https://doi.org/10.1109/JPROC.2017.2787688.
27. Rayan, Z., Alfonse, M., Salem, A.B.M., Machine Learning Approaches in Smart Health. *Proc. Comput. Sci.*, 154, 361–8, 2018.
28. Naseer Qureshi, K., Din, S., Jeon, G., Piccialli, F., An accurate and dynamic predictive model for a smart M-Health system using machine learning. *Inf. Sci.*, 538, 486–502, 2020, https://doi.org/10.1016/j.ins.2020.06.025.
29. Javed, A.R., Fahad, L.G., Farhan, A.A., Abbas, S., Srivastava, G., Parizi, R.M., Khan, M.S., Automated cognitive health assessment in smart homes using machine learning. *Sustain. Cities Soc.*, 102572, https://doi.org/10.1016/j. scs.2020.102572.
30. Ali, F., El-Sappagh, S., Islam, S.M.R., Kwak, D., Ali, A., Imran, M., Kwak, K.S., A smart healthcare monitoring system for heart disease prediction based on ensemble deep learning and feature fusion. *Inf. Fusion*, 63, 208–222, 2020, https://doi.org/10.1016/j.inffus.2020.06.008.
31. Subasi, A., Khateeb, K., Brahimi, T., Sarirete, A., Human activity recognition using machine learning methods in a smart healthcare environment, in:

Innovation in Health Informatics: A Smart Healthcare Primer, pp. 123–144, Elsevier, 2019, https://doi.org/10.1016/B978-0-12-819043-2.00005-8

32. Mohan, S., Thirumalai, C., Srivastava, G., Effective heart disease prediction using hybrid machine learning techniques. *IEEE Access*, 7, 81542–81554, 2019.

33. Pardakhe, N.V. and Deshmukh, V.M., Machine Learning and Blockchain Techniques Used in Healthcare System. *2019 IEEE Pune Section International Conference*, PuneCon, 2019.

34. Din, I.U., Guizani, M., Rodrigues, J.J.P.C., Hassan, S., Korotaev, V.V., Machine learning in the Internet of Things: Designed techniques for smart cities. *Future Gener. Comput. Syst.*, 100, 826–843, 2019.

35. Cello, M., Degano, C., Marchese, M., Podda, F., Smart transportation systems (STSs) in critical conditions, in: *Smart Cities and Homes: Key Enabling Technologies*, pp. 291–322, Elsevier Inc., 2016, https://doi.org/10.1016/B978-0-12-803454-5.00014-6

36. Amini, S., Gerostathopoulos, I., Prehofer, C., Big data analytics architecture for real-time traffic control, *2017 5th IEEE International Conference on Models and Technologies for Intelligent Transportation Systems (MT-ITS)*, pp. 710–715, 2017.

37. Xu, H., Lin, J., Yu, W., Smart transportation systems: Architecture, enabling technologies, and open issues, in: *Springer Briefs in Computer Science*, pp. 23–49, Springer, 2017, https://doi.org/10.1007/978-981-10-3892-1_2

38. Chen, W. *et al.*, Big data for social transportation. *IEEE Trans. Intell. Transp. Syst.*, 17, 3, 620–630, 2016, https://doi.org/10.1109/TITS.2015.2480157.

39. Reddy, D.V.S. and Mehta, R.V.K., Study on computational intelligence approaches and big data analytics in smart transportation system, in: *Springer Briefs in Applied Sciences and Technology*, pp. 95–102, Springer Verlag, 2019, https://doi.org/10.1007/978-981-13-0059-2_11

40. Yanxia, Z., Maoran, Z., Nan, J., Urban smart logistics platform based on FPGA and machine learning. *Microprocess. Microsyst.*, 103474, 2020, https://doi.org/10.1016/j.scs.2020.102572

41. Majumdar, S., Subhani, M.M., Roullier, B., Anjum, A., Zhu, R., Congestion prediction for smart sustainable cities using IoT and machine learning approaches. *Sustain. Cities Soc.*, 64, 102500, 2021.

42. Nallaperuma, D., Nawaratne, R., Bandaragoda, T., Adikari, A., Nguyen, S., Kempitiya, T., De Silva, D., Alahakoon, D., Pothuhera, D., Online Incremental Machine Learning Platform for Big Data-Driven Smart Traffic Management. *IEEE Trans. Intell. Transp. Syst.*, 20, 12, 4679–4690, 2019.

43. Li, D., Deng, L., Cai, Z., Franks, B., Yao, X., Intelligent Transportation System in Macao Based on Deep Self-Coding Learning. *IEEE Trans. Ind. Inform.*, 14, 7, 3253–3260, 2018.

44. Polson, N.G. and Sokolov, V.O., Deep learning for short-term traffic flow prediction. *Transp. Res. Part C: Emerg. Technol.*, 79, 1–17, 2017.

45. Yamin Siddiqui, S., Adnan Khan, M., Abbas, S., Khan, F., Smart occupancy detection for road traffic parking using deep extreme learning machine. *J. King Saud Univ. Comput. Inf. Sci.*, 34, 3, 727–733, 2020. https://doi.org/10.1016/j.jksuci.2020.01.016

46. Hadjidimitriou, N.S., Lippi, M., Dell'amico, M., Skiera, A., Machine Learning for Severity Classification of Accidents Involving Powered Two Wheelers. *IEEE Trans. Intell. Transp. Syst.*, 21, 10, 4308–4317, 2020.

47. Lu, X., Ota, K., Dong, M., Yu, C., Jin, H., Predicting Transportation Carbon Emission with Urban Big Data. *IEEE Trans. Sustain. Comput.*, 2, 4, 333–344, 2017.

48. Boukerche, A. and Wang, J., Machine Learning-based traffic prediction models for Intelligent Transportation Systems, in: *Computer networks*, vol. 181, p. 107530, 2020.

49. Sun, Q., Li, H., Ma, Z., Wang, C., Campillo, J., Zhang, Q., Wallin, F., Guo, J., A Comprehensive Review of Smart Energy Meters in Intelligent Energy Networks. *IEEE Internet Things J.*, 3, 4, 464–479, 2016.

50. Cooper, J. and Carvallo, A., The Advanced Smart Grid: Edge Power Driving Sustainability. (n.d.). Retrieved December 21, 2020, Published by Artech House, Inc. with a Product Code of B-ART-031, 266 pp, https://www.sae.org/publications/books/content/b-art-031/.

51. Lehpamer H. *Introduction to Power Utility Communications*. Artech House, 2016. Retrieved December 21, 2020, from https://www.google.co.in/books/edition/Introduction_to_Power_Utility_Communicat/_W6uDgAAQBAJ?hl=en.

52. Babar, M., Tariq, M.U., Jan, M.A., Secure and resilient demand side management engine using machine learning for IoT-enabled smart grid. *Sustain. Cities Soc.*, 62, 102370, 2020.

53. Ashrafuzzaman, M., Das, S., Chakhchoukh, Y., Shiva, S., Sheldon, F.T., Detecting stealthy false data injection attacks in the smart grid using ensemble-based machine learning. *Comput. Secur.*, 97, 101994, 2020.

54. Pallonetto, F., De Rosa, M., Milano, F., Finn, D.P., Demand response algorithms for smart-grid ready residential buildings using machine learning models. *Appl. Energy*, 239, 1265–1282, 2019.

55. Ahmad, T. and Chen, H., Potential of three variant machine-learning models for forecasting district level medium-term and long-term energy demand in smart grid environment. *Energy*, 160, 1008–1020, 2018.

56. Taherian, H., Aghaebrahtmi, M.R., Goldani, S.R., Application of a customers' behavior learning machine for profit maximisation of a retail electric provider in smart grid. *Proceedings - 2019 IEEE 13th International Conference on Compatibility, Power Electronics and Power Engineering*, CPE-POWERENG, 2019.

57. Ioaneş, A. and Tirnovan, R., Power Grid Health Assessment Using Machine Learning Algorithms. *2019 11th International Symposium on Advanced Topics in Electrical Engineering*, ATEE, 2019.

3

Application of Machine Learning Algorithms and Models in 3D Printing

Chetanpal Singh

Victorian Institute of Technology, Melbourne, Australia

Abstract

These days, three-dimensional printing is creating a huge hue in the manufacturing industry and also accumulating attention from various fields because of its capability to fabricate different parts having complex features; this advanced printing is known as Additive Manufacturing (AM). The AM processing parameter is highly effective on the microstructure that is printed, and the final product also depends upon the performance on these, controlling the AM processing parameters is quite tactful. There is no need for definite models to develop and mitigate the physical problems that are underlying as machine learning is successful for recognizing difficult patterns and regression analysis. Due to the presence of effective computational power, and sophisticated algorithm structure, the machine learning (ML) algorithm includes the neural network (NN) that is widely used to perform variable tasks on the large data set that are present at the moment. The neural network algorithm is attached to various parameters of the additive manufacturing chain, such as quality evaluation, *in situ* monitoring, and model design and the progress of these mechanisms is evaluated in this project. The application of Machine Learning in 3D printing of several aspects is discussed in the review article. There are also highlights of Machine Learning in 3D printing for potential uses and limitations.

Keywords: Additive manufacturing, machine learning, 3D printing, artificial neural networks, algorithms, *In situ* monitoring

Email: Chetanpal.singh@vit.edu.au

Budati Anil Kumar, S. B. Goyal and Sardar M.N. Islam. *Cognitive Computing Models in Communication Systems*, (47–74) © 2022 Scrivener Publishing LLC

3.1   Introduction

Additive Manufacturing technology has the potential to bring revolutionary progress in the modern manufacturing industry as this is the most renowned and popular process of manufacturing. By using the 3D model data, this process manufactures a part by joining the material layer after layer. This process is used for designing customized and low volume products with complicated geometrical and material properties in a short period, and it is cost-effective, this feature helps in providing a manufacturing industry to have the advantage over the others [1]. The enhanced propagation provides seven well-defined subcategories, where most of them are capable of developing metallic parts. The AM technology has been upgraded to an extent where it can be used for fabricating prototypes to manufacturing end-use metallic parts in several sectors. The various sectors include biomedical, automotive, aerospace, and the defense system.

The technology faces challenges regarding the consistency of developing quality parts and process reliability parts, though there is a growth and advancement in this industry. The material properties and its shape are developed during the AM process, which are the major reasons for these challenges. Understanding the process needs materials, intricate design, and process interactions throughout a complicated multi-stage development process having five vital steps. For developing an acute quality part, these processes need to be handled precisely for accurate execution.

Machine Learning for AM

Developing and studying systems that can learn the patterns from the data automatically is the main aim of machine learning techniques. Tasks such as performance optimization, defeat detection, forecasting, regression, classification, and prediction can be efficiently done by models that are formulated by ML [2]. The effectiveness of the ML technique is determined by the data applied for training the Machine Learning model. The efficacy of the trained data is directly proportional to the efficacy of ML models.

There are two categories of ML techniques: supervised learning and unsupervised learning [3]. A training data with a labeled set offers a sample of the input values and the related true output value is present in the supervised learning. The model data trained by the ML algorithm gives an idea about the functional relationship between the output and input areas. The process of classification and regression is used by supervised learning [4].

Labeled training data sets are not available in unsupervised learning. Divergent conditions can be detected by the applications of unsupervised learning [5]. The benefits from the given scenario decide the utilization of the supervised or unsupervised ML approach.

Different ML algorithms can be further classified by the high-level classification that is provided by supervised and unsupervised models. Support Vector Machines (SVM), as well as Neural Networks (NN), are two ML models that are used for classification and regression [6]. Identifying a hyperplane that segments the data into various classes is facilitated by the SVM model. A network of nodes "neuron" and weighted ages within nodes assisted in the computational model of NN. Raw data that can make accurate predictions can be identified by the NN, and thus makes it powerful. Places where identification of the features in the input data is intricate the features of NN help to solve the AM problems.

Audio and image processing are the two most complex tasks that can be evaluated easily, by deep learning neural networks of ML algorithms. As deep learning systems provide different stratified layers of processing note that helps in the identification of complex features within the data that is added.

CNN: also known as Convolutional Neural Networks (CNN) that are essential for image data processing and is a robust deep learning model. The matrix represents image pixel data is processed by a special processing layer, which is composed of CNN [7]. The intricate features are extracted from a specific image, shapes, texture, and edges that help in the classification of that image. With the CNN process, this task can be easily accomplished.

ANN: as the model interacts with the outcome of a given input, the ANN is considered to be a supervised ML. It contains well-defined outputs and inputs for the manufacturing process, therefore, ANN efficient for the 3D printing process [8]. This method can represent complex and extremely nonlinear relations between inputs and outputs, as it contains a robust assessing skill. ANN has three layers, namely, input layer, hidden layer, and output layer, and neurons are included in every layer. ANN contains parameters which are called "weights" that help in connecting the magnitude between the neurons that are present in each layer [9].

A. Research Objective

Applications of ML in AM technology in domains like 3D printing (Figure 3.1), *in situ* monitoring for quality control the research development, process optimization, and security of attack detection are presented in this

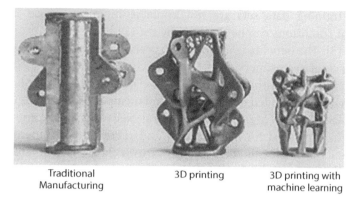

| Traditional Manufacturing | 3D printing | 3D printing with machine learning |

Figure 3.1 3D printing with machine learning [1].

article. Issues such as service analysis, safety of risk detection, and cloud service platform are also summarized in this project.

B. Research Motivation

AM is now the manufacturing domain that means it is knowledge-sparse but data-rich. It is an intricate and monotonous process to extract knowledge from the huge amount of AM data that are available. To evaluate the high dimensional and complex data, advanced computational, as well as analytical tools, are required. There can be an alteration of data into shrewd knowledge by developing the domain of Machine Learning (ML).

ML techniques can effortlessly carry out several tasks such as identifying implied knowledge and detecting connections between massive manufacturing data sets, producing vast data into actionable knowledge, etc. [10]. This literature enlightens readers on the state-of-the-art features of the mechanism of ML techniques used in 3D printing.

3.2   Literature Review

An intricate multi-physics process is bestowed in 3D printing. If the stimulation process is carried out before commencing any experiment, it shows better results. The relation between the printed workpiece and parameter process is evaluated in several studies [11]. Machine learning is adopted in the domain of 3D printing for several data-driven models. The data that has been provided during the learning automatically acknowledges the correlation between the inputs and outputs.

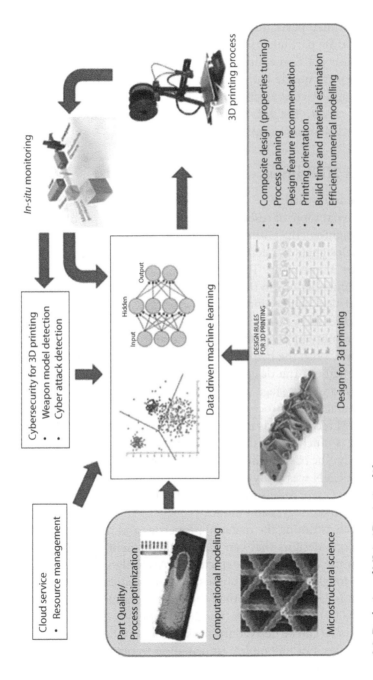

Figure 3.2 Deploying of ML in 3D printing [2].

A. Applying Machine Learning in 3D printing

The ML algorithm monitors various essential parts having huge impacts on the 3D printed parts' quality in the final process. The major facts are *in situ* monitoring, part quality process, optimization that analyzes the quality of the parts [1]. Some more related facts help in developing an efficient design. They are nozzle path planning, cloud service platform, printability checking, service evaluation, slicing acceleration, and detection of the security of attack. The ML algorithms that are used for performing 3D printing are discussed in this section.

Design for 3D Printing

Summarized knowledge of the merits and demerits of 3D printing techniques is a vital topic of research. This is the foremost process of fabricating and designing. The entire process of designing is time-consuming and repetitive. Designers can design efficiently if there is a data-oriented design available for 3D printing. The CAD (computer-aided design) model features recommendations in the email technique which speeds up the entire process and also the decision making to design.

The feature recognition of the CAD model helps in analyzing the manufacturability of 3D printing and therefore ml algorithms have been implemented. With the help of Heat Kernel Signature and the multi-scale clustering method, the designers can easily identify any important possible fault at an early stage and thus analyze any constraints that existed in the manufacturing process for a particular CAD model [12]. Another paper by [13] recommends that the CNN method for optimizing the build orientation is much better due to its consistency in predicting build time and accuracy. The baseline linear regression model does not provide search results. The CNN was analyzed and showed better results in offering consistent and accurate results in predicting the build-time when compared to the baseline linear regression model.

Tasks such as tuning the material properties and the capability for generating unique designs that can outrun the present composites that are available in the data set were depicted by ANN algorithms [14]. The visibility and toughness of the composite were predicted by CANN. ANN stimulation is 250 times faster than the FE stimulation that includes training (n = 80,000) and predictive (n = 20,000) phases. The high accuracy of the ANN model can be derived from a small amount of trained data. There are possibilities, but incomplete information to obtain an efficient design for the composite.

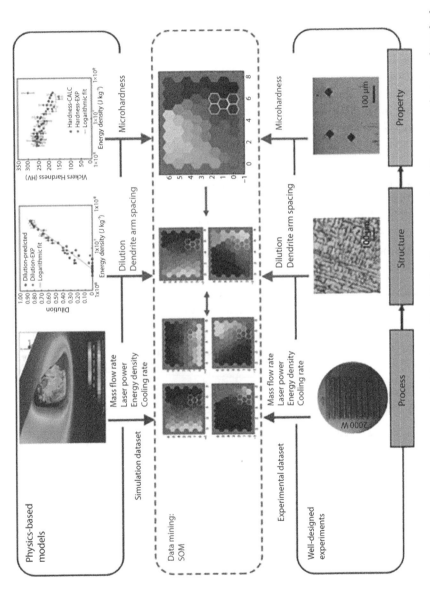

Figure 3.3 Use of ML in process structure properties (PSP) relationship with the direct energy deposition process for Inconel 718 [16].

The properties of the final printed parts can be easily predicted by the data-driven models. A deep learning-based framework was recommended by [15] to evaluate the stress distribution inside the real-time cured layer of SLA. Professionals generated a 3D model database having numerous geometric features at the foremost. To train the DL network, data labels were generated by using FEA simulations on 16700 3D printed models. It was found that the single-stream CNN in as well as artificial neural network (ANN) is outperformed by to stream convolutional neural network (CNN). The identification of the process structure properties (PSP) (Figure 3.3) relationship with the direct energy accumulation process for Inconel 718 was attempted by [16] that uses SOM, as an unsupervised ML technique (Table 3.1). The visualized SOM provides stimulation and

Table 3.1 Using ML algorithms in design for 3D printing.

ML technique	Description	Reference
Heat Kernel Signature and the multi-scale clustering method	Identifying any important possible fault in the manufacturing process for the CAD model at the initial stages	[12]
CNN method	Predicting build time and accuracy	[13]
CANN	• visibility and toughness of the composite were predicted • high accuracy of the ANN model can be derived	[14]
FEA simulations	Evaluate the stress distribution inside the cured layer of SLA in real-time	[15]
SOM	Stimulation and validation that has been obtained from multiple objective optimizations of the parameter process	[16]
CNN	Detecting the gun printing at a primary stage	[17]
ANN	Quick decision-making process	[18]
ANN (DLEANN)	Determining an optimum printing orientation that mitigates the exerting of support structures on the user preferred features	[19]

validation that has been obtained from multiple objective optimizations of the parameter process retrieved from the massive and high-dimensional dataset.

Illegal products such as guns that are developed through AM can be easily detected by a trained CNN; this was established by [17]. Identifying the gun printing at a primary stage and seizing the manufacturing process within the time can be done after the construction of CNN, which is then integrated into the printers. The author had gathered a dataset of 61,340 two-dimensional (2D) images of 10 classes including non-gun and gun objects to project the results of the 3D model. Two convolutional layers, two pulling layers, and a single fully connected layer are being developed to compose the CNN model. It is possible to decrease the classification error rate to 1.84% according to the experimental results.

Ref. [18] proposed that the design feature database allows rendering design features and ideas to inexperienced designers. Designers can make decisions faster in an ongoing decision stage using the ANN technique in 3D printing having feature recommendations characteristics in the present CAD model. In determining an optimum printing orientation that mitigates the exerting of support structures on the features preferred by users were used by [19] in double-layered extreme ANN (DLEANN). The first layer of DLEANN help scene classifying the evaluation of the relative score within the various part orientation; the regression to make a global school code for all printing direction is mentioned in the second layer. As there is no support, it was easy for the method to locate the optimum printing decisions with minimum visual artifacts.

Detection Attack Security

The sharing of the file and cloud manufacturing are gaining a considerable amount of hue in recent years because 3D printing is the only technology that will help to bring an industrial revolution 4.0 [2]. The malicious alteration of the process parameters can lead to attacks on the system that results in unwanted flaws in the products, and therefore, the cybersecurity of the 3D printing technology must be enhanced.

Ref. [20] used a supervised learning algorithm, called the nearest (kNN) neighbors algorithm, an unsupervised abnormal detection algorithm, and a random forest algorithm to detect malfunctions. This helps in identifying vulnerable attacks in the FFF technique under all possible circumstances. The optical camera helps to capture images transformed into a grayscale plot. Grayscale indicates standard deviation, and several pixels higher than the limit are evaluated and extracted from the grayscale value distribution are

Table 3.2 Using ML algorithms security of attack detection.

ML technique	Description	Reference
• k Nearest Neighbors (kNN) • an unsupervised abnormal detection algorithm • random forest algorithm	• to inspect and detect an abnormality in the FFF technique • Accuracy with kNN (87.5%) • Accuracy with random forest (95.5%) • Accuracy with unsupervised abnormal detection algorithm (96.1 %).	[20]
Anti-weapon detection algorithm	Avoiding printing and distribution of illegal and restricted items	[21]

some of its features (Table 3.2). The random forest (95.5%) and kNN (87.5%) are not able to render high accuracy as compared to an unsupervised anomaly detection learning algorithm that provides an accuracy rate of (96.1%).

Difficulties faced by several users in accessing and developing several 3D parts have been reduced due to (Figure 3.4) the file-sharing feature. If the 3D models of some illegal and dangerous weapons are uploaded on the internet and are fabricated using 3D printers, then it will create havoc and a threat in the community. An anti-weapon detection algorithm was brought forward to avoid printing and distribution of illegal and restricted items [21]. Facets and vertices are removed to develop pictures of random points from the 3D mesh that has been proposed in this algorithm.

In Situ Monitoring

The first-hand information related to the quality of the product during the AM process can be analyzed by *in situ* monitoring for data acquisition with the help of multiple sensors. Complete closed-loop control of the manufacturing process can be obtained if the real-time data can be inspected precisely and synchronously. The *in situ* quality monitoring for SLM that uses NNs and Acoustic Emission (AE) is represented by [22] (Figure 3.5) in a study. The NN algorithm is a spectral convolutional neural network (SCNN) that is an extended part of a traditional CNN, fiber Bragg grating sensor used for recording AE signals. The relative energies can find frequency bands of the wavelet packet transformation works as the input features of the model. The high, medium, and poor quality of the printed layer depicts the output feature of the model. The high, medium, and poor qualities of the work are stated as 83%, 85%, and 89% regarding the classification accuracy with the help of SCNN respectively (Table 3.3).

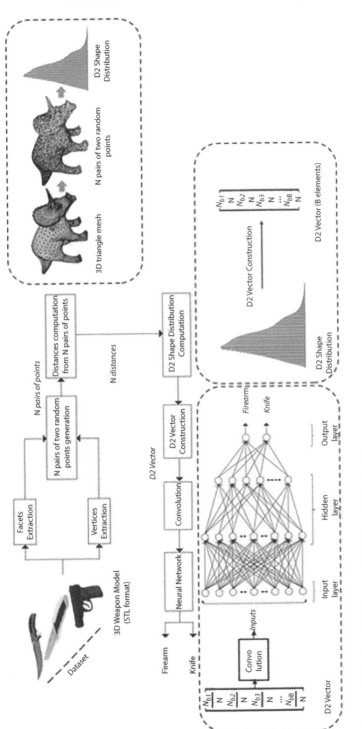

Figure 3.4 3D model of weapon detection with ML [21].

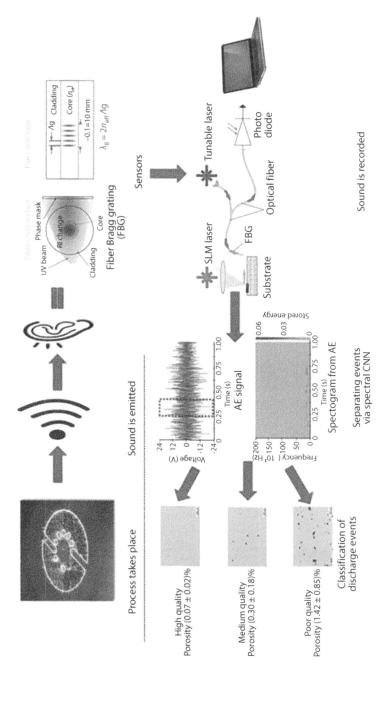

Figure 3.5 Workflow of using AE and SCNN for *in situ* monitoring [22].

Table 3.3 Use of ML algorithms in *In Situ* monitoring.

ML technique	Description	Reference
SCNN and Acoustic Emission (AE)	To check the quality of the printed layer for SLM	[22]
CNN	High accuracy of 92.7% for extracting melt pool, splatter data, and plume and real-time monitoring	[23]
SVM with Principal Component Analysis (PCA)	Moderate accuracy of 90.1% for extracting melt pool, splatter data, and plume and real-time monitoring	[23]
SVM	Low of 89.6% for extracting melt pool, splatter data, and plume and real-time monitoring	[23]
CNN, Histogram of Oriented Gradients (HOG), bag-of-words (BoW), clustering, and SVM	• To identify defects like balling, under melting, and key holding and to extract the melt pool features with the help of Scale Invariant Feature Transform (SIFT) • MsCNN has higher accuracy but is 75% slower than BoW	[24, 25]

The SVM (89.6%) as well as the integration of SVM with Principal Component Analysis (PCA) (90.1%) does not provide a higher accuracy rate of classification in extracting melt pool, splatter data, and plume as CNN (92.7%) [23]. For an accurate image recovery process, [23] has developed a vision system having a camera with high speed. Three major objects can be detected with the help of the system such as plume, splatter, and melt pool. The author's knowledge of the physical mechanism of a process to enter them into the traditional ML algorithm helps in extracting these objects successfully. As the CNN model offers a higher rate of accuracy of 92.7% in the identification of quality level, therefore, the author recommends that the feature extraction process is not required in this model [23]. The CNN model can achieve real-time monitoring in industrial applications, which is believed by several experts (Figure 3.6).

Detection of the defects must be processed by computer vision since most of the institute monitoring uses cameras to obtain data related to the

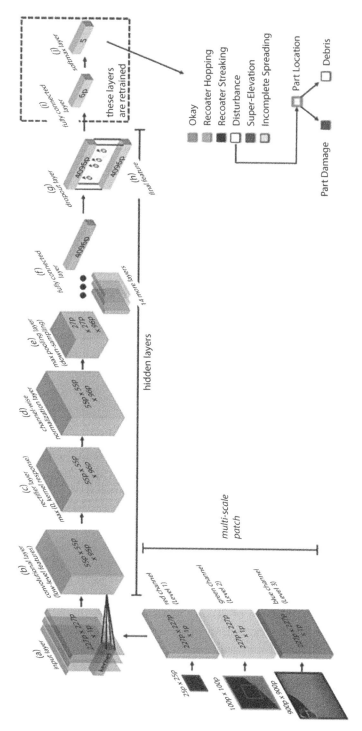

Figure 3.6 CNN based model for *in situ* monitoring [25].

printing condition. Several techniques are being used, but the ML technique that is the most effective in computer vision is CNN. Several ML techniques were used like clustering, bag-of-words (BoW), SVM, and Histogram of Oriented Gradients (HOG) to acknowledge any defects like balling, under melting, and key holding, to extract the melt pool features with the help of Scale Invariant Feature Transform (SIFT) that were used by [24]. Detection of abnormalities such as recoater streaking, recoater shopping, super-elevation, incomplete spreading, par failure, debris was attempted by them using the CV and ML technique.

The algorithm failed to predict recoater streaking with higher accuracy of 50.6%, and it also failed to predict any abnormalities with 100% accuracy [26]. The MsCNN is eligible to render high classification accuracy, but is more computationally expensive and also 75% slower than the BoW technique even when integrated with multiscale CNN [25]. The K Nearest Neighbor (KNN) and multi-layer perceptron (MLP) is highly effective if compared to Self-Organizing Error-Driven Neural Networks (SOEDNN) in identifying the penetrable defects accurately [27].

Cloud 3D Printing Service Platform

In the revolution of the industry to 4.0, 3D printing can be made popular with the help of cloud platforms as this is an essential element in the industrial sector. Hardware and software resources are infused in the server-based computing model. The formation of a comprehensive pool of resources can be effectively done in this platform, as this technique helps to share the resources to a public repository, which includes printing services as well as 3D models [2]. Intelligent resources that are based on time, cost, quality, and accuracy are demanded and evaluated by the extensive assessment of the terminal printers that help to manage these resources can be learned by the machine learning algorithm that helps to render efficient results. Intelligent customization of products that helps in reducing the entry barrier for public users can be enabled by the ML as it includes feature recommendation of design that allows doing all these tasks properly. Adaptive as well as collective management of resources are formulated by the use of resource allocation algorithms [10]. This features insurance-effective management of the models. Different quantization and Hamming distance algorithms help to quantify the quality of service and also enhances the accuracy of service selection. This can be done by using optimization algorithms that are based on various numbers.

Correlation Between Process Parameters' and Parts' Final Characteristics

It is imperative to optimize the parameter process in 3D printing. So it is effective in forming a correlation between the characteristics of 3D printed parts and process parameters. The 3D printing process is intricate and time-consuming to relate all the factors with each other reasonably because this relation has a high nonlinear feature, which means it requires several input parameters for the final process. An elemental nonlinear feature model needs to be used, and therefore, ANN is the most recommended [28]. To define an effective relationship between input and output for process optimization, several operating parameters were chosen for different outputs.

The properties and characteristics of 3D printed parts are affected by the process parameters. The parameters related to the database data can be selected for a specific 3D printing process and material can be obtained from the database of the process-structure-property relationship [16]. The large and high-dimensional dataset achieved from validation and simulation with experimental results, which was assisted by the visualized SOM helps to achieve optimizations of multiple objectives of the process parameters (Table 3.4).

B. Potential Challenges for the Implementation of ML Algorithms and Their Solutions

All the challenges that were faced while implementing the ML algorithm in 3D printing and all potential use of the ML in this mechanism have been explained meticulously.

Table 3.4 Using ML in correlation between process parameters' and parts' final characteristics.

ML technique	Description	Reference
ANN	To define an effective relationship between input and output for process optimization	[28]
SOM	Achieving multiple objective optimizations of the process parameters.	[16]

Building and Construction

The materials that can be made using 3D printing for construction and building need to have certain properties like good tensile and compressive strength, toughness and resistance against cracks, superior setting strength in a short setting time etcetera, and one method to do so is by the implementation of the ML technique. This technique has access to a large database of materials along with their features and properties which can be utilized in the aspects of design, the type of material, and the process [29]. The quantity can be surveyed using ML, and an accurate estimation of the materials required and the budget to be allocated for it can be done. Using the available data, newer 3D printing models can be created. For the technique to be a success, good knowledge about robotic synchronization and the mechanical behavior of the material is of utmost importance. ML technique can be used for the optimal consumption of material along with the cost and time reduction for a plan.

Tissue Engineering

The 3D printing method for printing the bio link to develop a tissue-like structure is an important feature of bioprinting required for tissue engineering [18]. The ML technology acknowledges the large data sets of materials and designs and evaluates the various mixture compositions of the bio-inks that help to design a new scaffold structure, which suits a specific purpose. The ML algorithm can perform multiple objective optimizations regarding the printing of bio-inks. To concurrently optimize process variables, material, and designed additive manufacturing of the silicone elastomer with the help of freeform reversible embedding was applied in the advanced machine learning by [30].

Medical

Better treatment planning communication and enhanced education and training are generated by the AM anatomical models. The image segmentation steps denote the position of the model. There is no need to manually extracting the data of interest as it enables a tailor-made model for the patient that helps to save time and effort [31]. The training of ML algorithms to learn large datasets is performed by tuning the material of multi-material printing like Polyjet. It is essential to train the personalized anatomical models with the large data set of all organ systems that help in acknowledging the ML algorithm, though it is difficult.

Data Acquisition Techniques

The data that is acquired is of utmost importance for the ideal results to be obtained from the ML technique so that it can give proper insights and accurate results of what is being sought. Since the majority of the data is dependent on the sensors, it should have a superior refresh rate and higher resolution than normal. The melt pool of the sensors should have a good thermal gradient and transfer of heat. According to [20], if the images are blurred, the accuracy of the result gets affected.

Although there are several sensors present, the different techniques of monitoring have their limitations which affect the production. For example, for checking the temperature of a melt pool only the surface is considered without providing any information about the transfer of heat and flow direction of the fluid [10]. Only expensive cameras with faster sensors can detect laser scans as well as the rapid cooling of the pool. Calibrating the emissivity of it can be slightly problematic. Using a thermal or optical camera for the detection of defects in layers can be done as an inexpensive process. However, this detects imperfections in layers and not what lies between them. For the detection of these internal issues, CT Scan and XPCI can be used, the detection is not done in real-time. Moreover, these are technique-sensitive, costly, and take up a lot of time [13]. The output of the sensors should remain consistent irrespective of the printing stress.

Computational Cost

The cost of a project is based on numerical simulations, and the one that is driven by data and supported by ML has proven to be more efficient than the physics-based one. The prediction of stress management by a particular lattice structure takes a mere 0.47s using ML whereas it can stretch up to 5–10 hours for other methods. Another article compared the stress prediction time for FEA and CNN, which is based on data, and it was reported that the CNN methods took milliseconds while FEA took a few minutes [32]. When a large dataset is used for computation, it can take time and become expensive as well. In a study by [8], ANN was employed which was knowledge-based and had 4 modules that took up 12 lesser neurons than the classical ANN model and were more homogenous and efficient as well.

If monitoring *in situ* and closed-loop approaches is the priority, computational cost can be important for it as well. The detection of defects is done in real-time and spontaneously so that the total build-time is not compromised and the rate of production remains the same. The time taken by BoW and MsCNN was compared by [25] to detect any anomaly that could be present. The former had a computational time of around 4s which was lesser than MsCNN which stood at 7 s. Both were considered fast as previously it used to happen in minutes. If inspection of the melt pool is the main aim, the ML technique is required as the dataset created due to it is larger and the computational efficiency also has to be higher.

Literature Gap

As ML techniques are becoming a part of the AM applications, this opens several doors for applications in the future. To give an example, unsupervised learning exercises did not gain much impetus, but the use of an unlabeled type of AM dataset can bring in a change and increase its popularity rapidly. However, proper training needs to be done to operate with the ML technique. The continuous integration between AM and ML techniques can improve the supervised ML as well.

Any condition that has not been previously diagnosed is difficult to detect using the ML technique. To improve the situation, more data related to scenarios that are frequently encountered should be generated so that the operating conditions improve [5]. The reason for making the switch from AM to ML technique is because various problems related to accuracy and accessibility are more commonly encountered in AM. Moreover, AM technique is not as efficient as ML in handling and computing huge datasets which have a high volume, resolution as well as velocity.

Problems related to data analysis are noticed whenever there are problems related to data structure and integration and fusion of data is to be done. Generation of appropriate data can also become troublesome and costly. If the available data is of poorer quality, the ML algorithm gets disturbed by it as well [29]. The poor-quality data is mainly due to low-resolution cameras with a field of view that is restricted maximally along with a high temporal set load. All of these factors combine to give inferior results, which can be a problem for the ML technique in general.

3.3   Methods and Materials

Production of industrial parts of the highest quality can be done by additive manufacturing, but the application of it in the mass production of finished goods can be a huge challenge, especially when the AM technique has to be scaled down [3]. However, using the AM machine smartly can help in improving the mechanical properties of the products.

The steps that can be followed for 3D printing are:

i.   A CAD model is developed by the software for CAD.
ii.   Conversion of CAD to stereolithography which is a drawing of the CAD Model itself in wedge-shape.
iii.   Using a slicer to slice the files into thin cross-sections according to requirements.
iv.   Codes for Computer Numerical Control (CNC) are used to print a 3D printed model from the layers that are sliced accordingly. The results provided by the CNC are of better quality and the movements of the heads for deposition are completely jerk-free [33].
v.   Treatment of the surface, sintering, and other post-processing steps are applied at the end.

The ML model can work along with the AM machines to generate builds of extravagant geometry that are usually difficult to manufacture using the subtractive framework, which is based on deformation [34]. Hollow objects can be dealt with in a more suitable fashion using this hybrid technique as any limitation related to access to the internal features can be overcome by the AM technique. A closed-loop architecture for the integration of AM and ML techniques has been shown in Figure 3.2. The ML system identifies the correlation between multiple models using sensors in an offline mode, and similarly, the process control of the AM data can be done in real-time.

A. Offline ML Model
The best method for the integration of AM and ML algorithms in an offline mode is by (Figure 3.7) Offline Training itself as shown below. It is a four-step procedure that involves:

- **AM algorithm filming**: it is an effective procedure to determine which type of characteristics will be good for a build based on the layer of powder during the entire process of laser scanning. Both scanning and spreading of powder are two integral steps [6]. A film of the build, by printing different geometric shapes like cylinders and bars, pits, divots, and other shapes which are not seen by the human eye, is done.
- **Sensory collection**: the properties of the build using multiple perspectives can be captured by sensors. Every layer of the sample is measured by different sensors. The Infrared camera is used to capture the thermal images by fusing process as a part of the procedure [12]. This is significant

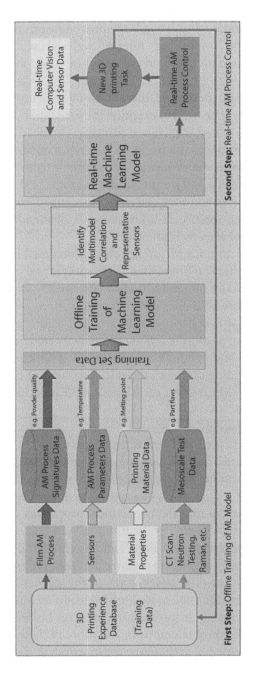

Figure 3.7 Offline ML model for integrating AM and ML (Gobert *et al.* 2018) [6].

because it can affect the different properties related to strength, microstructure, stress, etcetera. In case the data is not of good quality, it can be improved by pre-processing using spatial smoothing, filtering as well as clustering. Thus, online data can be refined and be made available in real-time.

- **Collection of mesoscale information**: A neutron testing procedure will be used to examine the final build. A scanner can be used to find the flaws in printing. Certain 3D printers can function optimally using certain types of powders and parts only, and the products that are built from are rough from the outside and porous from the inside [13]. Once the data is collected and analyzed from the scanned images using a 3D printer, mesoscale information is obtained, which is generally not seen by humans.

The algorithm for ML architecture is obtained by observing the mechanical properties of the sample and correlating them to the laser signatures that are obtained by scanning the powder layers [29]. Any defects in the pattern are detected by ML and it is collaborated by the AM algorithm as well. The data that is collected using the sensors are compared to mechanical and printed properties, and it resulted in some sensors standing out from the rest. This kind of correlation has also played a role in executing multiple tasks in real time.

B. Real-Time AM Process Control

Huge amounts of data are generated in real-time using the AM machines, and it is supplemented by ML techniques effectively, which learns and adapts to the control system in the process. When a collection of samples are given using appropriate labels by experts, multitasking is learned and executed in a manner so that the mechanical properties can be detected and any defects can be reported prematurely as well [24]. Certain sensors are selected to get the data in real-time, and it is correlated to the function of the offline DNN model in such a manner that the defects and properties can be seen in real-time. The observation of the data and the layers are done by the sensors in real-time as well, which forms an integral part of the ML technique. This results in premature detection before anything happens and the yield that is obtained from it is more likely to be 100 percent [1]. When certain remedial actions are recommended, the option of "go" or "no go" is also decided.

Layers of roughness and porosity of desire are obtained by using the data from the smart printers. It involves the selective fusing and powder spreading technique according to the parameters set by the AM model. The ML model is used to check for the variations in physical properties related to the size, shape, and texture of the powder particles [18]. These properties are also correlated to the microstructural features that are present to get better outcomes from the build.

A 3D printer that has a closed-loop model based on the ML technique can optimize the procedures by adjusting the parameters based on the properties of the products. The training of the model is based on the number of samples that are printed by it. Over some time, it gains enough data to make predictions in advance and in real-time and also suggests changes that can be brought about for better results [17]. Thus, the process of inspection is eliminated when working using these 3D model printers. It results in a breakthrough in productivity by making substances that are of superior physical properties and lesser-known errors. The database of the 3D printing is increased using the AM model as the training that is obtained over time is sufficient to identify any issues that might be arising and also suggestions to correct them [23]. Ultimately, the same process of real-time detection and potent solution to any issues that may arise definitively is provided by the ML model. Machine learning becomes an integral part of machine learning as well and it is used to gain new data, learn based on previous experiences and become better and smarter, improve the overall process of manufacturing and also automatically correct any defects which are a part of the quality control method as a whole [2]. Thus, lesser hiccups are encountered, and the final product that is obtained by it is better than before.

3.4 Results and Discussion

- Datasets Optimization

The better the quality and structure of data provided during the training, the more enhanced is the process of the ANN model. However, executing this process of collection and organizing data can become quite difficult. Another technique to amplify a dataset is an artificial generative method [35]. The training data is kept as a reference, and new random data are generated automatically using an autoencoder. The extension used here is a variational autoencoder. Adversarial nets and autoencoders are certain other procedures to enhance the generation of datasets as well [8].

The efficiency of the NN model is based on the amount of data generated and analyzed based on what is accessible by it. Certain huge datasets can be used effectively for training. This includes the use of MNIST for the recognition of optical characters, ImageNet for the recognition of images, and Youtube-8M for the classification of video. NN is powerful in these aspects [7]. However, one disadvantage of AM is that huge datasets are not available, and collecting the same for training can turn out to be expensive. These limitations prevent the organizations from creating their dataset as well, which are of open-source type. Therefore, it is imperative to work with smaller datasets in this aspect.

- Issue of Overfitting and Underfitting

The ability to generalize is something that the NN algorithm wants. It involves the prediction of output based on measurements done by an algorithm using sets of unknown data. One problem that is consistently seen is that of overfitting and underfitting.

Overfitting involves the forceful inclusion of all the data into the training set. This can make the whole database vulnerable as a whole, mainly due to the presence of outliers and noisy data [8]. Underfitting is the opposite of overfitting as a reasonable relationship between the data and the training set is not derived. Regularization and the exception of dropouts are some of the methods to control overfitting as well as underfitting.

A proper estimation of the output based on the available input data is instrumental for achieving the objectives of the ANN model. However, the performance can get slightly compromised due to the problems related to overfitting and underfitting. Overfitting involves the fitting of the complete dataset into the set used for training which makes it more susceptible to errors and noises [7]. Underfitting results in the failure of building appropriate relationships between the training set and data. If the correct number of neurons is chosen for each dataset, all these difficulties can be easily averted.

3.5   Conclusion

There are several utilities of using the ML technique in 3D printing and these start right from the designing process to the optimization of the process as well as complete monitoring. Numerical simulations that are data-driven can be tracked using the ML algorithm. It can also be used for recommending designs in the future, premature anomaly detection as well as cybersecurity. When the data is of higher dimensions, the ML technique has been known to overpower the conventional ones pretty considerably. Proper monitoring and control of feedback can be done by using advanced ML models in the future. Other challenges and issues that can be faced by the model have also been discussed in detail. This can enhance the performance of the 3D printing applications and help ML to grow in an even more formidable manner.

The research articles that have been reviewed in this paper have been published after 2017. This shows that the ML algorithm is just the beginning, especially where the collaboration with AM technique is concerned. Any problems that arise in the AM domain have been known to be solved effectively by the ML technique. The collaboration and research involving these two domains have been opportunistic and have been identified by continuous *in-situ* monitoring and control. The ML algorithm can be used in this aspect when the data of the AM model is complex and superior dimensionally. For example, the availability of datasets that are labeled resulted in the upscaling of supervised learning methods. Thus, future intensive collaborations between these two fields are inevitable.

This particular paper has proven time and again that there are many applications based on the AM domain that have benefited due to the introduction of the ML technique.

However, many other avenues can be explored still. In AM models, deep learning can be used on CAD models to make certain predictions based on attributes like the time for build and getting structural support. There are certain aspects of the domain that can benefit from the entire process and result in the early detection of faults to prevent failures of any kind. CNN can identify both micros as well as macro failures according to layers using data that is optically sensitive. Similar opportunities are sure to present themselves in the future as well.

It is imperative that the new opportunities arising out of the AM cycle are identified which are likely to arise when an advantage for the same is sought. The fusion of the in-data sensor is one aspect that needs to be looked at in more detail. The integration of data that can be optical, thermal, acoustic, and other related features can create something more holistic and accurate as it uses real-time data and the feedback is controlled. The AM datasets continue to emerge and develop, and the convergence with the ML techniques will play a significant role in making it formidable in the future.

References

1. Razvi, S.S., Feng, S., Narayanan, A., Lee, Y.-T.T., Witherell, P., A Review of Machine Learning Applications in Additive Manufacturing, in: *Proceedings of the ASME 2019 International Design Engineering Technical Conferences and Computers and Information in Engineering Conference*, CA, USA, 2019.
2. Banadaki, Y.M., On the Use of Machine Learning for Additive Manufacturing Technology in Industry 4.0. *J. Comput. Sci. Inf. Tech.*, 7, 2, 61–68, 2019.
3. Alabi, M.O., Nixon, K., Botef, I., A Survey on Recent Applications of Machine Learning with Big Data in Additive Manufacturing Industry. *Am. J. Eng. Appl. Sci.*, 11, 3, 1114–1124, 2018.
4. Joshi, M., Flood, A., Sparks, T., Liou, F.W., *Applications of supervised machine learning algorithms in additive manufacturing: a review.* Preprints, pp. 1–11, 2021. https://utw10945.utweb.utexas.edu/sites/default/files/2019/017%20Applications%20of%20Supervised%20Machine%20Learning%20Algori.pdf
5. Goh, G.D., Sing, S.L., Yeong, W.Y., A review on machine learning in 3D printing: Applications, potential, and challenges. *Artif. Intell. Rev.*, 54, 63–94, 2021, https://doi.org/10.1007/s10462-020-09876-9
6. Gobert, C., Reutzel, E., Petrich, J., Nassar, A., Phoha, S., Application of supervised machine learning for defect detection during metallic powder bed fusion additive manufacturing using high resolution imaging. *Addit. Manuf.*, 21, 517–528, 2018, https://doi.org/10.1016/j.addma.2018.04.005
7. Qi, X., Chen, G., Li, Y., Cheng, X., Li, C., Applying Neural-Network-Based Machine Learning to Additive Manufacturing: Current Applications, Challenges, and Future Perspectives. *Engineering*, 5, 4, 721–729, 2019.
8. Mahmood, M.A., Visan, A., II, Ristoscu, C., Mihailescu, I.N., Artificial Neural Network Algorithms for 3D Printing. *Materials*, 14, 163, 1–29, 2021.
9. Goldberg, Y., *Neural Network Methods for Natural Language Processing*, vol. 10, pp. 1–311, 2017.
10. Wang, J., Ma, Y., Zhang, L., Gao, R.X., Wu, D., Deep Learning for Smart Manufacturing: Methods and Applications. *J. Manuf. Syst.*, 48, 144–156, 2018.
11. Jin, Z., Zhang, Z., Demir, K., Gu, G.X., Machine Learning for Advanced Additive Manufacturing. *Matter*, 3, 1541–1556, 2020.
12. Shi, Y., Zhang, Y., Baek, S., De Backer, W., Harik, R., Manufacturability analysis for additive manufacturing using a novel feature recognition technique. *Comput. Aided Des. Appl.*, 15, 941–952, 2018.
13. Williams, G., Meisel, N., Simpson, T., McComb, C., Design repository effectiveness for 3D convolutional neural networks: Application to additive manufacturing. *ASME. J. Mech. Des.*, 141, 11, 111701, 2019, https://doi.org/10.1115/1.4044199
14. Gu, G., Chen, C., Richmond, D., Buehler, M., Bioinspired hierarchical composite design using machine learning: Simulation, additive manufacturing, and experiment. *Mater. Horiz.*, 5, 939–945, 2018.

15. Khadilkar, A., Wang, J., Rai, R., Deep learning–based stress prediction for bottom-up SLA 3D printing process. *Int. J. Adv. Manuf. Technol.*, 102, 2555–2559, 2019.

16. Gan, Z., Data-Driven Microstructure and Microhardness Design in Additive ManufacturingUsing a Self-Organizing Map. *Engineering*, 5, 730–735, 2019.

17. Li, H., Ma, X., Li, Z., An, Q., Wang, Y., Rathore, A.S., Song, C., Xu, W., Image Dataset for Visual Objects Classification in 3D Printing. *arXiv.* abs/1803.00391, 1–4, 2018.

18. Conev, A., Litsa, E.E., Perez, M.R., Diba, M., Mikos, A.G., Kavraki, L.E., Machine learning-guided three-dimensional printing of tissue engineering scaffolds. *Tissue Eng Part A.*, 26, 23–24, 1359–1368, 2020.

19. Gu, G., Chen, C., Buehler, M.D., De novo composite design based on machine learning algorithm. *Extreme Mech. Lett.*, 18, 19–28, 2018.

20. Wu, M., Song, Z., Moon, Y., Detecting cyber-physical attacks in CyberManufacturing systems. Mach. Learn. Methods *J. Intell. Manuf.*, 30, 1111–1123, 2017.

21. Pham, G., Lee, S.-H., Kwon, O.-H., Kwon, K.-R., Anti-3D Weapon Model Detection for Safe 3D Printing Based on Convolutional Neural Networks and D2 Shape Distribution. *Symmetry*, 10, 4, 1–90, 2018.

22. Wasmer, K., Le-Quang, T., Meylan, B., Shevchik, S., *In situ* quality monitoring in AM using acoustic emission: a machine learning approach. *J. Mater. Eng. Perform.*, 28, 2, 666–672, 2019.

23. Zhang, Y., Hong, G., Ye, D., Zhu, K., Fuh, J., Extraction and evaluation of melt pool, plume and spatter information for powder-bed fusion AM process monitoring. *Mater. Des.*, 156, 458–469, 2018.

24. Scime, L. and Beuth, J., Using machine learning to identify *in-situ* melt pool signatures indicative of flaw formation in a laser powder bed fusion additive manufacturing process. *Addit. Manuf.*, 25, 151–165, 2019.

25. Scime, L. and Beuth, J., A multi-scale convolutional neural network for autonomous anomaly detection and classification in a laser powder bed fusion additive manufacturing process. *Addit. Manuf.*, 24, 273–286, 2018b.

26. Scime, L. and Beuth, J., Anomaly detection and classification in a laser powder bed additive manufacturing process using a trained computer vision algorithm. *Addit. Manuf.*, 19, 114–126, 2018a.

27. Jafari-Marandi, R., Khanzadeh, M., Tian, W., Smith, B., Bian, L., From *in-situ* monitoring toward high-throughput process control: cost-driven decision-making framework for laser-based additive manufacturing. *J. Manuf. Syst.*, 51, 29–41, 2019.

28. Pasquet, I., Baco-Carles, V., Chamelot, P., Gibilaro, M., Massot, L., Tailhades, P., A multimaterial based on metallic copper and spinel oxide made by powder bed laser fusion: A new nanostructured material for inert anode dedicated to aluminum electrolysis. *J. Mater. Process. Technol.*, 278, 116452, 2020.

29. Yu, C. and Jiang, J., A Perspective on Using Machine Learning in 3D Bioprinting. *Int. J. Bioprinting*, 6, 1, 253, 2020.

30. Menon, A., Póczos, B., Feinberg, A., Washburn, N., Optimization of Silicone 3D Printing with Hierarchical Machine Learning. *3D Print. Addit. Manuf.*, 6, 181–189, 2019.

31. van Eijnatten, M., van Dijk, R., Dobbe, J., Streekstra, G., Koivisto, J., Wolff, J., CT image segmentation methods for bone used in medical additive manufacturing. *Med. Eng. Phys.*, 51, 6–16, 2018.

32. Koeppe, A., Hernandez Padilla, C., Voshage, M., Schleifenbaum, J., Markert, B., Efficient numerical modeling of 3D-printed lattice-cell structures using neural networks. *Manuf. Lett.*, 15, 147–150, 2018.

33. Mahmood, M., Han, C., Chu, H., Sun, C., Wu, W., Lin, W., Liu, L., Lai, J., Mihailescu, I., Lin, J., Effects of roll pattern and reduction ratio on optical characteristics of A1008 cold–rolled steel specimens: Analytical approach and experimental correlations. *Int. J. Adv. Manuf. Technol.*, 111, 2001–2020, 2020.

34. Chioibasu, D., Mihai, S., Mahmood, M., Lungu, M., Porosnicu, I., Sima, A., Dobrea, C., Tiseanu, I., Popescu, A., Use of X-ray Computed Tomography for Assessing Defects in Ti Grade 5 Parts Produced by Laser Melting Deposition. *Metals*, 10, 1408, 2020.

35. Géron, A., *Hands-On Machine Learning with Scikit-Learn, Keras, and TensorFlow: Concepts, Tools, and Techniques to Build Intelligent Systems*, O'Reilly Media, Inc, Sebastopol, CA, USA, 2019.

4

A Novel Model for Optimal Reliable Routing Path Prediction in MANET

S.R.M. Krishna[1*], S. Pothalaiah[2†] and R. Santosh[3]

[1]*MVSR College of Engineering, Hyderabad, India*
[2]*Dept of ECE, Vignana Bharathi Institute of Technology, Hyderabad, India*
[3]*Vasavi College of Engineering, Hyderabad, India*

Abstract

Accurate prediction of the path between the source and the destination nodes in a mobile ad hoc network (MANET) is essential and significant. The main challenge in dynamic MANETs is the mobility of the nodes, which are free moving from one place to another. A MANET does not have a fixed infrastructure, so different models have been proposed, such as rough sets and fuzzy sets, the technique for order preference by similarity to ideal solution (TOPSIS) scheme for classification, and the analytical hierarchical process (AHP) technique for obtaining the optimal paths rank-wise to be better with superior gradation of correctness. Hybrid optimization techniques are used to increase the accuracy toward better prediction. To predict the best route between the source and the destination, the proposed hybrid scheme, called rough set TOPSIS fuzzy-based analytical hierarchy process (RTF-AHP), are applied to predict the optimal paths among the set of random paths derived. The simulation of MANET was done with the ad hoc on-demand distance vector (AODV) routing protocol. The performance of the RTF-AHP model was compared with soft computing techniques. The simulation results were examined with the simulation parameters CPU execution time, throughput, and delay of the RTF-AHP model to give better accuracy in determining the optimal paths in MANETs.

Keywords: AHP, classification, fuzzy sets, performance, rough sets, ranking, routing, TOPSIS

*Corresponding author: krishna.murali564@gmail.com
†Corresponding author: pothalaiahs@gmail.com

Budati Anil Kumar, S. B. Goyal and Sardar M.N. Islam. Cognitive Computing Models in Communication Systems, (75–90) © 2022 Scrivener Publishing LLC

4.1 Introduction

Obtaining the optimal routing path prediction is a challenging issue mainly because of the larger broad network fast actions in the present time in many areas. Furthermore, the estimate of optimal paths has standing for MANETs [4, 16, 21]. Nonlinear or linear classification models and data-driven models [25] have been used in classification studies in many areas of science and engineering. Machine learning algorithms have been proposed for nonlinear processes, which are multifaceted in nature, mostly with difficulties in the data classification of the fuzzy set usage [12, 13]. Other techniques including rough sets [22, 25] and technique for order preference by similarity to ideal solution (TOPSIS) [23] have been found to be effective in the classification of routing paths in dynamic networks and in the determination of optimal paths, for which there are various enhanced intelligent models such as genetic algorithm (GA) [16–18] and swarm intelligence ant colony optimization (ACO) [11–13], with lack of trustworthiness establishment in the routing. All those models are non-hierarchical, which consume a lot of time in any optimal network routing operations such as in predicting the optimal path. However, the rough set TOPSIS fuzzy-based analytical hierarchy process (RTF-AHP) technique is hierarchical in nature, and so it performs well in determining the best paths at optimal times when compared to existing techniques. In addition, RTF-AHP predicts the optimal paths on rank base. Therefore, it basically overcomes the dynamic nature of a mobile ad hoc network (MANET) [16–18].

The analytical hierarchy process (AHP) scheme [1, 6–9, 25–29] was proposed by Thomas L. Satty [10]. It is not only hierarchical but also keeps the advantages of GA and ACO, but it resolves the major issues of GA and ACO in the context of optimal routing with consideration of exclusive priority of performance metrics including battery power, signal, and signal strength.

In the present study, AHP was chosen to forecast the optimal reliable routing paths in a dynamic network. The classified routing paths were made as alternatives for the input of the AHP technique [1, 3–5]. Classifying various routing paths from a network can be achieved using different classification models available [22, 25]. However, the existing models will not offer deeper, accurate results in classifying routing paths to achieve the final object for predicting the best optimal routing path in a timely basis.

Relying on basic classification models is very risky because such models do not offer accurate results.

The optimized difference protocols by hybrid techniques create a hybrid tool. The hybrid scheme [7–9, 11] is effective and efficient in improving classification with the MANET multipath route. Therefore, in the present work, fuzzy and rough sets offer more accuracy in filtering the routing paths derived from any dynamic MANETs. The filtered routes between the source and the destination were input into the model of AHP. The mathematical sets were used in the rough sets [22] to contract with indeterminate data. To simplify the knowledge about node some classification rules are required. In this study, rough sets were used to filter the routing paths derived using the ad hoc on-demand distance vector (AODV) protocol.

4.2   Analytical Hierarchical Process Technique

The AHP is a structural method [10] used to obtain multiple standard choices created mathematically. Multiple criteria [6] are the metrics on various parameters involved in finding the best path [8] for efficient data transmission in MANETs.

The AHP scheme was chosen to select one of the choices when more than one is available. It is also a method used to derive ratio measures from paired comparisons [1].

To analyze the ordering of routes, the solution alternatives and other criteria [2] were used, the Figure 4.1 shows. The performance measures C1, C2, C3, C4, and C5 were applied to create the criteria C1, C2, C3, C4, and C5. Alternatives A1, A2, A3, A4, and A5 were drawn from a variety of classified route paths detailed in subsequent sections.

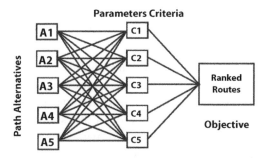

Figure 4.1 Analytical hierarchical process (AHP) architecture flow.

4.3 Mathematical Models and Protocols

This section briefly discusses the various mathematical set models and protocol application on a network model in generating inputs from the AHP model.

4.3.1 Rough Sets

The rough set theory (RST) [14–19, 22, 25, 28] was used to deal with uncertain data. Nodes doesn't require any preliminarily data to classify it.

4.3.1.1 Pawlak Rough Set Theory Definitions

Definition 1
Consider the Pawlak approximation space (U, R) [22]. Universe U is not $\varnothing$. An equivalence relation with U is R U/R. The group of all equivalence classes of R is denoted by U/R, and an equivalence class of R containing a member x U is denoted by $[x]R$. The lower and upper boundary approximations of X for every $X \subseteq U$ are defined as follows for any $X \in U$:

Let A be the target set, then rough set R is defined as the ratio of the lower approximation to the upper approximation.

$$R = |\underline{A}|/|A| \tag{4.1}$$

Upper approximation refers to elements that may or may not belong to set A, whereas lower approximation refers to elements that might or might not belong to the target set. A boundary region of A in the universe is the difference between the upper and lower threshold approximations.

$$\text{Boundary region} = |A| - |\underline{A}| \tag{4.2}$$

A reduct is a subset of elements that differentiate all of the data in an information system despite containing any redundancy. The core of the system, or notion, is described as a collection of parts based on indispensable traits or attributes that are required. In this study, classification rules were used to identify five optimal paths from a wide range of options using the above-mentioned five performance criteria.

4.3.2   Fuzzy TOPSIS

The membership function was used to analyze the data using fuzzy sets. The membership function is a criterion for the selection of an AHP model alternative [12, 19–21, 26, 28].

Definition 4: Fuzzy Set
Fuzzy set [12] A is defined as the set that has a pair, (U,m), where U is a set and m is a membership function of the fuzzy set.

$$A = \{y,m\}, y \in U$$

where m: $U - >[0,1]$ is the membership function of A and m is the degree of pertinence [24] of y in A.

For any value "y" in the setup that is not included in the fuzzy set, then $m(y)$ returns a zero value. If "y" is completely in the fuzzy set, then $m(y) = 1$, and then the set is called core [13]. If the $m(y)$ value lies between 0 and 1, then the set is said to be supportive of the set and y is called a fuzzy member [23] of the fuzzy set. The value of $m(y)$ is not accurate and called as the linguistic value, otherwise bivalent in the classical set [20] (Table 4.1).

Table 4.1   Metric values from the performance metric equations.

Nodes	Battery power	Trustworthiness	Signal strength	Mobility
1	0.75	0.81	0.55	0.23
2	0.72	0.75	0.82	0.25
3	0.32	0.45	0.44	0.20
4	0.83	0.77	0.80	0.22
5	0.65	0.72	0.73	0.35
6	0.77	0.65	0.67	0.29
7	0.64	0.55	0.71	0.38
8	0.71	0.65	0.63	0.15
14	0.81	0.47	0.49	0.22
15	0.87	0.53	0.46	0.24
23	0.70	0.80	0.66	0.18

The fuzzy TOPSIS method was proposed by Chen to solve multicriterion choice creation problems under uncertainty [23]. Linguistic variables are used by the decision makers, D_r ($r = 1,..., k$), to assess the weights of the criteria and the ratings of the alternatives. Thus, W_r^j describes the weight of the jth criterion, C_j ($j = 1,..., m$), given by the rth decision maker. Similarly, x_{ij}^r describes the rating of the ith alternative, A_i ($i = 1,..., n$), with respect to criterion j, given by the rth decision maker.

4.4 Routing Protocols

The MANET routing protocol has been classified into a proactive and reactive routing protocol based on the selection of routes.

4.4.1 Classification of Routing Paths

From the previous sections, the performance metric values were derived from the NS2 trace file after simulation of the network. The metric values that were extracted using the performance metric equations mentioned in Section 4.4.1 are listed in Table 4.2, which are noted as C1 (number of hops), C2 (battery power), C3 (signal strength), C4 (trustworthiness), and C5 (mobility).

This study describes the results obtained for five performance metric value equations. Here, we used NS2[ ] with the AODV protocol simulator to retrieve inputs from each metric.

Filtering the optimal possible routes from the network was done by the application of rough sets with the following classification rules with rough sets [ ]:

a) The average trustworthiness of the path should be >50%;
b) The average mobility of the path should be <30%;
c) The average battery power of the path should be >70%;
d) The average signal strength should be >45%; and
e) The average number of hops should be ≤4.

After evaluating the upper and lower boundary values of the possible routing path sets using the above classification rules, the final filtered routed nodes were indicated in bold format.

Table 4.2 describes all paths obtained for the network shown in Figure 4.3 for MANET with the AODV protocol. For the generation and performance

Table 4.2 All possible routes from nodes 1 to 12.

⇨ **R1**	N1	N2	N6	N11	N12		
⇨ **R2**	N1	N4	N7	N11	N12		
⇨ **R3**	N1	N3	N4	N6	N11	N12	
⇨ **R4**	N1	N3	N5	N4	N8	N12	N12
⇨ **R5**	**N1**	**N3**	**N4**	**N8**	**N12**		
⇨ **R6**	N1	N3	N5	N4	N7	N11	N12
⇨ **R7**	N1	N3	N5	N4	N8	N12	
⇨ **R8**	N1	N3	N5	N8	N10	N12	
⇨ **R9**	**N1**	**N3**	**N5**	**N9**	**N8**	**N12**	
⇨ **R10**	N1	N3	N5	N9	N10	N12	
⇨ **R11**	N1	N3	N5	N9	N8	N10	N12
⇨ **R12**	N1	N3	N4	N8	N10	N12	
⇨ **R13**	**N1**	**N3**	**N5**	**N4**	**N7**	**N12**	
⇨ **R14**	N1	N2	N4	N3	N5	N9	N12
⇨ **R15**	**N1**	**N2**	**N4**	**N8**	**N10**	**N12**	

of various routing paths, calculation of the metric input values in this study was done using the NS2[ ] toolbox.

4.5   RTF-AHP Model

The RTF-AHP model was developed for the prediction of optimal paths with reliable network metric features. The input parameters for this model were described in a previous section.

4.5.1   Rough TOPSIS Fuzzy Set Analytical Hierarchical Process Algorithm

The RTF-AHP algorithm considers paths (PT); five parameters (PR), C1, C2, C3, C4 and C5; and five alternatives (AT) as inputs for ranking the paths. The number of paths (n) to be ranked considered here is 5. C_{old} refers to Table 4.2, C_{new} refers to Table 4.2, and the total is the column of Table 4.2. The parameter d refers to the distance between the pair of sets CI (consistency index), RI (random index), and CR (consistency ratio). **Input:** An instance of a model (PT, PR, or AT).

 Initialize the value n.
while condition for all nodes **do**
if condition using the roughest classification rules is malicious, **then**
  Avoid nodes from the network.
 end if
end while

$$\text{Alternative matrix } C_{ij} = \frac{1}{C_{ij}} \tag{4.7}$$

Normalize the criteria evolution matrix:

$$N = \frac{C_{old\,i,j}}{\text{Total}_{i,j}} \forall_{ij} \tag{4.8}$$

$$\text{Criteria weighting AW} = \lambda_{max} \times W \tag{4.9}$$

$$\text{Consistency measure}_i = \sum \frac{C_{old\,i,j} \times C_{new\,j}}{C_{new\,j}\ \text{AVG}} \tag{4.10}$$

$$\lambda_{max} = \text{Avg[Consistency Measures]} \tag{4.11}$$

$$\text{CI} = \lambda_{max} - \frac{n}{n-1} \tag{4.12}$$

$$\text{CR} = \frac{\text{CI}}{\text{RI}} \tag{4.13}$$

if CR < 0.10, **then**
Proceed
else
Repeat procedure from first.
end if
while $i = 1, \ldots, n$, **do**

$$D_i^+ = \sum d\left(V_{ij}, V_j^*\right) \qquad (4.14)$$

$$D_i^- = \sum d\left(V_{ij}, V_j^-\right) \qquad (4.15)$$

end while
while $i = 1, \ldots, n$, **do**

$$CC_i = \frac{D_i^-}{D_i^- + D_i^+} \qquad (4.16)$$

end while
while $i = 1, \ldots n$, **do**
max <− CC_i
　　while $j = i, \ldots n$, **do**
　　if max < CC_j, **then**
　　max <− CC_j **end if**
　　end while swap(max, CC_i)
　　end while

The above RTF-AHP algorithm gave results of the optimal path in the minimum time period compared to other models because of its hierarchical evolution modeling and filtering or classifying possible routing paths. Moreover, this technique will give the order of the rankings for optimal paths in the best and the worst order, unlike other models.

4.6   Models for Optimal Routing Performance

The prediction accuracy for optimal paths in terms of time, throughput, packet delivery ratio (PDR), and trustworthiness of the RTF-AHP model was compared with that of the GA and ACO models.

4.6.1 Genetic Algorithm Technique

The NS2 tool box was used to develop the GA for predicting the optimal path from a network. Generally, the accuracy of GA [16–18, 20, 34, 35] simply depends upon the fitness function. However, GA was designed simply based on node distances, with no performance metric considerations like the RTF-AHP model. Therefore, the RTF-AHP generates reliable optimal paths compared to other models.

4.6.2 Ant Colony Optimization Technique

ACO is a swarm intelligence (SI) technique. SI [11–13, 21] is the property of the collective behavior of decentralized, self-configuring, and natural or artificial systems. SI is a new property to solving problems by observing the behaviors of various animals or insects [12]. One of the most used successful optimization methods with SI property [24] is ACO, which takes motivation from the behavior of some ants. This model is simply an extension of GA, which was designed with the view of probability function. Even though this technique is better than GA, it is also limited to generating routing paths without metric factors.

4.6.3 RTF-AHP Model Architecture Flow

In this section, the process flow of the RTF-AHP model place from the generation of the input to finally the output is briefly described in Figure 4.2.

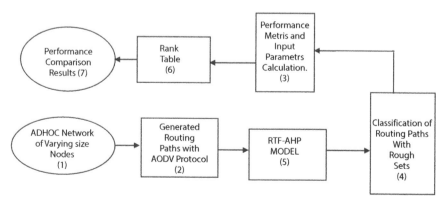

Figure 4.2 Structure of the rough set TOPSIS fuzzy-based analytical hierarchy process (RTF-AHP) model.

4.7   Results and Discussion

To generate a variety of routing pathways from a dynamic network sample, the following Table 4.3 lists the various parameters that can be set *via* the simulator environment. The NS2 [15] trace file was used to obtain all simulator results.

When the network size is raised by "*n*" nodes, Figure 4.3 series shows the observed and computed CPU consumption or execution time to create the first 5, 10, 15, and 20 ranked alternatives or routing options.

The aforesaid findings were compared to new optimized models, i.e., GA and ACO.

According to Figure 4.3 series, the CPU execution time for the RTF-AHP model dropped by approximately 40%, 45%, 55%, 50%, and 70% when compared to the time consumption of the GA and by around 30%, 35%, 40%, 30%, and 20% when compared to that of ACO for 10%, 20%, 30%, 40%, and 50% nodes of a simulated network. According to the results of the preceding investigation, the RTF-AHP model generated.

From Figure 4.4 where the best alternatives or routing paths are 5, 10, 15, and 20 using a) the rough set TOPSIS fuzzy-based analytical hierarchy process (RTF-AHP) model, b) the genetic algorithm (GA) model, and c) the ant colony optimization (ACO) model for network size increments of 10–50.

From the Figure 4.5 examination of noticed when best alternatives or directing paths P1, P2, P3, P4, and P5 are produced with a) the rough set TOPSIS fuzzy-based analytical hierarchy process (RTF-AHP) model, b) the genetic algorithm (GA) model, and c) the ant colony optimization (ACO) model for 10, 20, 30, and 40 hubs.

Table 4.3 Simulation parameters.

Parameter	Value
No. of nodes	25
Data packet size	1,000 bytes
Environment area	1,800 × 840
Transmission range	250 m
Traffic type	CBR (constant bit rate)
Routing protocols	AODV
Time delay	0.0347 ms

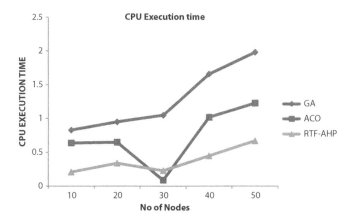

Figure 4.3 Comparison of the observed and computed CPU execution times with number of nodes.

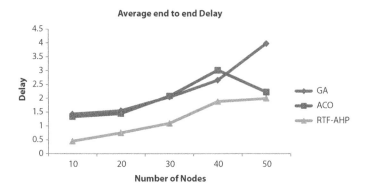

Figure 4.4 Comparison of the measured and simulated CPU execution time period vs number of nodes.

Figure 4.5 series gives the observed and processed average throughput values of the five other options or steering paths—P1, P2, P3, P4, and P5—for the 10, 20, 30, and 40 nodes of a network simulation. Corresponding to each upside of the throughput values of varying network sizes, it is seen that the RTF-AHP model offered high throughput for every path, in contrast with the existing ACO and GA models. From Figure 4.6 series shows that the throughput values of the RTF-AHP model for each of the directing paths P1, P2, P3, P4, and P5 expanded by around 30%, 55%, 63%, 43%, and 40% of the normal throughput created by GA and 30%, 55%, 60%, 45%, and 47% of what ACO generated. The above investigation presumes that

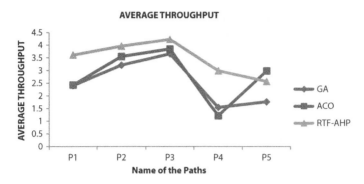

Figure 4.5 Throughput vs Name of the paths.

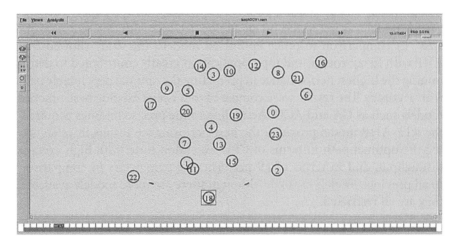

Figure 4.6 Data transmission through path 2-18-22.

the RTF-AHP model produced ideal steering paths in the least amount of time and with precise outcomes, i.e., with less CPU consumption time and high throughput, not at all like the GA and ACO models.

When the RTF-AHP prediction method was used for a network of 20 nodes, the accuracy and efficiency in determining a trustworthy or reliable routing path increased by 70% (for best path R3) compared to that of other existing models such as GA and ACO, while the average mobility accuracy of all routing paths reduced by 25%.

The RTF-AHP model predicted the network size of 30 nodes. In comparison to existing models such as GA and ACO, its accuracy and efficiency in determining a trustworthy or reliable routing path showed an increase of 25% (for best path R1), while the average mobility accuracy of all routing paths was lowered by 15%.

The various routing pathways were developed with AODV simulation on a MANET of 24 nodes, in which the source was 2 and the destination was 23, as shown in the 1, 2, and 3 series in Figure 4.6. Using the RTF-AHP model, numerous alternatives were identified and filtered as a result of such a simulation. P1, P2, P3, P4, and P5 are examples of different alternatives.

4.8   Conclusion

We introduced an RTF-AHP hybrid model for the problem of forecasting an optimum reliable routing path for a MANET in this paper. The suggested model was put to test on an ad hoc network with different network sizes. In comparison to other optimized models, the study showed that AHP with fuzzy, rough, and topic application greatly contributed to determining the highest performance in predicting the optimal dependable path with accuracy. The results were compared to those of existing best-practice models such as GA and ACO. According to the precise findings acquired, the RTF-AHP model provided the best performance results in establishing the optimal path in terms of CPU execution time, with high average throughput, and in terms of all performance parameters in comparison to all previous models created. Although there are more models available, they are all restricted.

References

1. Albayarak, E. and Erensal, Y.C., Using analitic hierarchy process to improve human performance. *J. Intell. Manuf.*, 15, 491–503, 2006.
2. Saini, V.K., AhP, Fuzzy sets and TOPSIS based reliable route selection for MANET. *IEEE Conf.*, 2014.
3. Qadri, N. and Liotta, A., A comparative analysis of routing protocols for MANETs. *IADIS International Conference Wireless Applications and Computing*, University of Essex, Colchester, UK, 2008.
4. Perkin, C.E. and Royer, E.M., Adhoc on demand distance vector routing. *Proc. Workshop Mobile Computing systems and Applications*, pp. 90–100, Feb. 1999.

5. Chan, F.T.S. and Kumar, N., Global Supplier development considering risk factors using fuzzy extended AHP-based approach. *Omega*, 35, 4, 417–431, August 2007.

6. Liu, D., Duan, G., Lei, N., Wang, J.S., Analytic hierarchy process based Decision modeling in CAPP development tools. *Int. J. Adv. Manuf. Technol.*, 15, 1999.

7. Blum, C., Beam-ACO—Hybridizing ant colony optimization with beam search: an application to open shop scheduling. *Comput. Oper. Res.*, 32, 6, 1565–1591, 2005.

8. Juang, C.F., Hung, C.W., Hsu, C.H., Rule-based cooperative continuous ant colony optimization to improve the accuracy of fuzzy system design. *IEEE Trans. Fuzzy Syst.*, 18, 1, 138–149, February 2010.

9. Juang, C.F. and Lo, C., Zero-order TSK-type fuzzy system learning using a two-phase swarm intelligence. *Fuzzy Set. Syst.*, 159, 21, 2910–2926, Nov. 2008.

10. Patil, A.P., Kanth, K.R., Sharanya, B., Kumar, M.P.D., Malavika, J., Design of energy efficient routing protocol for MANET based on AODV. *IJCSI*, 8, 4, 1, July 2011.

11. Riley, G.F. and Henderson, T.R., The ns-3 network simulator. in: *Modeling and tools for network simulation*, pp. 15–34, Springer, Berlin, Heidelberg, 2010.

12. Biradar, A. and Thool, R.C., Performance evaluation of mobile ad-hoc networks routing protocols to employ genetic algorithm. *3rd World Congress on Information and Communication Technologies(WICT 2013)*, Hanoi, Vietnam, IEEE, December 15-18 2013.

13. Abhishek, R. and Das, S.K., QM2RP: A QoS-based mobile multicast routing protocol using multi-objective genetic algorithm. *Wirel. Netw.*, 10, 3, 271–286, 2004.

14. Nikhil, K., Agarwal, S., Sharma, P., *Application of genetic algorithm in designing a security model for mobile adhoc network*, CSIT, 2012.

15. Per Kins, C.E. and Bhagwat, P., Highly dynamic destination sequenced distance vector routing (DSDV) for mobile computer. *SIGCOMM*, ACM, 1994.

16. Jindal, J. and Gupta, V., Fuzzy improved genetic approach for route optimization in MANET. *Int. J. Adv. Res. Comput. Sci. Software Eng.*, 3, 1, 782–790, January-February-2018.

17. Varsheney, T., Katiyar, A., Sharma, P., Performance improvement of MANET under DSR protocol using swarm optimization. *IEEE Conf.*, 2014.

18. Zeng, A. *et al.*, A fuzzy rough set approach for incremental feature selection on hybrid information systems. *Fuzzy Sets Syst.*, 258, 39–60, 2015.

19. Junior, F.R.L., Osiro, L., Carpinetti, L.C.R., A comparison between Fuzzy AHP and Fuzzy TOPSIS methods to supplier selection. *Appl. Soft Comput.*, 21, 194–209, 2014.

20. Patil, A.P., Kanth, K.R., Sharanya, B., Kumar, M.P.D., Malavika, J., Design of energy efficient routing protocol for MANET based on AODV. *IJCSI*, 8, 4, 1, 215–220, July 2011.

21. Jones, T. and Forrest, S., Fitness distance correlation as a measure of problem difficulty for genetic algorithms, in: *Proc. 6th International Conf. on Genetic Algorithms*, Kaufman, Los Altos, CA, pp. 184–192, 1995.

22. Erensal, Y.C., Oncan, T., Demircan, M.L., Determining key capabilities in technology management using fuzzy analytic hierarchy process: A case study of Turkey. *Inf. Sci.*, 176, 18, 2755–2770, 2006.

23. Chang, D.Y., Applications of the extent analysis method on fuzzy AHP. *Eur. J. Oper. Res.*, 95, 649–655, 1996.

24. Bozbura, F.T. and Beskese, A., Prioritization of organizational capital measurement indicators using fuzzy AHP. *Int. J. Approx. Reason.*, 44, 2, 124–147, 2007.

25. Vaidya, O.S. and Kumar, S., Analytic hierarchy process: An overview of applications. *Eur. J. Oper. Res.*, 169, 1–29, 2006.

26. Merkle, D. and Middendorf, M., Modelling ACO:composed permutation problems, in: *ANTS 2002: Proc. Of the Third International Workshop on Ant Algorithms, Lecture Notes in Computer Science*, vol. 2463, pp. 149–162, Springer, Berlin, Germany, 2002.

27. Dorigo, M., *Optimization, learning and natural algorithms (in Italian)*, Ph.D. Thesis, Dipartimento di Elettronica, Politecnico di Milano, Italy, 1992.

28. Jones, T. and Forrest, S., Fitness distance correlation as a measure of problem difficulty for genetic algorithms, in: *Proc. 6th International Conf. on Genetic Algorithms*, Kaufman, Los Altos, CA, pp. 184–192, 1995.

29. Goldberg, D.E., Simple genetic algorithms and the minimal deceptive problem, in: *Genetic Algorithms and Simulated Annealing*, Pitman, London, UK, pp. 74–88, 1987.

5

IoT-Based Smart Traffic Light Control

Sreenivasa Rao Ijjada[1] and K. Shashidhar[2]

1Department of EECE, GITAM deemed to be University, Visakhapatnam, India
2Department of ECE, LORDS Institute of Engineering and Technology,
Hyderabad, India

Abstract

Managing traffic issues in the cosmopolitan cities is a very challenging task for policemen. Moving through traffic is very important in urban and highly populated areas and in big cities. The traditional methods that we follow today are unable to handle such a day by day increase of road traffic in cities, and to handle these situations efficiently the concept of smart cities, has risen. We need to use the technology we have today. The main goal of this chapter is to create a traffic system that depends on density which handles the situation better than existing methods. As a solution, we have to use an Internet of Things (IoT) technology in the traffic control system based on the density constraint algorithm. This algorithm will solve problems created by traditional methods which are not as effective. As per previous discussion, we control our traffic signal system by calculating according to the speed limit of the respective road and distance between two consecutive signals. The system takes traffic density as input from cameras and sensors. Depending on this input, output signals are monitored. The algorithm is used to calculate the traffic density by the input from sensors. An additional feature is that, RFIDs are used to identify the emergency vehicles like ambulance, fire brigade, etc. by making mandatory RFID tags in emergency service vehicles. In serious events like fire in a vehicle or fire accident on a road there are some sensors that can find out these cases. We also have an application which is interlinked to a city's traffic database and forwards the issue to department about vehicle fire and tags the whereabouts of the incident. The user will also receive a notification about these situations. The municipalities or the equivalents of any city can always look at the density of traffic at any signal also things like the annual traffic flow which will help them in plans like road expansion etc. We create an application where the user can access the speed range and real-time traffic information.

*Corresponding author: sijjada@gitam.edu

Budati Anil Kumar, S. B. Goyal and Sardar M.N. Islam. Cognitive Computing Models
in Communication Systems, (91–106) © 2022 Scrivener Publishing LLC

We control our traffic signals using Raspberry Pi where the data is being received from Google maps application programming interface (API), where the information will be stored on server data base (DB). Our application will display the data from server regarding the user's location.

Keywords: IOT, API, wamp server, online database

5.1 Introduction

In our luxurious, comfortable, and high-speed life, we have many problems. One of the biggest problems is between all traffic congestion. It results in decreasing the efficiency of the individual as well as society by wasting their valuable time in waiting at traffic signal points. Large number of vehicles, the low structure, and the inconsistent distribution of the traffic signaling system are the major reasons for these traffic congestions at urban areas [1]. It finally results in the increasing pollution due to engines remain on during these conditions. At certain conditions, without any gain large number of natural resources has been consumed. However, we need to reduce all the problems stated above to certain level by implementing sensor-based traffic systems, that IoT based and dynamic in nature helps in reducing all these problems.

Rise in traffic due to increase in population is becoming a big problem especially in urban areas. To examine the traffic, we consider three things namely velocity, density, and number of automobiles [2]. This is our proposed solution; our new algorithm will calculate the traffic based on number of vehicles present on the road. The algorithm can help minimize traffic by sharing the number of vehicles along different routes, thereby reducing the burden on civilian roads. There are many avenues and approaches to do this [3]. But in our algorithm, we will manage the traffic lights based on traffic density. Nowadays being stranded in traffic is a very big problem. Our algorithm will provide us with a solution which will reduce the cases of being stranded in traffic. Our algorithm is controlled by a microprocessor also called as Raspberry Pi3. This also reduces accidents, not wasting our fruitful time, better understanding traffic through our web application. The infra-red (IR) sensors emit infrared rays helps in calculating density [4]. The system has on-road IR sensors which respond if any vehicle tries to move over IR sensors on the road. Microprocessor monitors the IR sensors and measures the vehicle density that passes on the road. Depending on vehicles density at different lanes, the Raspberry Pi will evaluate the situation and gives an output though traffic lights. The sensors and output lights are separated at least by a few meters [5]. So depending up on the number of cars, Raspberry Pi will evaluate the situation and gives real time updates to traffic lights. The Infra-Red devices will calculate the density. Our raspberry pi will control the traffic lights because each one of them are linked to raspberry pi and will calculate the output according to density which is identified by IR device. The IR devices constantly observe the density and it will be their decision to give the green signal or not. Green signals will be given when they notice higher number of cars. This is our algorithm which works seamlessly across multiple junctions.

5.2   Scope of the Proposed Work

Traditional traffic systems used at present are traffic signs and markings by the traffic personnel, individual traffic signals at junctions. Everyone who operates the motor vehicles need a specific and matching education in understanding rules and regulations, that helps in simple management of traffic and reduces accidents. This is controlled and monitored by the driving-licensing authorities and they are responsible in making everyone knowledgeable. We have certain rules and regulations like, stop sign should consist red light and octagonal background shape. Every traffic signal should follow these rules and administered by standards. These standards are designed to easy recognition of the motorist and helps in understanding easily and clearly visible up to certain eyesight. These standards help in easy recognition and following appropriate rules constantly and taking certain decisions regarding it. Our traditional traffic signal system follows the transferring signals from on lane to another lane by fixing time for each signal. This makes traffic congestion and waiting at lanes due to wasting of time at lanes having no traffic. It also creates a problem by wasting time at every signal due to lack of inter-connectivity.

The modern traffic systems that we are proposing will, calculate time depending on the input received from the sensors which are fixed at positions in all different lanes. IR trans-receivers end the IR rays to identify any obstacles present, basing on the information received from sensors; Raspberry Pi has calculated the time for every signal present at the junction and set the time for signals.

The transportation industry is disrupted by the IoT by building smart transportation infrastructure. It helps in improvement of security, safety, emergency services, traffic management, etc. Intelligent transportation system automates entire transportation sector. We can also add live tracking by implementing GPS feature in it. It improves the delivery system. Implementing ITS can automate the entire transportation system. Increasing accidents and congestion requires a better transportation system that consists of sensors, microprocessor. These results in improvement of delivery, logistics, fleet management, and all sectors depend on the transportation sector.

5.3   Proposed System Implementation

A Wamp server screen shot is shown in the Figure 5.1, it is selected for the linking the online monitoring systems. The implementation process is as given below.

Go to URL: http:/www.wampserver.com/en/download-wampserver-64bits/for download and install the Wamp Server latest version. It is used to maintain a local server between database and web page created.

System analysis is the procedure where one can understand the difference between the existing system and proposed system of the same. This helps in the understanding the system being implemented to an address the shortcomings in the current system or whether further specifications are required or not.

a) Existing system: The current systems used to control the trafic is programmed to give the equal time slots for all the roads eventhough no traffic/vehicle in a particular road. This existing system has its own advantages and disadvantages like makes much waiting other signals and some misses signal in fraction of seconds. The existing traffic signal picture is shown in the Figure 5.2.

Figure 5.1 Wamp server screen shot.

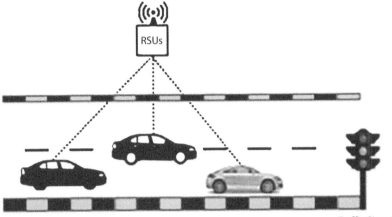

Figure 5.2 Existing system diagram.

b) Proposed System

The proposed system for the traffic control which is implemented based on the IoT is shown in the Figure 5.3. This can be demonstrated with three layers as below.

1. First layers gain data and assembling the layer
2. Second one evaluates the information and gives a decision as the output
3. Last layer is about displaying output and providing the results to the user in the best way.

c) Expected working model: Figure 5.4 represents the traffic network system animated diagram. This system uses IR (Infra-Red)/Ultrasonic sensors, and Surveillance camera and IoT core processor. IR components are more common and critical components in the systems which are used to detect the density of the traffic or number of vehicles on each lane of road.

IR ultrasonic sensors will measure the length by ejecting a specific wavelength sound wave which will bounce when it hits a moving object and returns to the receiver. But this only works to a range of 0.2–4 meters.

Length = $((l \times m) / 0.2 \times 10)$;
Where, l = sound velocity;
m = consumed time

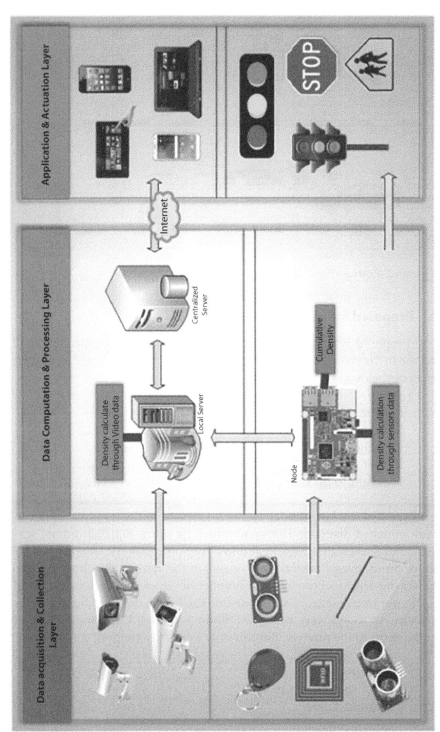

Figure 5.3 Expected IoT-based traffic control system model.

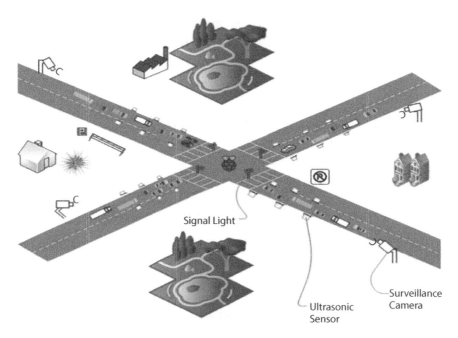

Figure 5.4 Traffic network system animated diagram.

We know that there will be three IR devices separated by a few meters are interlinked to every junction road to measure the density of vehicles. The IR device reading will be in binary digits 1 or 0. The measuring of density will only be done after the results from each IR device which is present at that junction road.

$$\sum_{i=1}^{3}(Pi) = P_i + P_{i+1} + P_{i+2}$$

P will denote the combination of duo of ultrasonic gadgets. We can observe the conditions of the devices and the output they have given.

Table 5.1 Results from duo of ultrasonic devices.

Condition/sensors	P1	P2	P3	Status
Condition 1	1	0	0	Low
Condition 2	1	1	0	Medium
Condition 3	1	1	1	High

The Raspberry pi will get the conclusions from US devices through a native server which will help it to determine the aggregate density by making use of Table 5.1.

d) Sample code

Part (I) When no emergency vehicle detected

```
if (Traffic Density == high)
    if (Rush interval ==Yes)
        Time = ((α eˣ sinθ) + β) + γ
    else
        Time = (α eˣ sinθ) + (cosθ * γ) + β
    else
    if (Rush Interval == Yes)
    Time = (α eˣ sinθ) + γ
```

e) System modeling and design: Through this phase we make sure that the architecture, blocks, UI, parts, and raw data will attempt to meet the requirements needed. This is a significant step for system growth. The main aim of this program is to examine model design perceptive view. The categorical model of a system is to check on the portrayal of information pass, controls, and I/O of the model. This can be done by comparing with the existing model.

Physical Design

The physical model portrays the I/O processes of the design. This also includes how the data is fact cross checked, processed, and validated. We're not searching for real and concrete ones, though. For example, if we take a smart phone, it receives its inputs from human feather touch and output through built-in display or external display or a printer etc. via its touch sensitive display. But the actual hardware is its CPU and Graphics unit.

f) Flow chart: The proposed model flow chart is shown in the Figure 5.5. The Use Case Names that are used in our project are as follows:

- status of signal
- set signal
- analyze traffic flow
- assign time

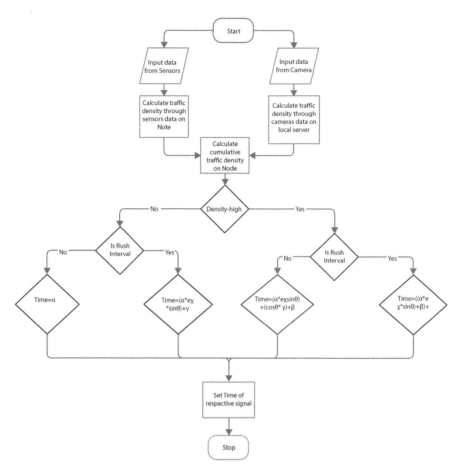

Figure 5.5 Flow chart diagram.

5.4   Testing and Results

a) Functional testing and test objectives: We test the algorithm against the utilitarian essentials on software basis. All the features will be thoroughly analyzed by giving a known set of data which we already know the results and we cross check them with the results produces by our algorithm. This analyzing test whether the conditions are accomplished by our algorithm.

- To find the density in roads
- Controlling traffic signals at a junction
- If density high, calculate time for signals

- Store the signals status in local database
- Display status of signals on web page

5.5   Test Results

- Signal lights are controlled automatically
- Density has detected and time is calculated according to density level as shown in algorithm
- Signals status has been stored in database through local server
- Signals status has been shown successfully on web page

Non-functional testing: As in the above step we checked the utilitarian test now we will prefer a non-utilitarian aspect of our software application. This will test various aspects like preparedness and keenness which could be never done in above evaluation.

Test objectives: System must be responsive and user interface should look good.

Test results: Interface looks good, and application is very responsive.

Traffic signals hardware output: First the prototype hardware tested with the code for a single signal at a junction. The picture shown in Figure 5.6 depicts the output of green, yellow, red lights at a signal. The signal has

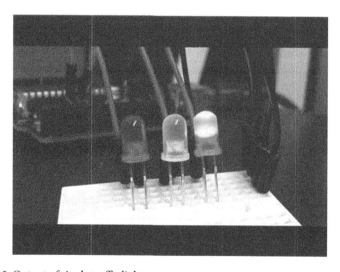

Figure 5.6 Output of single traffic light prototype.

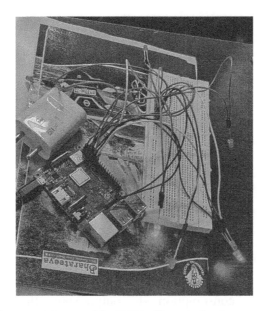

Figure 5.7 Hardware prototype model of IoT traffic control system.

been transferring continuously between three lights. According to the signals vehicles on that lane will follow traffic rules.

Timings for the traffic lights have been calculated based on the density, according to the algorithm that we have mentioned. Now signals are controlled by the raspberry pi according to density. Figure 5.7 shows the hardware prototype model of IoT traffic control system.

Database outputs: Here we used database that has been created through MySQL to store the status of signals which helps in displaying data in web page. The data stored in this database have been sent to web page through local server that has been created through Wamp server. Figure 5.8 shows the status of traffic signals stored in database.

Outputs from the webpage: The data stored in database are retrieved to the web page through the local server that has been created using Wamp server. This picture shows the four traffic signals at a junction in an inactive state. This picture depicts the signals at traffic junction and is in active state with zero density, i.e., no vehicles are recognized at any lane. This output shows the status of signals present at the traffic junction when recognized density. This helps in knowing the status of signals at every traffic junction before we reach or go to that location. This helps in minimizing the wastage of time by waiting in traffic. This also helps in reducing pollution and

Figure 5.8 Status of traffic signals stored in database.

minimizes the fuel consumption. This output shows the status of signals present at every traffic junction when recognized density at some signals. This helps in knowing the status of signals at every traffic junction before we reach or go to that location. This helps in minimizing the wastage of time by waiting in traffic. The traffic statuses are shown in the Figures 5.9–5.12.

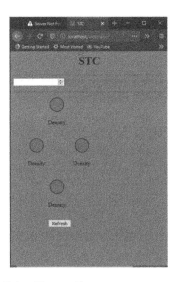

Figure 5.9 Status of traffic lights (Output 1).

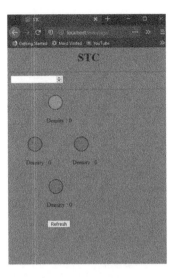

Figure 5.10 Status of traffic lights when density is 0 (Output 2).

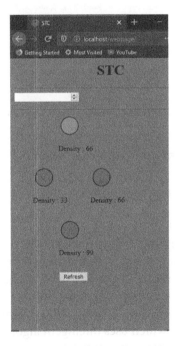

Figure 5.11 Status of traffic lights when density is not zero (Output 3).

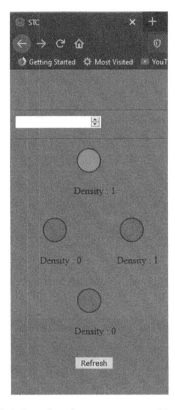

Figure 5.12 Status of traffic lights when density is not zero (Output 4).

5.6 Conclusions

This paper grants an impressive quick fix for rise of traffic problems in urban areas. As our existing methods were not enough to cope with the ever-increasing traffic the humanity is facing, here we tried to develop a state of art traffic management system which will beat the old methods we are using by a significant margin. This will work by evaluating the traffic density and it also interlinks all the junctions to the local server database which in return make our algorithm more effective. The main ambition of this paper is to recommend a well-equipped traffic management algorithm which takes help of IoT which uses intelligent algorithms to provide better results. Our proposed algorithm is outperforming the accuracy of previous traffic management algorithms. By paying a look at our website the civilians can have information regarding the traffic in the city.

Our algorithm gives conclusions based on flexible, density, and supremacy conditions. It also provides access to website which will be useful to roads authority for expansion of roads. With the help of IoT we can get drastic improvements in logistics, automobile parking, courier services, tragic accidents, etc. Civilian road blockades, fire accidents, and emergency situations can be better handled by our smart algorithms than our existing system. And we can also anticipate that the prices of sensors will reduce in future.

Internet of Things is overwhelming the transportation sector by creating smart transportation system. It helps in improvement of security, safety, emergency services, traffic management, etc. Intelligent implementing GPS feature in it. It improves the delivery system. Implementing ITS can automate the entire transportation system. Increasing accidents and congestion requires a better transportation system that consists of sensors and microprocessor. These result in improvement of delivery, logistics, fleet management, and all sectors that depend on the transportation sector.

References

1. Lee, W.-H. and Chiu, C.-Y., Design and Implementation of a Smart Traffic Signal Control System for Smart City Applications. *Sensors*, 20, 508, 2020.
2. Javaid, S., Sufian, A., Pervaiz, S., Tanveer, M., Smart traffic management system using Internet of Things. *20th International Conference on Advanced Communication Technology (ICACT)*, IEEE xplore, 2018.
3. Rath, M., Smart Traffic Management System for Traffic Control using Automated Mechanical and Electronic Devices. *IOP Conf. Series: Materials Science and Engineering*, vol. 377, p. 012201, 2018.
4. Chandana, K.K.1., Meenakshi Sundaram2, Dr. S., Cyana, D. sa1, Swamy 1, M.N., Navya, K., Eng. Technol., J., A Smart Traffic Management System for Congestion Control and Warnings Using Internet of Things (IoT). *Saudi J. Eng. Technol.*, 2, 5, 192–196, May, 2017.
5. Kumari1, A., Patil2, D., Maurya3, V., Phalle4, S., Hule5, S., Smart Traffic Management System Using Resource Sharing. *Int. Res. J. Eng. Technol. (IRJET)*, 04, 04, 335–338, Apr -2017.

6

Differential Query Execution on Privacy Preserving Data Distributed Over Hybrid Cloud

Sridhar Reddy Vulapula[1]*, P. V. S. Srinivas[2] and Jyothi Mandala[3]

[1]Department of IT, Vignana Bharathi Institute of Technology,
Hyderabad, Telangana, India
[2]Department of CSE, Vignana Bharathi Institute of Technology,
Hyderabad, Telangana, India
[3]Department of CSE, Christ University, Bangalore, Karnataka, India

Abstract

Hybrid cloud is proposed as a solution for ensuring security and privacy for data outsourced to cloud. Hybrid cloud uses a mix of both private and public cloud with distribution of sensitive information to private cloud and insensitive information to public cloud. Though data distributed over multi storage provides enhanced security and privacy, query performance is distorted. This work proposes a privacy preserving data distribution with goal of ensuring reduced query latency for data distributed over hybrid clouds without any compromise to the security and privacy. The proposed solution also provides different queries results for the query depending on the access control provided to the users.

Keywords: Hybrid cloud, privacy, query, perturbation, cryptography, access control, security, data distribution

6.1 Introduction

Enterprise are rapidly offloading data storage to cloud due to various benefits like reduced capital and operational expenditure, higher availability, etc. Storage offloading to cloud also introduces various challenges of security and privacy. Towards ensuring the security and privacy, many mechanisms

---

Corresponding author: vsridharreddy19@gmail.com

Budati Anil Kumar, S. B. Goyal and Sardar M.N. Islam. Cognitive Computing Models in Communication Systems, (107–122) © 2022 Scrivener Publishing LLC

have been proposed. These mechanisms are in categories of: Anonymization, Randomization, Cryptographic Techniques, Diversification, and Aggregation. But these approaches have limits on scalability and performance. Recently, hybrid cloud is proposed to address these limits on scalability and performance. Hybrid cloud combines both trusted private cloud and un-trusted public cloud. Sensitive information like keys, sensitive attributes, etc., is distributed to private cloud. Insensitive information is distributed to public cloud. Though hybrid cloud is promising solution to ensure security and privacy, it has performance bottlenecks in query processing.

Since the data is distributed over multiple stores, query processing spans across multiple stores. Query processing on multi store systems consists of three steps: query rewriting, optimization and execution, and translation and execution [1]. Each data store has different capabilities and these heterogeneous data capabilities make query optimization difficult. In the presence of heterogeneous cost modeling and strong environmental variations like failure of data store and variable latency in data access it becomes difficult to optimize the queries. Unlike SQL, there is no simple cost model for multi storage systems and this makes query optimization very difficult for hybrid cloud.

This work proposes query optimization strategy for data distributed over hybrid cloud without any compromise to the security and privacy of data distributed over hybrid clouds. The structured data is distributed across multiple cloud providers with consideration of multiple objectives of security, privacy, and query performance. The data distribution is made dynamic considering the heterogeneous processing capabilities of cloud providers. Fine grained access control over result of the queries is done, such that there is no leakage of information beyond the access control provided to the query users. Following are the contributions of the solution:

1. Data transformation strategy enabling differential query results for same query depending on access control of users
2. A multi-objective data distribution strategy over hybrid cloud with joint consideration for security, privacy, and query performance
3. Differential query results for the same query depending on access provided to the users

6.2   Related Work

Fabian *et al.* [2] proposed a scheme for data partitioning across semi-trusted clouds using cryptographic secret sharing. Though the method provides stronger security, the query execution performance is poor. Before executing any queries, the shares distributed across multiple clouds need to reassembled and this creates a huge overhead and query latency. Achampong *et al.* [3] proposed a scheme for encrypting the data using attribute-based encryption (ABE) before offloading to a cloud. Before execution of any queries, the data need to be decrypted and this creates query latency. Sun *et al.* [4] proposed a searchable encryption scheme based data offloading scheme for cloud. The data to be stored in cloud is encrypted using the searchable encryption scheme and the access to search is controlled using ABE. But the scheme does not provide any differential control over query results. Yang *et al.* [5] proposed a privacy preserving data partitioning solution for cloud. The solution also implemented a cryptography-based hybrid search over the partitioned data. But the solution has restrictions over the types of queries and query latency is higher. Kao *et al.* [6] proposed privacy preserving data perturbation scheme based on grouping adjacent data values. Query results are inaccurate without restoration and restoration results in query inefficiency. Li *et al.* [7] proposed a multi cloud data offloading architecture with private cloud as access interface and public cloud for data storage. The architecture supports fuzzy keyword search to speed up the query but at compromise of accuracy of query result. Zhang *et al.* [8] proposed a privacy preserving data publishing system using an extended quasi-identifier-partitioning scheme. The solution is able to provide differential privacy for query but at compromise of loss of information. Lyu *et al.* [9] proposed a two-stage data perturbation scheme called RG + RP. The higher dimensional data are transformed to lower dimensional data in a distance preserving manner. The data are more suitable for distance based queries but are not suitable for exact queries. Chen *et al.* [10] proposed a geometric data perturbation scheme involving three stages of random rotation, translation, and noise addition to ensure privacy preserving data storage in cloud. The perturbation ensures only distance preservation and suitable only for distance based queries. Yuan *et al.* [11] optimized the query execution using fast indexing mechanism. An encrypted high-performance index is constructed by processing the dataset and kept in a cloud. The query is encrypted and search against encrypted index is done to provide query result. Majeed *et al.* [12] proposed a secure data transformation scheme for cloud in which original values of data are replaced with average values. This data transformation is one way and transformation cannot be brought to original state. Though the query execution is faster in this work, the results are in average and not exact value.

Ramadhan *et al.* [13] proposed a query execution approach for data distributed across multiple data stores. The query is split to sub queries and each of the sub queries are executed on different stores. The results are then merged using join operations. The scheduling of queries is based on cost model. Forresi *et al.* [14] proposed a query processing model for data distributed across multi stores. The approach supports both relational and document-based data models. The query is mapped to execution plan and executed on the data stores. The results are then merged, but the approach does not select the best execution plan based on cost and execution time. Kranas *et al.* [15] exploited the parallel processing capabilities to speed up the query processing in multi stores. The query is transformed to a parallel execution plan. The transformation made by the optimizer involves replacing table scans with parallel table scans, and adding shuffle operators to make sure that, in stateful operators (such as Group By, or Join), related rows are handled by the same worker. Parallel table scans will divide the rows from the base tables among all workers. The solution works only on relational table model which is partitioned across multiple stores. Also parallelism is considered without any cost factor; due to this resource cost for execution of query can be higher. An adaptive query execution plan with goal of reducing response time and monetary cost is proposed by Wang *et al.* [16]. The query is converted to a multi stage query execution plan. Each stage is executed and plans for further stages are adjusted based on the response time and monetary cost. But the method is suitable for certain queries and there is privacy control on query execution.

6.3   Proposed Solution

The architecture of proposed solution is given in Figure 6.1. The proposed solution involves the following components:

1. Data transformation
2. Data distribution in hybrid clouds
3. Query execution

6.3.1   Data Transformation

The data to be uploaded by the owner is in tabular format with each column representing an attribute.

The data owner defines the sensitive attribute in the data. This sensitive attribute must be transformed. The transformation must be done in such a way to provide differential view to user as desired by the data owner.

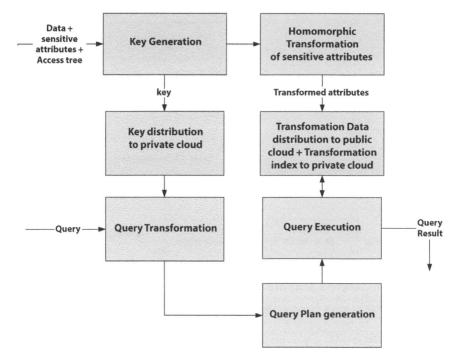

Figure 6.1 Proposed architecture.

This differential view is based on generalization. As seen from Figure 6.2, actual survey area is a sensitive information which needs to presented at various level of generalization for different user as desired by the data owner. At the topmost level of generalization, the survey area must be presented as complete transformed to the user. At the lowest level of generalization, the actual survey area is presented to the user. At the intermediate levels, the generalization label as desired by owner is presented to the user. Domain expert designs the generalization tree for all sensitive attributes and keeps the sensitive index in the private cloud. The data owner defines the access tree T (Figure 6.3). When a data user's attributes match the partial access structure, he can decrypt the data that associate with that level.

The access index of form $\{\langle T_1, Level\ x \rangle, \supset \langle T_n, Level\ x \rangle\}$ where for each tree, the level of view for the user is defined. This access index is maintained in the private cloud. Homomorphic encryption keys generated for each level $\{ck_{l0}, ck_{l1}, ..ck_{ln}\}$ are encrypted using AHAC CP-ABE algorithm [17].

AHAC CP-ABE encryption algorithm takes the access tree for each level and the homomorphic keys for each level as input and encrypts

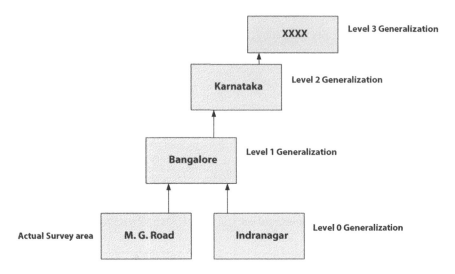

Figure 6.2 An example of generalization tree.

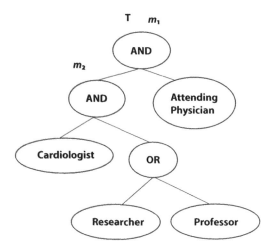

Figure 6.3 Access tree.

the homomorphic keys. AHAC CP-ABE decryption takes the level attributes and the encrypted homomorphic keys as input and provides the corresponding homomorphic key for the levels matching to level attributes and the level (It). From the symmetric key, the encrypted token $eck_{l0}, eck_{l1}, ..eck_{ln}\}$ at level is decrypted using the corresponding key ck_{lt}

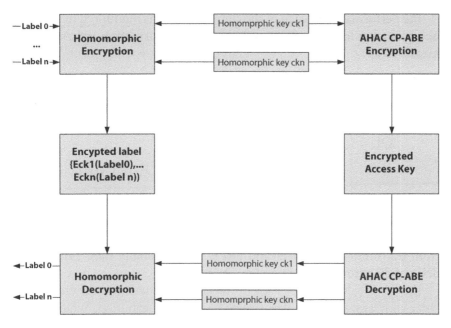

Figure 6.4 Encryption and decryption of keys using AHAC.

with homomorphic decryption algorithm. The encryption and decryption flow using AHAC CP-ABE is given in Figure 6.4.

Each of the sensitive attribute or column in the dataset is replaced with columns for each level and the attribute values in those columns are replaced with homomorphically encrypted labels of the corresponding levels. By this way a single column is replaced to N transformed columns where N is the number of levels. A mapping is maintained between the original attributes and the transformed columns are kept in a transformation index. This transformation index is kept in the private cloud.

6.3.2 Data Distribution

The hybrid cloud has single private cloud and multiple public clouds. The dataset rows can arrive in different batch from owner and this must be transformed. While the transformation index and keys are maintained in the private cloud, the transformed data must be kept at public cloud. With availability of multiple cloud providers with different security and performance, it becomes necessary to select the best among the public cloud for offloading transformed data.

The performance of each of the cloud provider is monitored in terms of query latency for each query per volume of information returned. It is measured as

$$QL = \begin{cases} \displaystyle\sum_{i=0}^{\infty} f_i(a).f_i(b) , x = 0 \\ \displaystyle\sum_{i=0}^{\infty} f_i(a).f_{2x+i}(b) + \sum_{i=0}^{\infty} f_i(b).f_{2x+i}(a), x > 0 \end{cases}$$

Where a, b are forward (query) and backward directions (query retrieval) from transmitter to receiver and f(z) is the probability mass function of delay of direction z.

The QL is calculated for each of the cloud provider and the cloud provider with least value of QL is selected for data distribution. When data is distributed, the information about data distribution is kept in a distribution index. This distribution index is maintained in the private cloud.

6.3.3   Query Execution

The query given by user is first transformed at the private cloud. Before transformation, the attributes of the user is passed to AHAC CP-ABE decryption algorithm to get the level of the user and the corresponding homomorphic key (Lx)

The query is formed of:

Select Attribute from Data where [Attribute1==value 1 (and | or) Attributen==value n]

The attributes in the query are replaced with the actual transformation columns. The value given for matching in the query is homomorphically encrypted with the key Lx. The transformed query is of the form:

Select T(Attribute) from Data where [T(Attribute1)==HE(value 1,Lx) (and | or) T(Attributen)==HE(value n,Lx)]

Where HE is the homomorphic encryption and T is the transformation of attribute to corresponding column using the transformation index in private cloud.

The transformed query is given to multi-clouds where the rows corresponding to Data are maintained. The rows are found using the distribution index maintained in the private cloud.

Each of the multi-clouds provides receiving the transformation query, executes the query, and returns the result to the private cloud. Private cloud does the joining of the result and the return of the result to the querying user.

Since attributes in the query are replaced with transformed columns based on access level of the user, for the same query, different results are returned at various generalization levels depending on the access level provided by the owner. By this way differential query processing is enabled in this work. Also when user provides attribute value not in his access level, the query will fail; thus, there is stronger control on what information can be viewed the user.

6.4   Novelty in the Proposed Solution

The proposed solution has following novelties:

1. Data owner has more control on what access he wants to provide to the users. Using the generalization level, fine-grained information can be provided to user depending on his access level.
2. Data distribution to multi cloud is controlled based on the past query execution performance. Thereby query latency is reduced.

6.5   Results

The performance of the proposed privacy-preserving data distribution in hybrid cloud is compared in different aspects of:

1. Perturbation efficiency
2. Data storage and retrieval efficiency
3. Security against attacks

The performance of the proposed solution is tested against arrhythmia dataset [18].

The perturbation efficiency of the proposed solution is compared against geometric data perturbation (GP) proposed in [20] and RG + RP algorithm proposed in [19]. The original data and the perturbed data are clustered using K-means clustering algorithm. The clusters of original and perturbed are compared in terms of clustering accuracy.

The clustering accuracy is calculated as:

$$ACC = \frac{1}{N} \sum_{i=1}^{k} \left(\left| Cluster_i\left(P\right) \right| - \left| Cluster_i\left(P'\right) \right| \right)$$

where P is the original data, P' is the transformed data, k is the number of clusters, and N is the number of items in the dataset. The value of k is varied in the K-mean clustering and the results for clustering accuracy are given below:

K	Clustering accuracy in RG + RP [19]	Clustering accuracy in GP [20]	Proposed
2	66.23	65.89	68.52
3	66.56	71.25	75.62
4	73.33	74.59	78.85
5	67.22	79.58	82.34

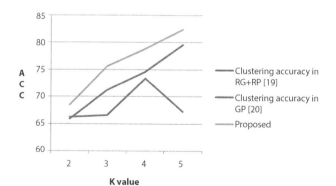

The average clustering accuracy in proposed solution is 8% higher compared to RG + RP [19] and 3.51% higher compared to GP [20]. Use of homomorphic encryption in proposed solution has ensured better distance preservation in the proposed solution. Due to this accuracy is higher in the proposed solution.

The data upload time which includes data transformation and data distribution to cloud is measured for various volumes of data and the result is given below.

	Upload time (sec)		
Size (MB)	Proposed	GP [20]	RG + RP [19]
20	15	18	21
40	26	34	37
60	48	59	63
80	87	110	120
Average	44	55.25	60.25

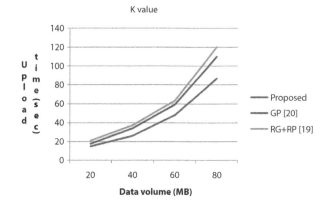

The average upload time in proposed solution is 20.36% lower compared to GP [20] and 36.93% lower compared to RG+RP [19]. Comparatively lower transformation head and migrating to cloud with least latency has reduced the data upload time in the proposed solution.

The query retrieval time is measured for different volume of data and the result is given below:

	Retrieval time (sec)		
Size (MB)	Proposed	GP [20]	RG + RP [19]
20	14	19	22
40	24	35	38
60	43	61	64
80	78	112	122
Average	39.75	56.75	61.5

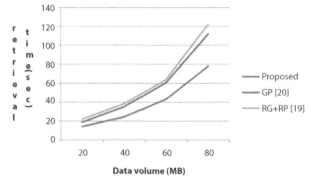

The average retrieval time in the proposed solution is at least 29.95% lower compared to GP [20] and 35.36% lower compared to RG+RP [19]. The data retrieval time is faster, because query execution is done in encrypted domain without any de-transformation in the proposed solution.

The security of the proposed solution is evaluated in terms of difficulty level of estimating the original data from the perturbed data by an attacker who steals the perturbed data from the cloud.

Variance of difference-based approach is used for estimating the difficulty level. Let the difference between the original column data and the estimated data be a random variable Di. Without any knowledge about the original data, the mean and variance of the difference present the quality of the estimation. Since the mean of difference can be easily removed if the attacker can estimate the original distribution of column, we use only the variance of the difference (VoD) as the primary metric to determine the level of difficulty in estimating the original data.

Let X_i be a random variable representing the column i, X_i' be the estimated result of X_i and difference $D_i = X' - X$. Let mean of D be $E(D_i)$ and variance be $Var(D_i)$. VOD for column i is $Var(D_i)$. VOD is measured for each column and average VOD is given as privacy measure (pm).

$$pm = \frac{\sum_{i=1}^{N} VOD_i}{N}$$

A guess is launched for 5 hours on the perturbed data and the privacy measure (pm) is measured for every 1-hour interval and plotted below:

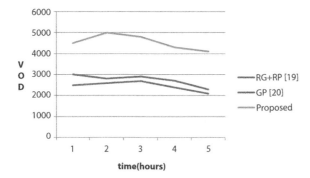

The VOD is higher in the proposed solution compared to RG + RP [19] and GP [20]. Higher VOD indicates that it is very difficult to find a nearest estimation of original data from the perturbed data. The VOD has increased in the proposed solution due to generalized level transformation before homomorphic encryption.

6.6   Conclusion

In this work, a privacy preserving data distribution method with goal of ensuring reduced query latency for data distributed over hybrid clouds without any compromise to the security and privacy is proposed.

The scheme uses multiple concepts of generalization based transformation, homomorphic encryption, AHAC CP-ABE, and different query results. The proposed solution is able to provide at least 29.95% lower query execution time compared to existing works without any compromise to privacy and security. Also the approach is able to provide differential query processing for same query depending on access control rights offered to query user. The query plan is formulated only for optimization of query latency in this work. Extending the work for multi cloud with different cost and query plan formation with cost factor is in scope of future work.

References

1. Bondiombouy, C. and Valduriez, P., *Query Processing in Multistore Systems: an overview. [Research Report] RR-8890*, p. 38, INRIA Sophia Antipolis - Méditerranée, France, 2016.
2. Fabian, B., Collaborative and secure sharing of healthcare data in multi-clouds", Information systems, Algorithms 2014, in: *Energy Efficient Routing in Wireless Sensor Networks Through Balanced Clustering*, Nikolidakis, S.A., Vergados, D.D., Douligeris, C. (Eds.), 2013.
3. Achampong, E. and Dzidonu, C., Optimising attribute-based encryption to secure electronic health records system within a cloud computing environment, *International Journal of Computer Science*, 3, 27-34, 2016.
4. Sun J, Wang X, Wang S, Ren L., A searchable personal health records framework with fine-grained access control in cloud-fog computing. *PLoS ONE* 13(11):e0207543, 2018.
5. Yang, J., Li, J., Niu, Y., A hybrid solution for privacy preserving medical data sharing in the cloud environment. *Future Gener. Comput. Syst.*, 43-44, 2, 7486, 2015.
6. Kao, Y.-H., Lee, W.-B., Hsu, T.-Y., Lin, C.-Y., Tsai, H.-F., Chen, T.-S., Data perturbation method based on contrast mapping for reversible privacy-preserving data mining. *J. Med. Biol. Eng.*, 35, 6, 789-794, 2015. 35.10.1007/s40846-015-0088-6
7. Li, J., Li, J., Chen, X., Liu, Z., Jia, C., Privacy preserving data utilization in hybrid clouds. *Future Gener. Comput. Syst.*, 30, 98–106, 2014.
8. Zhang, H., Zhou, Z., Ye, L., Du, X., Towards privacy preserving publishing of set-valued data on hybrid cloud. *IEEE Trans. Cloud Comput.*, 6, 2, 316–329, 1 April-June 2018.
9. Lyu, L., Bezdek, J., Law, Y.W., He, X., Palaniswami, M., Privacy-preserving collaborative fuzzy clustering. *Data Knowl. Eng.*, 116, Issue C, 21–41, 2018. 10.1016/j.datak.2018.05.002.
10. Chen, K., Sun, G., Liu, L., Towards attack-resilient geometric data perturbation, *Proceedings of the Seventh SIAM International Conference on Data Mining*, Minneapolis, MN, 26-28, April 2007. 10.1137/1.9781611972771.8.
11. Yuan, X., Wang, X., Wang, C., Weng, J., Ren, K., Enabling secure and fast indexing for privacy-assured healthcare monitoring via compressive sensing. *IEEE Trans. Multimed*, 18, 10, 2002–2014, Oct. 2016.
12. Majeed, A., Attribute-centric anonymization scheme for improving user privacy and utility of publishing e-health data, *Journal of King Saud University - Computer and Information Sciences*, 2018.

13. Ramadhan, H., Indikawati, F., II, Kwon, J., Koo, B., MusQ: A multi-store query system for IoT data using a datalog-like Language. *IEEE Access*, 8, 58032–58056, 2020.

14. Forresi, C., Gallinucci, E., Golfarelli, M. *et al.*, A dataspace-based framework for OLAP analyses in a high-variety multistore. *VLDB J.*, 30, 1017–1040, 2021.

15. Kranas, P., Kolev, B., Levchenko, O., Pacitti, E., Valduriez, P., Jimenez-Peris, R., Patiño-Martínez, M., Parallel query processing in a polystore. *Distrib. Parallel Database*, 39, 4, 939–977, Dec 2021.

16. Wang, C., Arani, Z., Gruenwald, L., d'Orazio, L., Adaptive time, monetary cost aware query optimization on cloud database systems. *International workshop on Scalable Cloud Data Management (SCDM@BigData)*, Seattle, United States,. 3374–3382, Dec 2018.

17. He, H., Zheng, L., Li, P. *et al.*, An efficient attribute-based hierarchical data access control scheme in cloud computing. *Hum. Cent. Comput. Inf. Sci.*, 10, 49, 2020.

18. https://archive.ics.uci.edu/ml/datasets/Arrhythmia

19. Lyu, L., Bezdek, J.L., Wei, Y., He, X., Palaniswami, M., Privacy-preserving collaborative fuzzy clustering. *Data Knowl. Eng.*, 116 Issue C, 21–41, Jul 2018. 10.1016/j.datak.2018.05.002

20. Sridhar Reddy, V. and Thirumala Rao, B., A Combined clustering and geometric data perturbation approach for enriching privacy preservation of healthcare data in hybrid clouds. *Int. J. Eng. Syst.*, 11, 1, 201–210, Oct 2017.

7

Design of CMOS Base Band Analog

S. Pothalaiah[1], Dayadi Lakshmaiah[2]*, Bandi Doss[3], Nookala Sairam[4] and K. Srikanth[5]

[1]Professor of Electronics and Communication Engineering Dept., VBIT, Hyderabad, India
[2]Professor of Electronics and Communication Engineering Dept., Sri Indu Institute of Engineering and Technology, Hyderabad, India
[3]Professor of Electronics and Communication Engineering Dept., CMR Technical Campus, Hyderabad, India
[4]Professor of Electronics and Communication Engineering, KPRIT, Hyderabad, India
[5]Professor of Electronics and Communication Engineering, SIIET, Hyderabad, India

Abstract

A complementary metal–oxide semiconductor (CMOS) less-energy receiver baseband analog (BBA) Base band analog continuous analog circuit design found on irregular filter and level of the gain is described. The most effective allocation of the gain, noise figure (NF), and the input-referred third-order intercept point (IIP3) of every block was carried out to decrease utilization of power by using the specified guidelines of the analog block. The BBA receiver strip was manufactured on 0.18-μm CMOS generation and 30 dB of IIP3 with 55 dB of gain, and 31 dB of NF was acquired at energy utilization of 4.86 mW. It was used to decrease the consumption of power. The use of the Miller capacitance in the receiver BBA improved the phase margin for the operational amplifier (op-amp). This circuit was designed with micrometer CMOS generation with good gain and NF, which is very useful in communication systems.

Keywords: Gain, noise figure and phase margin

*Corresponding author: laxmanrecw@gmail.com

Budati Anil Kumar, S. B. Goyal and Sardar M.N. Islam. Cognitive Computing Models in Communication Systems, (123–136) © 2022 Scrivener Publishing LLC

7.1   Introduction

For the requirements of higher battery life and lower price results for wireless personal area networks (PANs) that are IEEE802.15.4, a complementary metal–oxide semiconductor (CMOS) lessen energy single chip receiver draws high consideration [1]. For a lower price and lower energy solution, the direct conversion receiver (DCR) is one of numerous receiver constructions.

In a DCR, as represented in Figure 7.1, band blockers without filtering go to baseband levels. For this reason, excessive linearity and overall execution of the analog circuit are needed for dealing with interferers. Additionally, the band interferer is going to limit the accepted gain of the radiofrequency (RF) front-end, and the consequence noise results problems. Considering that the input-referred third-order intercept point (IIP3) and the noise are linear to the utilization of direct current (DC) energy, it is a great task to acquire reduced excessive linearity and lower disturbance overall completion at less energy utilization.

This paper proposed the ultimate allocation of noise figure (NF), IIP3, gain of filtering, and gain level in a baseband analog (BBA) chain and proposed reducing modern utilization of the total BBA chain for the needed requirement.

The receiver BBA circuit was created and manufactured using the 0.18-μm CMOS technology. The receiver BBA with a low-energy layout approach was fully defined and the manufacturing outcomes were stated.

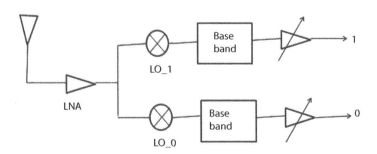

Figure 7.1 Base band analog (BBA) circuit for direct conversion receiver (DCR) low-noise amplifier (LNA).

7.2 Proposed Technique of the BBA Chain for Reducing Energy Consumption

The IIP3 and NF overall working of the RX (receiver) rely on the blocks of linearity and external and internal disturbances, in addition to the gain. Here filtering observed with the of gain level hold back of channel relaxes, interferes linearity necessity of gain level. However, a low-noise channel selection filter is compulsory.

Here gain level observed by means of filtering level loosen LPF noise necessities stressful excessive proportionality amplifier, the shape of the quality disturbance overall working results in the waste proportionality achievement; in addition, a shape with the excessive gradually rising results in horrific noise completion.

To maximize the performance of linearity and noise, greater delivery of power is needed for use inside the constructing block; this is not a good method because current utilization needs to be reduced. A satisfactory method to constructing the highest quality BBA chain is to change the filter and advantage levels [2]. This permits higher alternates between the NF and linearity for every level.

The energy consumption is reduced for the desired requirement, the dealings among linearity, NF in power utilization want to be understandable. In this paper, the more level BBA chain includes one cell filter and a gain feature. The BBA chain version includes two cells, shown in Figure 7.2, which may be extended to two or more levels [4–12].

The metal–oxide semiconductor field-effect transistor (MOSFET) $I - V$ output theoretically in channel is shown below.

$$I_d = (W/2L)\, \mu_{eff} C_{ox} (V_{GT}^2/1 + \theta\, V_{GT}^2) \tag{7.1}$$

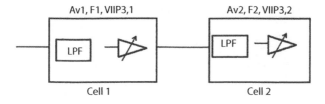

Figure 7.2 Base band analog (BBA) strip that changes the filters and gain levels. Low pass filter (LPF).

where $\theta = 1/(E_{sat} \times L)$ and $V_{GT} = V_{GS} - V_t$. W is the width, E_{sat} is the saturation, V_t is the thermal voltage, L is the length, C_{ox} is oxide capacitance, and I_d is the drain current.

Analyzing [3], the input IIP3 of the MOSFET can be determined as below.

$$V_{IIP3} \approx (8V_{GT}/3\theta) = KV_{GT} \tag{7.2}$$

$K = 8/3\theta$-(4) by utilizing the link in (4). The IIP3 PGA filter with feedback(f/b) is shown by:

The above circuit shows the two-stage op-amp with an active load and transistor of the first stage followed by the second stage. These levels are the gain stage and the filter stage, respectively. Figure 7.3 displays the design of a two-level op-amp utilized in programmable amplifiers and filters. Here, primary level transistors are categorized and well to decrease flicker disturbance frequency. By use of Miller capacitance 1.2 Pico farad, and resistor 11 kilo ohm are produces zero for left plane and also improve the phase margin for op amp. Here, the I_{total} drain for the op-amp was identical up to 112 mA. One problem is for common mode CMFB design is stable performance, and for supply restoration Resistances are utilized [11, 12].

$$V^2_{IIP3} = KV_{GT}(1 + |A_o/A_v|)^3 \tag{7.3}$$

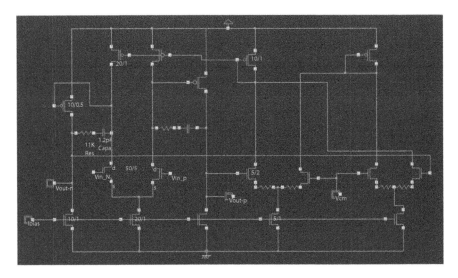

Figure 7.3 Two-level operational amplifier (op-amp).

where A_o is the gain of the open loop and A_v is the gain of the closed loop.

Here, both the "R" and the op-amp add to the noise in the resistor–capacitor (RC) filter. Figure 7.3 shows the utilization of the input noise of the two-level op-amp in this structure. It is defined by using the transistor and load of the first stage as below.

$$V^2_n/\Delta f = 8kT\gamma/g_{mn}(1 + (g_{mp}/g_{mn}))$$ (7.4)

where g_m is the transconductance.

Here, $\gamma \geq 3/2$. The NF of the above design w.r here to R_s is

$$NF = 1 + (1/g_m R_s)\,(\gamma + (1/A_v))$$ (7.5)

Here, the IIP3 and NF of every level are related to the current utilization by spurious-free dynamic range (SFDR), as below.

$$SFDR = (IIP3/F \cdot kTB)^{2/3} \approx (KI/kTB\,(\gamma + 1/A_v))^{2/3}(1 + |A_o/A_v|)^2$$ (7.6)

where K is the Boltzmann constant.

The current utilization of every level is

$$I = (1/2R_s K)\,(\gamma + 1/A_v)(V^2_{IIP3}/F)\,(1 + |A_o/A_v|)^{-3}$$ (7.7)

where A_o is the open-loop gain and A_v is the closed-loop gain.

The I_{total} utilization of the BBA chain is shown below.

$$I_{total} = \Sigma^2_{n=1}(1/2R_s K)\,(\gamma + 1/A_{vn})(V^2_{IIP3.n}/F_n)\,(1 + |A_o/A_{vn}|)^{-3}$$ (7.8)

Here, the dynamic range, DR (change in volume), of a cascaded level is determined by the n/f (NF), gain, and the IIP3 of every level, as follows:

$$1/DR = F/V_{IIP3} = (F_1 + ((F_2 - 1)/A^2_{v1})\,((1/V^2_{IIP3,1}) + (A^2_{v1}/V^2_{IIP3,2}))$$

$$= (1/DR_1) + (1/DR_2) + (F_1 A^2_{v1}/V^2_{IIP3,2}) + ((F_2 - 1)/A^2_{v1})\,(1/V^2_{IIP3,1})$$ (7.9)

Here, the DR of the total stages in cascaded level was increased using the following equation.

$$A^2_{v1} = ((F_2 \times V^2_{IIP3,2}) \, / \, (F_1 \times V^2_{IIP3,1}))^{1/2} \qquad (7.10)$$

In contrast to the amplifier, the third-order intermodulation consists of input tones. Here, two-tone interferers are present in the stop band and compressed or changed through the filter. With the aid of the preceding stages, the gain level and the IIP3 after the filter level were efficiently extended for the compression of interferers. Here, E_f is described by $VIIP_3^2$ (filtering before). $E_F = VIIP_3^2$ (after) using Equation 10, rewritten as below.

$$I_{total} = (1/2R_sK)\,(\gamma + 1/A_{v1})\,(4V^2_{IIP3}/F)\,(1+|A_o/A_{v1}|)^{-3} + ((1/2R_sK)$$

$$(\gamma + 1/A_{v1})\,(4V^2_{IIP3}/F \times E_f)\,(1 + |(A_{v1} \times A)/A_{total}|)^{-3}) \qquad (7.11)$$

where I_{total} is the total current, A_o is the open-loop gain, and A_v is the closed-loop gain.

The most reliable gain of Av_1 was acquired to reduce the current utilization for the design of the overall gain, NF, and IIP3. The common I_{total} utilization of the BBA chain vs. the cell gain is shown in Figure 7.4. The gain of channel A_{total} was 58 dB and the op-amp A_o was 77 dB. As displayed in Figure 7.5, the I_{total} utilization for BBA is stricken to desire gain of cell 1 because of trade-off among the IIP3 and NF.

Figure 7.6 shows the diagrammatic view of the RC filter with low-pass filters 1 and 2. These filters are the fourth- and second-order Butterworth

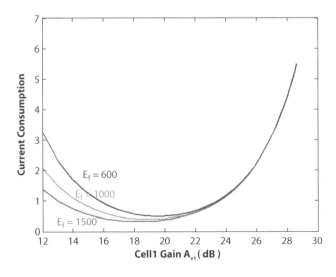

Figure 7.4 Current utilization vs. A_{v1}.

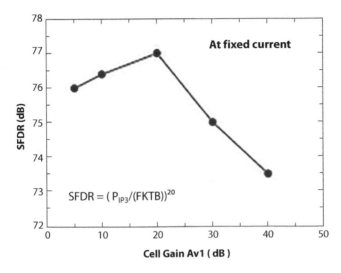

Figure 7.5 Simulation results for the transistor circuit-level spurious-free dynamic range (SFDR) *vs.* A_{v1} at a fixed I_{total} utilization.

(LPF$_1$) and Chebyshev (LPF$_2$) low-pass filters, respectively, due to the trade-off between group delay (GD) and stop band alteration. Because of the proportionality passive elements and the heavy-gain op-amps, the dynamic passive element filter is extremely proportional. These regular executions of LPF$_1$ and LPF$_2$ are shown Figures 7.6a and b, respectively.

The I_{total} utilization was decreased on A_{v1} of 20 dB, represented in Figure 7.4. E_f is steady component follows with respect to filter level and better E_f results in a decreased I_{total} utilization. However, the filter level is restricted with the aid of standard NF necessities.

The simulation outcomes of SFDR *vs.* A_{v1} are at constant I_{total} utilization, seen in Figure 7.5. The SFDR was acquired on a gain of 20 dB. For a decrease of "I" utilization, the common requirements end in identical outcomes and increase the normal SFDR in the specified "I" utilization.

The planned BBA chain is primarily shown in Figure 7.2. This is going to change the LPF levels along the PGA. With 35 dB of gain within the RF component, nearly gain 40 decibels of range for the receiver desires to supplied by the BBA chain. For this outcome, the PGA range is roughly between 18 and 53 dB with results of 2 dB. The most efficient proposed layout approach, with the greatest distribution of the layout parameters for every level with minimal current utilization at the needed requirement of the BBA, is detailed in the above table.

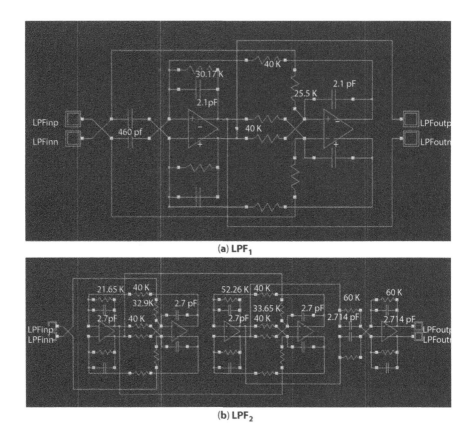

(a) LPF$_1$

(b) LPF$_2$

Figure 7.6 Diagrammatic representation of the resistor–capacitor (RC) filter. (a) Low-pass filter 1. (b) Low-pass filter 2.

7.3   Channel Preference Filter

This preference filter needs to offer the desired selection. A regular execution of the filter is for less disturbance in order to reduce the general receiving disturbances to determine the linearity sufficient to restrict the receiving of IIP$_3$. Here, the filter energy loss is an additionally essential parameter in low-energy applications.

Here PGA is programmable gain amplifier; these are used in receiver for communication of less power consumption of less power. On this layout, the fourth- and second-order Butterworth (LPF$_1$) and Chebyshev (LPF$_2$) low-pass filters were chosen due to the trade-off between GD and stop band alteration. Moreover, the first-order all-passing filter was needed for GD standardization. Because of the proportionality passive elements and the heavy-gain op-amps, the dynamic passive element filter was extremely

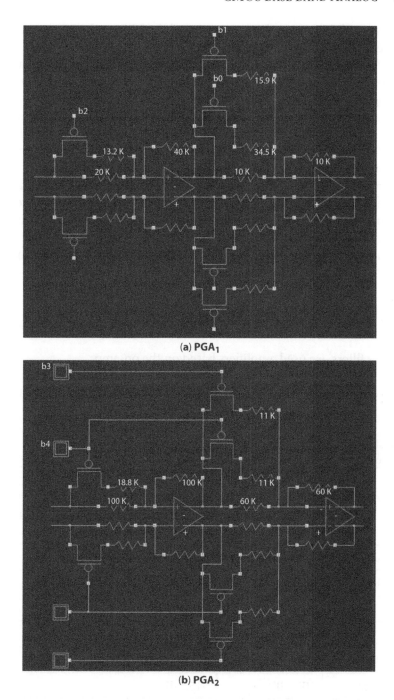

(a) PGA₁

(b) PGA₂

Figure 7.7 Diagrammatic representation of the programmable gain amplifier (PGA). (a) PGA$_1$. (b) PGA$_2$.

proportional. These regular executions of the LPF_1 and LPF_2 are seen in Figures 7.7a and b, respectively.

Every op-amp has to operate an R&C load, which calls for using a two-level op-amp. Figure 7.3 displays the design of the two-level op-amp utilized in programmable amplifiers and filters. Here, the primary-level transistors that decrease the flicker disturbance frequency are categorized. The use of a Miller capacitance of 1.2 pF and resistor of 11 kΩ produced zero for the left half-plane and also improved the phase margin for the op-amp. The I_{total} drain for the op-amp was identical up to 112 mA. One problem in CMFB design is its stable performance, and for supply restoration R's are utilized.

Every "C" here has a collection of digitally managed control utilized for making variable filters. Every unit capacitor within the filter has a five-bit collection of C's, and 50% varying variety was carried out to sufficiently conquer RC behavior changes. And variable speed of this process same as 3%, it is ideal sufficient.

7.4   Programmable Amplifier Gain

In these filters, we used amplifiers based on the op-amp.

Because of exceptional proportionality overall working, this PGA used on layout are seen in Figure 7.7. By swapping the f/b R's and the R's inside

Table 7.1 Power layout elements at essential base band analog (BBA) requirements.

		Cell 1		Cell 2	
		LPF_1	PGA_1	LPF_2	PGA_2
	Filter	2nd		4th	
Sub-block	Gain order (dB)	3 dB	6–20	3	0–32
Spec.	IIP_3 (dB)	21.5 dB	−3.5	16.5	−27
	NF	34 dB	31	49	46
	Filter level	6th			
BBA	Gain (dB)	12–58 db			
Spec.	IIP_3 (dB)	>15.5 dB			
	NF	<35.7 dB			

the frontward direction, the distinctive gains are found. All gain varieties between 12 and 58 dB with a period of 2 dB and gain segregation for the BBA are shown in Table 7.1. The gain of the PGA is in decibel modification proportionality with phrase management by means of a digitally managed five-bit transfer.

The maximum gain was approximately 58 dB in the baseband, the output (O/P) offset for the baseband filters desires to compensate with the D_{in}. For DC offset deletion, a servo meter was used. The offset of the DC was eliminated by using the measurement of the offset of the O/P and subtracting it from the input (I/P). In the PGA, we used a f/b integrator to maintain a steady high-pass F_C for distinct gain.

7.5   Executed Outcomes

The BBA design including a PGA and filters was fabricated with a D_{in} of 0.18 ml poly-6-metal complimentary MOS method. The microphotograph of the BBA can be seen in Figure 7.8. The BBA structure consists of a PGA and filters, and the bias design was 1.5 mm².

The receiver BBA response is shown in Figure 7.9 above. Here, the f_c (cutoff frequency) was sort of identical at different gains between 12 and 55 dB. The simulation response of the design is seen in and near the known measured value. The characteristics of this design, with different phrases, are displayed in Figure 7.10. The benefit of the amplifier gains with

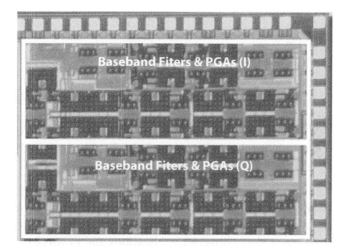

Figure 7.8 Microphotograph of the baseband design.

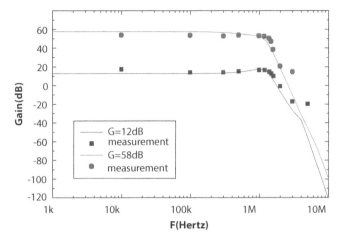

Figure 7.9 Graph between the frequency (in hertz) and gain (in decibels) of the receiver baseband analog (BBA).

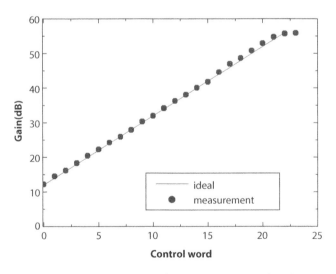

Figure 7.10 Gain programmable working of the receiver baseband analog (BBA).

programmable decibel modification proportionality with manage mistakes of gain was lower than 0.7 dB. We used a Butterworth filter for audio processing application. It was also used in various communication and control systems, as well as in data converter applications and in wireless PANs.

Table 7.2 Receiver baseband analog (BBA) execution report [13].

Noise figure at 50	31 dB
Gain	12–55 dB
IIP3 at 50	30 dBm
Ripple delay	80 ns
Channel rejection	72 dB
Current utilization	2.7 mA
V_s (supply)	1.8 V
Technology	1P-6M, 0.18mm

7.6 Conclusion

A low-energy CMOS receiver BBA design primarily depends on the filter and gain level. To reduce the current utilization, here, we used IIP3, NF, and gain for the known conditions of the BBA. The receiver BBA circuit was manufactured with 0.18-μm CMOS generation and an IIP3 of 30 dB, with a gain of 55 dB and a NF of 31 dB acquired with 4.86 mW of energy (power) utilization. BBA is used in communication systems (Table 7.2).

NF, noise figure; IIP3, input-referred third-order intercept point; BBA, baseband analysis; CMOS, complementary metal–oxide semiconductor; DCR, direct conversion receiver; LPF_1, low-pass filter 1; WPAN, wireless personal area network

References

1. Choi, P., *et al.*, An experimental coin-sized radio for extremely low power WPAN application at 2.4GHz. *IEEE ISSCC*, pp. 92–93, Feb. 2003.
2. Cojocaru, C., *et al.*, A 43mW bluetooth transceiver with–91dB msensitivity. *IEEE ISSCC*, pp. 90–91, Feb. 2003.
3. Soorapanth, T. *et al.*, RF linearity of short-channel MOSFETs. *1st International Workshop on Design of Mixed0Mode Integrated Circuit and Applications*, pp. 81–84, 1997.
4. Abidi, A.A., General relations between IP2, IP3 and offsets in differential circuits and the effects of feedback. *IEEE Trans. Microw. Theory Tech.*, 51, 5, 1610–1612, May 2003.

5. Harjani, R. and Harvey, J., DC coupled IF stage design for a 900-MHzISM receiver. *IEEE J. Solid-State Circuits*, 38, 1, 126–134, Jan. 2003.

6. Kim, J., Chang, S., Kim, S., Shin, H., A 1.2 GHz bandwidth baseband analog circuit in 65nm CMOS for millimeter-wave radio. *2019 International SoC Design Conference (ISOCC)*, pp. 301–302, 2019.

7. Kwon, I., Low-power design of CMOS baseband analog chain for direct conversion receiver. *Int. J. Circuit Theory Appl.*, 38, 111–122, 2008.

8. Kim, C.-W. and Lee, S.-G., A 5.25-GHz image rejection RF front-end receiver with polyphase filters. *IEEE Microw. Wirel. Compon. Lett.*, 16, 5, 302–304, May 2010.

9. Kwon, I., Low-power design of CMOS baseband analog chain for direct conversion receiver. *Int. J. Circuit Theory Appl.*, 38, 2, 111–122, Mar. 2014.

10. Moschytz, G.S., A comparison of continuous-time active RC filters for the analog front end. *Int. J. Circuit Theory Appl.*, 35, 5, 575–595, Sep. 2016.

11. Razavi, B., *Design of Analog CMOS Integrated Circuits*, Tata Mcgrow-Hill Edition, 2008.

12. Sedra, A.S. and Smith, K.C., ch. 8, in: *Microelectronic Circuits*, 4th ed., p. 852, Oxford University Press, 2017.

13. Hossain, W., Rouf, V., Rakib, R., Undergraduate Thesis, BUET, October 2017.

8

Review on Detection of Neuromuscular Disorders Using Electromyography

G. L. N. Murthy[1]*, Rajesh Babu Nemani[2]†, M. Sambasiva Reddy[1]‡ and M. K. Linga Murthy[1]§

[1]*Department of ECE, Lakireddy Bali Reddy College of Engineering, Mylavaram, Andhra Pradesh, India*
[2]*Department of ECE, Ideal Institute of Technology, Kakinada, Andhra Pradesh, India*

Abstract

Communication within the body is done via neurons that transmit or receive electrical impulses. These neurons also called as nerve cells controls the sense organs as well as muscle contraction. Atrophy of neurons will interrupt the information transfer between nervous system and muscles. The consequence of this is the weakening of muscles as well as their deterioration. The consequence of neuromuscular disorders (NMD) is the direct or indirect impairment of muscles with loss of sensation, difficulty in swallowing and breathing, loss of muscles, and weakness as the most frequently observed symptoms. Exposure to toxics, aging heredity, cancer, and genetic disorders are the fundamental reasons behind NMD. Added to all these, diabetes caused due to nonfunctioning of pancreas is the significant contributor. Over the entire world there is a sharp rise in number of diabetic cases that subsequently result in muscle disorder termed as diabetic neuropathy. Damage of neurons in the feet due to diabetes will result in ulcers, infections, as well as amputation. Amyotrophic lateral sclerosis (ALS), myopathy, Inclusion body myositis, myasthenia gravis, and Lambert-Eaton syndrome are a subset of disorders due to different reasons. Noninvasive detection of NMD is done by either lab tests, electromyography EMG), and magnetic resonance imaging (MRI). MRI provides structural analysis while EMG concentrates on functional analysis of muscles. EMG quantifies the electrical activity of the muscles by analyzing which, the nature and state of the disorder can be diagnosed.

**Corresponding author*: murthyfromtenali@gmail.com
†*Corresponding author*: rajeshbabu_n641@yahoo.co.in
‡*Corresponding author*: sambasivareddymula@gmail.com
§*Corresponding author*: lingamurthy413@gmail.com

Budati Anil Kumar, S. B. Goyal and Sardar M.N. Islam. Cognitive Computing Models in Communication Systems, (137–144) © 2022 Scrivener Publishing LLC

Manual analysis of the EMG data is time consuming and prone to error. Large population of data with different electrode positions need accurate conclusions leaving which the entire diagnosis and treatment planning will be affected there by necessitating automated analysis. The developments in signal processing have yielded sophisticated algorithms either for qualitative or quantitative investigation. Preprocessing techniques like windowing and filtering are basically meant for better representation while quantifiable inspection can be carried out by means of feature extraction. This paper presents a study of different neuromuscular disorders and their symptoms. It also reviews state of art techniques available for the detection of NMD. More emphasis will be laid on diabetic neuropathy as diabetic is the one of the most common causes for death throughout the world.

Keywords: Neuromuscular disorders, amyotrophic lateral sclerosis, myopathy, electromyography (EMG)

8.1   Introduction

Muscles play a vital role in the human body by controlling as well as balancing the body through contraction. Each muscle is made up of specific type of elastic tissue comprising small fibers. Each of this fiber is managed by synapses received from the nerve cells termed as neurons. The most prominent muscles in the human body are skeletal, smooth and cardiac muscles. Almost 30% to 40% of the human body mass is constituted by skeletal muscles [1–3], which are connected to bones for controlling the movements voluntarily meaning that human controls the time and the manner they work. Structural support and posture of the body are provided by this muscle and during starvation this muscle acts as an energy source. Unlike skeletal muscles, cardiac muscles are involuntary muscles located in the heart, which contract and relax for pumping the blood throughout the body [4]. Intestine, stomach, and other hollow organs will be consisting of smooth muscles that are meant for performing basic function. Movement of the food, getting rid of toxins through urinary system, and pushing a baby out of the uterus during pregnancy are some of the functions of the smooth muscles which are made from thin form of layers [5].

The neuromuscular system comprised of brain, nerves, and muscles coordinates the voluntary movement of the body, the failure of which leads to neuromuscular disorders there by affecting the peripheral nervous system. The muscles are controlled by nerve cells through messages and if the information transfer between nervous system and the muscles is interrupted due to unhealthy muscles or death of muscles, there will be muscle atrophy. The symptoms of neuromuscular disorders can be issues related to movement and balancing, difficulty in swallowing and breathing, twitching, and pain. These symptoms are exhibited at different parts of the body. Even though not specific, the reasons behind the neuromuscular disorders may be due to heredity, disorders in the immune system, ageing, or even exposure to heavy toxins. There are more than 150 types of these disorders and every year new types are getting discovered.

Neuromuscular disorders can be categorized as muscular dystrophy, peripheral motor neural disorders, motor neuron disease, neuromuscular junction diseases, myopathy, and metabolic diseases. The seriousness of these disorders varies from person to person irrespective of age and gender. Diagnosis of neuromuscular disorders is done by either blood tests that checks the chemical composition or through electromyography (EMG) magnetic resonance imaging (MRI). EMG and MRI provide functional and structural information respectively and are performed based on the need. Like ultra sound imaging, MRI is also used to identify the progression of neuromuscular disorders upon examination of distribution and involvement of biopsy sites [6, 7] and in majority of the cases can better detect inherited myopathies. The abnormalities in anatomy, mass lesion, volume as the signals from the muscle can be diagnosed through muscle MRI.

Electromyography performed by injecting an electrode in the form of thin needle into the muscle, records the electrical activity of the muscle. Injuries to the nerves, neuromuscular disorders, as well as progressive degenerative diseases can be diagnosed through EMG. In the development of devices for human computer interaction, hand control study of EMG signal plays a vital role [8].

8.2 Materials

A number of open source databases are available for analyzing the muscle condition that provide EMG data relevant to specific pathology or specific position of the muscle. Real, synthetic, and clinical signals were available under emglab [9]. Clinical signals corresponding to 10 healthy controls, seven subjects with myopathy and eight subjects with ALS are used to analyze the muscle condition. These signals were collected from five different places with varying levels of insertion. Another database [10] provides data samples categorized into normal, myopathy, and neuropathy, collected using 25-mm concentric needle electrode placed on tibialis anterior muscle. Even though these mentioned databases are relevant to clinical signals, other [11, 12] databases provide signals corresponding to either hand movements or signals recorded while performing any task.

8.3   Methods

With the evolution of machine learning, several algorithms were defined that can better analyze a real time signal based on large amount of data. Feature selection, feature extraction followed by classification is the process flow involved in these automated algorithms. Numerous classification algorithms were tested for better discriminating between the classes or groups of items present in each data sequence. These algorithms considered statistical, temporal, as well as spectral features in the process of pathology detection. Different classifiers are developed that can either distinguish between healthy or pathological subjects or even identify the nature of pathology. Various steps involved in the identifying and classification of neuromuscular disorders was depicted in Figure 8.1.

The input to the classifier will be raw EMG data that will be either filtered for removal artifacts or amplified to raise the signal strength as the basic amplitude level is varying between 0–10 mV. The artifacts in EMG signal occur during the passage through different tissues, electromagnetic radiation, and noise inherent for electronic equipment are the other contributors. Before numerous features are extracted in different domains, it is common practice to segment the EMG signal to be analyzed into either overlapping or non-overlapping frames using windowing. The computational complexity can be reduced by minimizing the feature space by

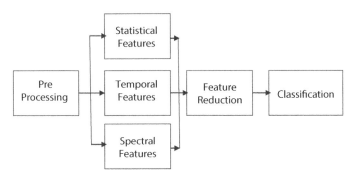

Figure 8.1 Process steps in the detection of neuromuscular disorders.

choosing the best features that yield better accuracy. Relief algorithm and ANNOVA test are some of the approaches used in this context which will be followed by the classification. Much work has been carried out in this context by incorporating the machine learning algorithms either individually or by developing hybrid algorithms.

An ANN based classifier was proposed in [13], in which multi-layer perceptron was used to discriminate between healthy as well as subjects with neuropathy or myopathy. Five different features were considered in the process and the classification accuracy relied on the manner in which the subject data was grouped. In [14], a classifier based on bagging ensemble was proposed. Statistical means at different levels are estimated from the wavelet coefficients in the process of dimensionality reduction followed by classification. The problem of over fitting is eliminated by the incorporation of bagging ensemble approach thereby demonstrating better performance than single classifiers. Mean and standard deviation of seven features have been used in [15] for discriminating between subjects with and without neuromuscular disorders. Support vector machine is being incorporated in the process of classifying the data into healthy and affected subjects that subsequently followed identifying the types of the pathology.

A binary classification algorithm was presented by [16] in which five distinct features, extracted from the wavelet coefficients are considered as feature set. Better accuracy was observed for k-nearest neighbor algorithm when feature set that is the conglomeration of four out of five features. Variable time scales with subsequent rise in the length were used in [17] for analyzing the EMG signal based on the multi scale entropy method. The complexity of the time series was estimated based on the sample entropy in the process of classification. Wavelet-based [18] algorithm was proposed for detection of neuromuscular disorders where spectral as well as statistical features were estimated from wavelet sub bands. Statistical features extracted from the EMG data were fed to an SVM classifier [19] after minimizing the number of features by applying relief algorithm that extracted the prominent features yielding better accuracy. An ANN-based classifier with 11 features has been used [20] to differentiate between healthy controls and pathological subjects. EMG data from biceps brachii was initially preprocessed and then applied to feature extraction algorithm. The role of motor unit action potential (MUAP) in identifying the neuromuscular disorders was discussed in [21]. The entire data has been segmented into windows of 120 points each and fed to ANN based pattern recognition algorithm.

8.4   Conclusion

This chapter is aimed at providing an insight into the automated diagnosis of neuromuscular disorders, which is the most sought problem in the ageing community in particular. Information about most popularly used databases was provided for detecting specific types of disorders neuropathy, myopathy, and amyotrophic lateral sclerosis. Various algorithms intended to analyze the raw data were reviewed based on three different categories. The EMG data considered in this chapter is restricted to disorder detection but the same can also be used for developing devices for human computer interaction as well as human support systems.

References

1. Wei, Y. *et al.*, The Canadian Neuromuscular Disease Registry: Connecting patients to national and international research opportunities. *J. Pediatr. Child Health*, 23, 1, 20–26, 2018.

2. Potikanond, S. *et al.*, Muscular Dystrophy Model. *Adv. Exp. Med. Biol.*, 1076, 147–172, 2018.

3. Dave, H.D., Shook, M., Varacallo, M., Anatomy, Skeletal Muscle, in: *StatPearls [Internet]*, Treasure Island (FL): StatPearls Publishing, 2021 Jan. Sep. 5, PMID: 30725921.

4. Saxton, A., Tariq, M.A., Bordoni, B., Anatomy, Thorax, Cardiac Muscle, in: *StatPearls [Internet]*, Treasure Island (FL): StatPearls Publishing, 2021 Jan. Aug. 11, PMID: 30570976.

5. Hafen, B.B., Shook, M., Burns, B., Anatomy, Smooth Muscle, in: *StatPearls [Internet]*, Treasure Island (FL): StatPearls Publishing, 2021 Jan–Jul 19, PMID: 30422452.

6. McDonald, C.M., Clinical approach to the diagnostic evaluation of hereditary and acquired neuromuscular diseases. *Phys. Med. Rehabil. Clin. N Am.*, 23, 3, 495–563, 2012.

7. Ortolan, P., Zanato, R., Coran, A., Beltrame, V., Stramare, R., Role of radiologic imaging in genetic and acquired neuromuscular disorders. *Eur. J. Transl. Myol.*, 25, 2, 5014, 2015.

8. Raez, M.B., MS, Hussain, Mohd-Yasin, F., Techniques of EMG signal analysis: Detection, processing, classification and applications. *Biol. Proced. Online.*, 8, 163, 11–35, 2006.

9. Nikolic, M., Detailed analysis of clinical electromyography signals EMG decomposition, findings and firing pattern analysis in controls and patients with myopathy and amytrophic lateral sclerosis, in: *PhD Thesis, Faculty of Health Science*, 2001.

10. Goldberger, A., Amaral, L., Glass, L., Hausdorff, J., Ivanov, P.C., Mark, R., Stanley, H.E., PhysioBank, PhysioToolkit, and PhysioNet: Components of a new research resource for complex physiologic signals. *Circ. [Online]*, 101, 23, e215–e220, 2000.

11. Malešević, N., Olsson, A., Sager, P. *et al.*, A database of high-density surface electromyogram signals comprising 65 isometric hand gestures. *Sci. Data*, 8, 63, 2021, .

12. Phinyomark, A. and Scheme, E., EMG pattern recognition in the era of big data and deep learning. *Big Data Cogn. Comput.*, 2, 21, 2018.

13. Elamvazuthi, I., Duy, N., Ali, Z., Su, S., Khan, A., Parasuraman, S., Electromyography (EMG) based classification of neuromuscular disorders using multi-layer perceptron. *Proc. Comput. Sci.*, 76, 223–228, 2015. 10.1016/j.procs.2015.12.346.

14. Subasi, A., Yaman, E., Somaily, Y., Alynabawi, H., Alobaidi, F., Altheibani, S., Automated EMG signal classification for diagnosis of neuromuscular disorders using DWT and bagging. *Proc. Comput. Sci.*, 140, 230–237, 2018. 10.1016/j.procs.2018.10.333.

15. Goen, A., Classification of EMG signals for assessment of neuromuscular disorders. *Int. J. Electron. Electr. Eng.*, 2, 3, 242–248, 2014. 10.12720/ijeee.2.3.242-248.

16. Belkhou, A., Achmamad, A., Jbari, A., Myopathy detection and classification based on the continuous wavelet transform. *J. Commun. Software Syst.*, 15, 336–342, 2019. 10.24138/jcomss.v15i4.796.

17. Ahammed, K. and Ahmed, M., Determination of neuromuscular diseases using complexity of electromyogram signals. *Neurosci. Int.*, 10, 8–12, 2019. 10.3844/amjnsp.2019.8.12.

18. Verma, A. and Gupta, B., Detecting neuromuscular disorders using EMG signals based on TQWT features. *Augment. Hum. Res.*, 5, 1–9, 2020. 10.1007/s41133-019-0020-7.

19. Hasni, H., Yahya, N., Asirvadam, V., Jatoi, M., Analysis of electromyogram (EMG) for detection of neuromuscular disorders. *International Conference on Intelligent and Advanced System (ICIAS 2018)*, 1–6, 2018. 10.1109/ICIAS.2018.8540619.

20. Ahmed, T. and Islam, Md K., EMG signal classification for detecting neuromuscular disorders. *Journal of Physics: Conference Series*, Bristol, vol. 1921, May 2021.

21. Christodoulou, C.I. and Pattichis, C.S., Unsupervised pattern recognition for the classification of EMG signals. *IEEE Trans. Biomed. Eng.*, 46, 169–178, 1999.

9

Design of Complementary Metal–Oxide Semiconductor Ring Modulator by Built-In Thermal Tuning

P. Bala Murali Krishna[1*], **Satish A.**[2], **R. Yadgiri Rao**[3], **Mohammad Illiyas**[4] **and I. Satya Narayana**[5]

[1]Electronics and Communication Engineering Dept., Chalapathi Institute of Technology, Guntur, India
[2]Electronics and Communication Engineering Dept., Caterpillar Inc., Whittington Way, Dunlap, IL, USA
[3]Humanities and Sciences Dept., HOD, Sri Indu Institute of Engineering and Technology, Hyderabad, India
[4]Electronics and Communication Engineering Dept., HOD, Shadan College of Engineering and Technology, Hyderabad, India
[5]TKRCET, Karmanghat, Hyderabad, India

Abstract

A ring modulator of 25 Gb/s by integrated thermal tuning was invented within a 130-nm complementary metal–oxide semiconductor procedure. Its high-speed section, employing a P–N junction that works at a carrier-depletion mode, enables 25 Gb/s modulation and has an extinction ratio >6 dB with only a 2-V peak-to-peak driving voltage. Its thermal tuning section allows the device to work in a broad range of wavelengths. The optical eye displays an elimination ratio greater than 6 dB. The modulation power stays predictable at <24 fJ/bit of circuit molding. Some advantages include high-performance scaling, many core computing systems calling for radical approaches to provide ultra-energy efficiency, and the high bandwidth density interconnection at a low cost. Silicon (Si) is a promising material because of its low latency, low power consumption, high bandwidth, and high density. For photonic solutions to succeed in intra/inter-chip applications, the communications link power consumption, including

Corresponding author: pbmk@city.ac.in

Budati Anil Kumar, S. B. Goyal and Sardar M.N. Islam. Cognitive Computing Models in Communication Systems, (145–154) © 2022 Scrivener Publishing LLC

all electronic circuits. Ring modulators are used in digital communication, in transmitters and receivers.

Keywords: MOS ring modulator, thermal tuning, small signal radio frequency, data modulation

9.1   Introduction

In the upcoming exascale calculation schemes, silicon (Si) photonics is a powerful technology designed for inter-chip infrastructures [1, 2]. A high-speed and effective Si modulator is a vital element within Si photonic applications. With regard to decreasing the power consumption and footprint, which is a challenge in exascale calculation schemes, the Si modulator operates from compressed to less capacitance and much less voltage modulation. Several modulator candidates have been improved in the past years, with carrier-injection Si micro-disk modulators [4], Si ring modulators [3], germanium Si quantum well modulator [6], Franz–Keldysh effect germanium Si modulators [5], hybrid 3-5 modulators [7], and with carrier-depletion Si ring modulators [8–10]. Among several candidates, the carrier-depletion Si ring modulators engaging the P–N diode in reverse-biased mode was chosen, which fulfilled all the required advantages, as well as the compatibility with complementary metal–oxide semiconductor (CMOS), compact dimension (5-m radius), less optical losses (approximately 3-dB ON-state losses), lower driving voltage (peak-to-peak voltage, V_{pp} = 1 V), very high speed (12.5 Gb/s), less capacitance (less than 40 fF), modulators with very high extinction ratios (greater than 7 dB), and integrated thermal tuning. Furthermore, most expressively, an array with a 1 × 8 carrier-depletion CMOS Si ring fused by a 40-nm CMOS driver chip consumes newly confirmed 80-Gb/s procedure by consumption of an ultra-low power of around <80 fJ/bit with the total energy of the driver circuit [11]. Furthermore, the tuning power of the ring resonator similarly reached an unexpected 10–20 interval decrease due to techniques used to weaken and eliminate Si substrates, with established tuning efficacies of 2.4 mW [12] and 3.9 mW [13] per free spectral range (FSR). Numerical analysis on the developed data in a CMOS plant specified that of ring resonators merely desires to adjust less fractions of the FSR in the connection of wavelength multiplexed (e.g., less than 1/8 of the FSR with eight-wavelength linkage) [14]. These kinds of exciting advancements have made the provider depletion-type Si ring modulator the most favorable candidate used for communication purposes, as in inter-chip communication. It similarly files a 25-Gb/s provider-depletion CMOS-type ring modulator incorporated by thermal fine-tuning. With modulations below 2 V V_{pp} not having more significance, the outcome of optical eye displays was greater than 6 dB polarization extinction ratio. The modulation power was less than 24 fJ/bit built in the takeout circuit model system.

9.2   Device Structure

The ring modulator was manufactured by Luxtera/Freescale 130-nm photonic CMOS technology. The math tool was enhanced in lieu of high-velocity modulation using Luxtera's PDK tool. Figure 9.1a shows the fabricated device. The ring waveguide comprises 67% of the ring and has a 7.5-m radius doped with a P–N junction (displayed in Figure 9.1b) meant for high-speed modulation, while the top proper 25% is an N-type doped as a Si resistor or device for thermal fine-tuning. There is a 2-m extensive gap with isolation, wherein the ring-type waveguide is not doped, between the P–N diode and the thermal resistor segments. More than one steel layers were used for the design of the electrodes. The ring waveguide has 380 nm width and 220 nm scratch depth, with an 80-nm-thick Si slab. The ring-type waveguide is broader than the bus-type waveguide (300 nm wide) used for lesser twisting damage and enhanced coupling phase equivalent. In the P–N junction, doping densities that were uneven due to impurity diffusion came about in the course of implantations and thermal cycles, are pretend besides decides by using the trade-off between the modulation efficacy and the rate.

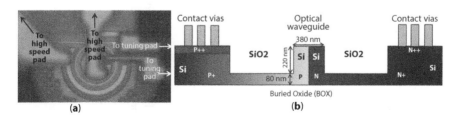

(a)   (b)

Figure 9.1 (a) Photograph of the ring modulator. The upper-right 25% of the ring was made as a Si resistor heater that provides wavelength tuning. (b) Cross-sectional diagram of the ring waveguide high-speed section. The color shading represents doping density variations from low (light colors) to high (dark colors).

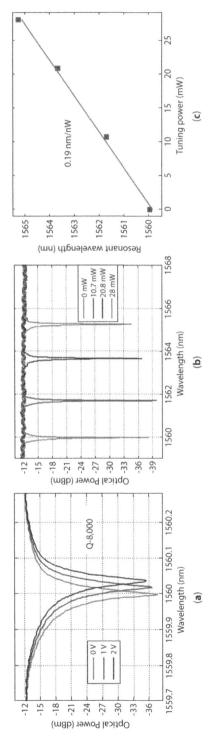

Figure 9.2 (a) P–N diode with diverse reverse biases practical to obtaining the resonance spectrum. (b) With an altered tuning power applied to the Si resistor on the ring to obtain the resonance spectrum. (c) Resonance wavelength versus tuning power representing a tuning efficacy of 0.19 nm/mW.

9.3   DC Performance

The resonance spectrum by altered direct current (DC) voltages is displayed in Figure 9.2a, pragmatic through the greater pad speed, the outcomes in the reverse bias toward the P–N junction diode. The value of the quality factor was approximately 8,000; in addition, the wavelength change from values of 0–2 V was 40 pm. It was activated at about 1,560.05 nm wavelength, and by a voltage fluctuation from 0 to 2 V, the ring-type modulator may reach greater than 10 dB of DC power extinction ratio by 4.5 dB optical damage in the ON mode.

The resonance spectrum with diverse tuning power realistic to the Si resistor within the ring is displayed in Figure 9.2b. The Si resistor has resistance of 750 Ω. The resonance wavelength against tuning is shown in Figure 9.2c, screening the tuning efficacy with 0.19 nm/mW; therefore, a tuning power of 66 mW is advantageous for tuning the total 12.6 nm free spectral range (FSR). By behind native substrate elimination method, a remarkable 20 times improvement in efficacy is probable [13].

9.4   Small-Signal Radiofrequency Assessments

The high-velocity conduct of a ring-type modulator may be considered with the use of a circuit model extracted with the aid of curve-becoming the restrained S11 records [8]. The extracted circuit and the circuit model standards at 1 V are displayed in Figure 9.3a and represent the capacitance values among the electrodes over the highest dielectric, the Rs and C_J model system of the power direction *via* the reverse biased P–N junction diode, the R_{Si} and COX design of the modern path *via* with the BOX, and Si management. Figure 9.3b suggests that a notable suitable curve has been accomplished. Primarily created on this extracted circuit design, the modulation strength was less than 24 fJ/bit modulated [14–18] *via* 25 Gb/s pseudo-random statistics with a 2-V fluctuation.

The modulator electric-to-optical (EO) frequency reaction was verified using a microwave network analyzer. The measured output results in Figure 9.3c suggest a 3-dB bandwidth of 17.5 GHz at 1 V, with the wavelength set to approximately 1,560.05 nm. The modulation bandwidth of the tool is within the resistor–capacitor (RC) limit, which is 30 GHz as predicted by the circuit model (by a 50 supply), and the photon's lifetime, which is 24 GHz based on the total measured good component.

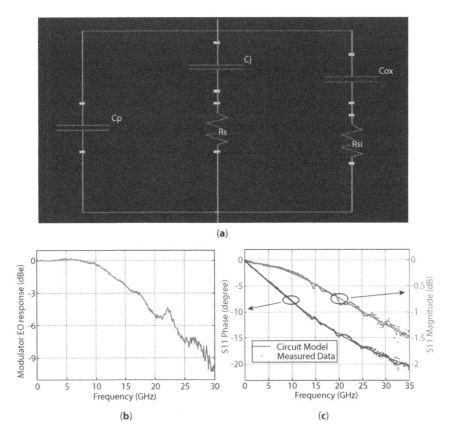

Figure 9.3 (a) Ring modulator with a small-signal circuit model and with circuit values at 1 V reverse bias. (b) Curve adjustments of the measured S11 values at 1 V using the circuit model in (a). (c) Modulator frequency response measured at 1 V.

9.5   Data Modulation Operation (High Speed)

To illustrate high-speed modulation, we used a 40-GHz electric probe to touch the high-speed pads of the ring modulator and connect the coaxial cable as a probe to a function generator device. The function generator device voltage values were fixed to fluctuate from a 0.5-V reverse bias toward the ring diode. Because of the microwave reflection by the capacitive-type ring diode (see S11 in Figure 9.3b) [19–22], a contemplated signal swinging of approximately −0.5 to +0.5 V may be predictable. The supply signal besides the carefully sign collectively assembled reflected a voltage modulation range from 0 to 2 V in the modulator diode.

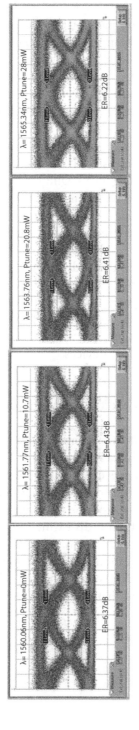

Figure 9.4 Optical eye of 25 Gb/s from the ring modulator with altered laser wavelengths and with altered tuning powers. The demonstrated timescale is 8 ps/div.

To exhibit the modulations in the specific wavelengths, DC-type probes were used to touch the tuning pads of the tool, besides connecting the probe to a DC generator with an examined voltage (V) and current (I). The optical bus-type waveguide of the ring modulator comprise two strident couplers that are straight up joined to an array of polarization maintaining (PM) fibers through sliced termination aspects. At the input side PM (polarization modes), the fibers are linked with a tunable laser; at the production side, they are driven near an erbium-doped fiber amplifier (EDFA). To boost up the signal, an optical filter was used for the eye diagram presentation. The increased or enlarged optical signal was fiber linked to a 30-GHz optical dome on an agility to digital range.

The calculated [23–25] eye diagrams through 25-Gb/s PRBS31 data modulation are displayed in Figure 9.4. Diverse alterations of power are useful for the integrated Si-type thermal resistor indirection in order to adjust the ring for modulation in diverse laser wavelength values. Despite certain noise of the EDFA and the widespread total of the eye diagrams with greater than 6 dB extinction ratio and the laser wavelength value regulated above the 5.3-nm range, it was shown that the device is capable of allowing without errors 25 Gb/s of communication within a wavelength division multiplexing connection. A ring modulator is used in communication in transmitter and receiver devices.

9.6　Conclusions and Acknowledgments

They have been verified with no errors of a 25-Gb/s alterable carrier-depletion ring modulator within a 7.5-µm radius. The device was designed in a typical CMOS plant. The less capacitance indicates an ultralow 24-fJ/bit modulation power. With the broad wavelength range and by alteration of the integrated thermal resistor device, the optical eye of the modulator was widened with a greater than 6-dB extinction ratio when modulated with a 2-V V_{pp} and 25-Gb/s data stream of PRBS31. These effects show that carrier-depletion Si ring modulators may allow very high-speed and ultra-low-energy wavelength division multiplexing (WDM) photonic contacts with dense footprints and that it is significant for upcoming exascale calculation arrangements.

References

1. Krishna Moorthy, A.V., Computer systems based on silicon photonic interconnects. *Proc. IEEE*, 97, 7, 1337–1361, 2009.
2. Miller, D.A.B., Device requirements for optical interconnects to silicon chips. *Proc. IEEE*, 97, 7, 1166–1185, 2009.
3. Manipatruni, S., High speed carrier injection 18Gb/s silicon microring electro-optic modulator. *LEOS*, pp. 537–538, 2007.
4. Watts, M.R., Ultra low power silicon microd is k modulators and switches, Group IV. *Photonics*, 8, 4–6, 2008.
5. Liu, J., Waveguide-integrated, ultralow-energy GeSi electro-absorption modulators. *Nat. Photonics*, 2, 433–437, 2008.
6. Roth, J.E., Optical modulator on silicon employing germanium quantum wells. *Opt. Express*, 15, 9, 5851–5859, 2007.
7. Tang, Y., Over 40 GHz traveling-wave electro absorption modulator based on hybrid silicon platform. *OFC, OWQ3*, 2011.
8. Li, G., Ultralow-power, high-performance Si photonic transmitter. *OFC, OMI2*, 2010.
9. Dong, P., Wavelength-tunable silicon micro ring modulator. *Opt. Express*, 18, 11, 10941–10946, 2010.
10. Dong, P., High-speed & compact silicon modulator based on a race trackres on a tor with a 1Volt drive voltage. *Opt. Lett.*, 35, 19, 3246–3248, 2010.
11. Zheng, X., Ultra-low power arrayed CMOS silicon photonic transceivers for an 80Gbps WDM optical link. *OFC, PDPA1*, 2011.
12. Dong, P., Thermally tunable silicon race trackres on a tors with ultra low tuning power. *Opt. Express*, 19, 20298–20304, 2010.
13. Cunningham, J.E., Highly-efficient thermally-tuned resonant optical filters. *Opt. Express*, 18, 19055–19063, 2010.
14. Krishnamoorthy, A.V., Exploiting CMOS manufacturing to reduce tuning requirements fores on ant optical devices. *IEEE Photonics J.* Accepted Publ. Special Issue Photonic Integration, 2, 35–38, 2011.
15. Kogge, P., Next-generation supercomputers. *IEEE Spectr.*, 4, 68–71, February, 2011, http://spectrum.ieee.org/computing/hardware/nextgeneration-super-computers. Pepeljugoski, P., Kash, J., Doany, F., Kuchta, D., Schares, L., Schow, C., Taubenblatt, M., Offrein, B.J., Benner, A., Low power and high density optical interconnects for future supercomputers, in: *Optical Fiber Communication Conference (OFC2010), Paper OThX2*.
16. Ho, R., Zheng, X., Schwetman, H., Lexau, J., Koka, P., Li, G., Shubin, I., Cunningham, J.E., Computer systems based on silicon photonic interconnects. *Proc. IEEE*, 97, 7, 1337–1361, 2009.

17. Xu, Q., Schmidt, B., Shakya, J., Lipson, M., High speed carrier injection 18Gb/s silicon micro-ring electro-optic modulator, in: *IEEE LEOS Annual Meeting*, pp. 537–538, 2007.

18. Rosenberg, J., Green, W.M., Rylyakov, A., Schow, C., Assefa, S., Lee, B.G., Jahnes, C., Vlasov, Y., Ultra-low-voltage micro-ring modulator integrated with a CMOS feed-forward equalization driver, in: *Optical Fiber Communication Conference 2011, Paper OWQ4*, 2011.

19. Trotter, D.C., Young, R.W., Lentine, A.L., Ultralow power silicon microdisk modulators and switches, in: *IEEE Conference on Group IV Photonics*, pp. 4–8, 2008.

20. Beals, M., Pomerene, A., Bernardis, S., Sun, R., Cheng, J., Kimerling, L.C., Michel, J., Waveguide-integrated, ultralow-energy GeSi electro-absorption modulators. *Nat. Photonics*, 2, 7, 433–437, 2008.

21. Lim, A.E.-J., Liow, T.-Y., Qing, F., Duan, N., Ding, L., Yu, M., Lo, G.-Q., Kwong, D.-L., Novel evanescent-coupled germanium electro-absorption modulator featuring monolithic integration with germanium p-i-n photodetector. *Opt. Express*, 19, 6, 5040–5046, 2011.

22. Feng, N.-N., Feng, D., Liao, S., Wang, X., Dong, P., Liang, H., Kung, C.-C., Qian, W., Fong, J., Shafiiha, R., Luo, Y., Cunningham, J., Krishnamoorthy, A.V., Asghari, M., 30GHz Ge electro-absorption modulator integrated with 3 μm silicon-on-insulator waveguide. *Opt. Express*, 19, 8, 7062–7067, 2011.

23. Chen, H., Peters, J., Westergren, U., Bowers, J., Over 40 GHz traveling-wave electroabsorption modulator based on hybrid silicon platform, in: *Optical Fiber Communication Conference 2011, Paper OWQ3*, 2011.

24. Young, I.A., Mohammed, E., Liao, J.T.S., Kern, A.M., Palermo, S., Block, B.A., Reshotko, M.R., Chang, P.L.D., Optical I/O technology for tera-scale computing. *IEEE J. Solid-State Circuits*, 45, 1, 235–248, 2010.

25. Shubin, I., Zheng, X., Pinguet, T., Mekis, A., Luo, Y., Thacker, H., Li, G., Yao, J., Raj, K., Krishnamoorthy, A.V., Highly-efficient thermally-tuned resonant optical filters. *Opt. Express*, 18, 18, 19055–19063, 2010.

10

Low-Power CMOS VCO Used in RF Transmitter

D. Subbarao[1], Dayadi Lakshmaiah[2]*, Farha Anjum[3], G. Madhu Sudhan Rao[4] and G. Chandra Sekhar[5]

*[1]Professor of Electronics and Communication Engineering Dept.,
Siddartha Institute of Engineering and Technology, Hyderabad, India
[2]Professor of Electronics and Communication Engineering Dept., Sri Indu Institute
of Engineering and Technology, Hyderabad, India
[3]Professor of Electronics and Communication Engineering Dept., HOD, Siddhartha
Institute of Engineering and Technology, Ibrahimpatnam Hyderabad, India
[4]Professor of ECE Dept., Bule Hora University, Ethiopia, South Africa
[5]Assistant Professor of Electronics and Communication Engineering, SIIET,
Hyderabad, India*

Abstract

A transmitter circuit based on complementary metal–oxide–semiconductor (CMOS) is regular knowledge. It operates through a European band of 863–873 MHz used for wireless sensor applications. Here, the binary frequency shift keying (BFSK) modulator is combined using the present transmitter. It uses the frequency hopping spread spectrum (FHSS) and is developed for a small variety of wireless applications and also for renovation mixers and energy amplifiers. In this document, two significant blocks are discussed: a voltage-controlled ring oscillator (VCO) and an original synthesizing design for a direct translation transmitter based on simple CMOS inverters. By using voltage control (V_{CTRL}), the VCO of the $f_{oscillation}$ is controlled. The reaction outcome of the present voltage-controlled oscillator demonstrated energy utilization, at the preferred fluctuation frequency and below a V_S = 3.3 V, at just 7.48 mW, as well as a phase noise lower than −126 dBc/Hz at an offset frequency of 10 MHz. The summer working through transconductance cells with a characteristic purpose of subtraction is attainable toward design

---

*Corresponding author: laxmanrecw@gmail.com

Budati Anil Kumar, S. B. Goyal and Sardar M.N. Islam. Cognitive Computing Models
in Communication Systems, (155–164) © 2022 Scrivener Publishing LLC

requirements. Low-power CMOS VCOs are widely used in communication in VLSI (very large-scale integration) chips and in optimization of the trade-off between phase noise and power consumption. VCOs are also used in radiofrequency (RF) transmitters.

Keywords: Summer, CMOS technology, wireless sensor, direct conversion transmitter, CMOS inverter, ring VCO

10.1 Introduction

Through increasing of WCS, require of speedy WLAN enhance important into current years, the need for speedy wireless local area network (WLAN) has become more important [1, 2]. In fact, behind huge advancements in the development of bright sensors, powerful microprocessors with communication protocols, wireless sensor networks achieve quick incorporation into a lot of applications. Wireless sensor networks (WSNs) are collected through small nodes communicating in small distances that perform detailed objectives. While deployed in surroundings, they converse wirelessly toward bringing together method and broadcast information regarding their physical atmosphere to an end of concentration. Sensors are used in several significant applications such as in telemedicine, correctness cultivation, armed supervision, ecological monitoring, and in home computerization and alarms. The growing attention during extremely ICs also systems imposes be brutal strain for little price, small power moreover minute sensors' dimension. In detail, to intend completely incorporated RF independent sensor meant used for characteristic applying alike as domicile mechanization also repeated indicator evaluation, sensors ought to work additional other 5 years below battery power deliver. The 863–873 MHz band, it offered only in Europe, be excellent pasture to check latest thoughts moreover concepts toward the improvement of a small power. This has led to several improvements in transmitter construction [3–5].

Moreover, while the broadcast range is extremely small, which is usually in the range of 50 m or lower, a small data-rate plus a small range communication system are required. So, the straight alteration design as an extremely integrated RF-IC execution, the 863–870 MHz range, it recognized through Electronic Communication Committee and novel worldwide ordinary for wireless connectedness Zigbee adapted be used toward attain strict transmitter necessities for the design.

10.2 Transmitter Architecture

A transmitter is a significant block in communication systems. It changes non-modulated functions to the RF through performance of three essential tasks: modulation, frequency rendition, and power amplification. There are two main transmitter architectures [5]. The first one is a two-step transmitter design where the non-modulated function is up-converted twice such that the power amplifier output spectrum is remote from the frequencies of the restricted turner; the second one utilizes I/Q modulations and carries out occurrence conversion in one step, as displayed in Figure 10.1. Since modulating function is frankly translated awake to an RF signal. Although the straight exchange construction had various well-known difficulties that prevented its extensive use [5, 6], it has been fine-renowned for it its minimalism also possible utilized used in solitary chip accomplishment. Additionally, it needs just the smallest amount of RF segment and no image-reject filter [7]. The characteristic straight conversion transmitter displayed in Figure 10.1 works as follows: a digital frequency-shift keying (FSK) modulator modulates information and incorporates into the fourth-order outputs a composite frequency hopping spread spectrum (FHSS) function on data transmission. Modulation is established on a direct digital frequency synthesizer [8]. Subsequently, a secure-frequency oscillator produces a set of four-phase local oscillator (LO) functions in quadrature with all others and awake changes the output (o/p) within 863 and 870 MHz in the single-sideband (SSB) mixer. Moreover, the higher or the lesser sideband is preferred with the oscillator of 866.5 MHz of the RF. Here, the intermediate f_c is positioned where the known band occurs. The o/p of the modulator simply needs between 0 and 3.5 MHz to enclose an

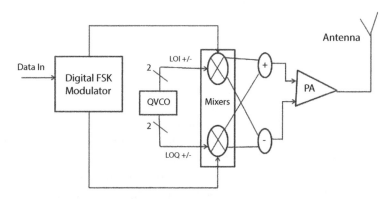

Figure 10.1 Direct conversion wireless sensor transmitter architecture.

area of 866.5 ± 3.5 MHz and a 7-MHz ISM (industrial, scientific, and medical) band [8]. Following up-conversion, a complete-discrepancy energy amplifier operates the antenna through and suppresses out-of-band signals and the hopped carrier at the transistor (T_x) o/p. Here, the results of two mixers were added by the use of summers for adding the in-phase mechanism and reject the quad apparatus of the adder/subtractor results. The final outcome is a suppressed carrier, a single side band (SSB) V_o of a frequency that is the added or the differentiated baseband and LO signals. The broadcast bandwidth of the binary frequency shift keying (BFSK) signal was calculated as 80 kHz, with the partition among adjoining channels equivalent to 40 kHz. To meet the FHSS prerequisite and the ETSI convention (smallest amount of division among adjoining channels of 25 kHz), the ISM band was divided into 58 channels, with each channel having a 120-kHz bandwidth [8, 9]. The FHSS device was selected for its low-power spectral concentration and because it is highly exempt from near-vanishing with interfering [8]. In addition, a decrease of transmitter power was achieved with the application of the FHSS method through the BFSK modulation approach [9]. The above addresses complementary metal–oxide–semiconductor (CMOS) knowledge plus allows extremely incorporated one chip explanation.

10.3   Voltage-Controlled Ring Oscillator Design

The proposed discrepancy ring VCO uses three cascaded delay cells and should produce the center frequency of the 863- to 870-MHz ISM band [8]. In the literature, ring oscillators are mainly used for combinations [7]. Although ring oscillators have a moderately elevated phase noise, they usually cover a regularity range with wider fluctuations, smaller die size, and lower power utilization. Because the incorporated oscillator should comply with significant specifications including low power utilization, low phase noise, and short expiry duration, a ring oscillator is the most appropriate for our application. The use of positive feedback reduces the delay time and therefore increases the velocity of operation. Two P-type metal–oxide–semiconductor (MOS) transistors (m5 and m6) specified *via* the $V_g(V_{CTRL})$ and two other P-type MOS cross-coupled transistors (m3 and m4) form the cell, shown in Figure 10.2. The VCTRL controls the o/p frequency, f, of the construction. Here, the divergence of the differential construction is supplied by a polysilicon resistance "R" to avoid the use of current mirrors, with a corresponding decrease in the design range. In addition, this improves the phase noise presentation. A comprehensive discussion can

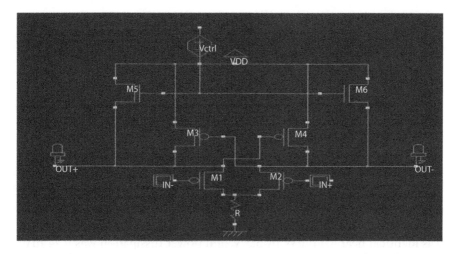

Figure 10.2 Proposed voltage-controlled ring oscillator (VCO) delay cell implementation.

be found in [10]. In detail, the I_s transistor is responsible for injecting the sparkle sound at choral f_c to the cross-coupled T_x, therefore reducing the phase noise presentation. In Figure 10.2, the N-type MOS T_x m1 and m2 formed input (i/p) pairs, increasing the g_m-to-C ratio and accomplishing superior frequency of the procedure. Here, the produced frequency was tuned by calculating the channel conductance of T_x m_5 and m_6 through the V_c. Furthermore, the value of R was slightly different from that of the $f_{oscillator}$, but it extensively disturbs the energy utilization and phase distortion. For this reason, the circuit parameters are affected by the R value, which was selected to remain a fine negotiation among control utilization plus phase noise. To complete the designed VCO, the dimension parameters of the delay phase were designed using theoretical analysis. The equations relating $f_{oscillation}$ and V_C with the design requirements were used to determine optimized parameters enchanting keen on explanation VCO performances those are energy utilization and stage distortion. As discussed in [1–8], the turn down of transistor extent returns to the working action of the design is distended, so the effective frequency also enlarged. However, at the same time, the energy utilization increase; therefore, new techniques are needed to reduce the dissolution energy. Therefore, it is essential a dispensation amid the working frequency plus the energy utilization. A microphotograph of the prototype, manufactured using a 0.35-μm CMOS process, is shown in Figure 10.2. The strip range, which includes pads with and without buffers, is 725 × 324.4 μm. As the VCO was hypothetical and not yet calculated, additional post-layout simulation was ended to make sure that yet through procedure is tinctions the design preserves his execution. Thus, to establish the tuned area and the proportionality of the projected VCO, a parametric examination in which the $f_{oscillation}$ was replicated for distinct V_C values was executed. The alteration area of the VCO design was from 381 MHz to 1.15 GHz when the V_c differed between 1.8 and 3.3 V. Considering 866.5 MHz as the mid-frequency, the imitation tuning difference, $\Delta f / \Delta f_0$, was 89%. The VCO showed good linearity for managing the voltage between 1.8 and 2.2 V, VCO grow be roughly MHz/V transitory response on a frequency of 866.51 MHz while control voltage equivalent toward 2 V, which is depicted in Figure 10.3. Managing the voltage, the power utilization of the VCO was only 7.48 mW, with the observable o/p signals, V_{out+} and V_{out-}, of the planned VCO showing large amplitudes. Therefore, power consumption changes through the control voltage, which was identical near 4.44 mW by 3.3 V, and power dissipation was 9.24 mW at a working frequency of 1.15 GHz below the control voltage of 1.8 V. The SSB phase noise of the VCO at a frequency of 866.521 MHz was 106 dBc/Hz at an offset frequency of 1 MHz and valve-126 dBc/Hz at an offset frequency of 10 MHz.

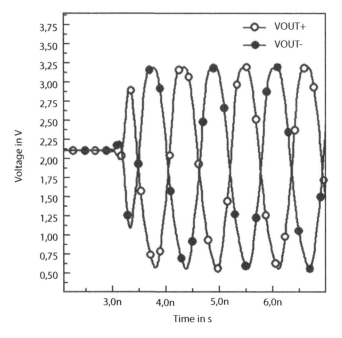

Figure 10.3 Transient response of the voltage-controlled ring oscillator (VCO) at 866.521 MHz [8].

10.4   CMOS Combiner

CMOS inverter is a resourceful circuit this is build balancing switches. Regarding the distinction between the mobility values (μ_N and μ_P) of the N-type and P-type MOS (NMOS and PMOS, respectively), a conventional inverter reaches stability while LN is uniform. LP is approximately WP = $[\mu_N \mu_P] W_N$, where W_N and W_P (L_N and L_P) are the channel diameters of NMOS and PMOS, respectively because situation, here electrical energy approach procedure while o/p junction OUT be open, low voltage kick-off be next to $V_{IN} = V_{OUT} = V_{DD}/2$. At approximately this exacting working point, the common-mode voltage (VCM) is equivalent to $V_{DD}/2$, and the NMOS and PMOS transistors together work in saturation mode. Therefore, a CMOS voltage regulator reproduces, on a tiny signal amplitude, a negative transconductance between V_{IN} and I_{OUT}. In this transconductance mode, the inverter small-signal o/p current is specified at a low frequency by $I_{out} = -g_m \times V_{IN}$, $g_m = g_{mN} + g_{mP}$, where g_m is the transconductance of the CMOS inverter and g_{mN} and g_{mP} are the gate-source transconductance of NMOS and PMOS in saturation mode, respectively. The proposed combiner (subtractor) topology is based on classical CMOS inverters. The subtractor shown in Figure 10.4 uses only 10 CMOS inverters. Because the circuit is fully differential, it was fashioned using two proportional branches, with each branch containing four inverters and the two branches connected by two extra inverters, each linked between one information source and the output of further information. Allowing for the trans-impedance g_{mi} of each inverter INVi in Figure 10.4 and choosing all g_{mi} as identical, outputs V_{OUT1} and V_{OUT2} can be simply generated, as described in the subsequent subsection. Inverters INV2 and INV4 here in each pathway can be averted as resistors $1/g_{m2}$ and $1/g_{m4}$, respectively, by linking the o/p and i/p nodes.

With the small frequency at node A_1, we obtain:

$$V_{A1} = I_{OUT1} * (1/g_{m2}) = -(g_{m1}/g_{m2}) . I_{IN1} \tag{10.1}$$

Because the g_m of each inverter is equivalent, voltage V_{A1} was near to $-V_{IN1}$. In conclusion, for the expression of o/p V_{OUT1} at node B_1, we have:

$$V_{OUT1} = (I_{OUT3} + I_{OUT6}) * (1/g_{m4}) \tag{10.2}$$

Since $g_{m3} = g_{m6} = g_{m4}$, then $V_{OUT1} = V_{IN1} - V_{IN2}$; a similar move toward was followed for the occurrence of o/p V_{OUT2} through bearing in mind nodes A_2 and B_2, as given by the equation.

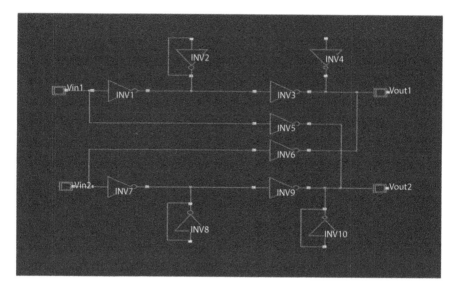

Figure 10.4 Proposed subtractor based on complementary metal–oxide–semiconductor (CMOS) inverters [9].

The circuit was fabricated *via* the 0.35-μm CMOS procedure, which has an exterior of 35 × 50 μm without pads. The simulation confirmed that, under 3.3 V voltage, the circuit works at frequencies up to 900 MHz with a dissolution current of 1.34 mA. To confirm the performance of the projected circuit and the equations previously obtained, applying in phase conflict blue and pink waves at nodes V_{IN1} and V_{IN2}, respectively, the two outputs, V_{OUT1} and V_{OUT2} (green wave in Figure 10.5), were well

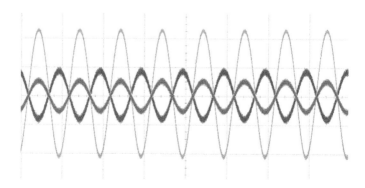

Figure 10.5 Temporary subtractor reaction at node V_{OUT2} for two in-segment competition input signals [8].

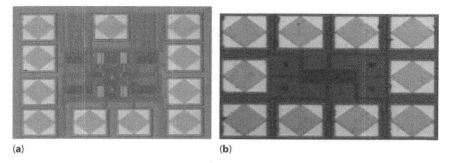

(a)   (b)

Figure 10.6 (a) Die microphotograph of the voltage-controlled ring oscillator (VCO) prototype. (b) Die microphotograph of the subtractor prototype [8].

within segment competition. This condition needs to obtain $V_{OUT1} = 2V_{IN1} = -V_{OUT2}$ and, thus, $V_{OUT2} = -2V_{IN}$.

10.5   Conclusion

An 836- to 870-MHz band, three-phase CMOS ring oscillator by means of positive feedback plus wide range of fine-tuning frequency be comprehensive in this document. The linearity of the VCO appears relatively good, and the outcomes of the post-layout simulation showed that the VCO has the advantages of extremely low-power dissipation and large voltage amplitude swing and is suitable for use in small area designs. For the first time, the possibility of latest elevated performances subtractor with simple CMOS inverters has been established in this paper. VCOs are used in RF transmitters in communication. These proposed circuits might facilitate analog design aimed at combining various analog functions (Figure 10.6).

References

1. Razavi, B., *RF microelectronics*, Prentice Hall PTR, Text Book PTR Publishers, 1998.
2. Lee, T.H., *The design of CMOS radio-frequency integrated circuits*, Cambridge University Press, 1998.
3. ECC, Strategic plans for the future use of the frequency bands 862-870 MHz and 2400-2483.5 MHz for short range devices. *European Conference of CEPT*, Helsinki, European Conference Paper, May 2002.

4. Mikkelson, J.H., Assessment of CMOS front end receiver architectures for GSM handset applications. *IEEE Symp. Communications Systems and Digital Signal Processing*, pp. 164–167, 1998.

5. Razavi, B., RF transmitter architectures and circuits. *IEEE Custom Integrated Circuits Conference*, pp. 197–204, 1999.

6. Razavi, B., *Design of analog CMOS integrated circuits*, McGraw-Hill, New York, USA, 2001.

7. Trabelsi, H., FPGA implementation of FHSS-FSK modulator. *Proceedings of the International Conference on Design & Technology of Integrated Systems in Nanoscale Era*, Tozeur Tunisia, 26-28 March 2011, pp. 1–5.

8. Bouzid, Gh., Wireless sensor transmitter design for spread-spectrum direct conversion. *J. Trans. Syst. Signals Devices TSSD*, 4, 3, 35–43, 2012.

9. Deen, M.J., Low power CMOS integrated circuits for radio frequency applications. *IEE Proc. Circuits Devices Syst.*, 152, 5, 502–508, Oct. 2015.

10. Naseh, S., Kazemeini, M., Jamal Deen, M., Very low-voltage operation capability of CMOS ring oscillators and logic gates. *J. Vac. Sci. Technol. A* (Special Issue), 24, 3, 763–769, May/June 2016.

11

A Novel Low-Power Frequency-Modulated Continuous Wave Radar Based on Low-Noise Mixer

Dayadi Lakshmaiah[1]*, Bandi Doss[2], J.B.V. Subrahmanyam[3],
M.K. Chaitanya, Suresh Ballala[4], R. Yadagirir Rao[5] and I. Satya Narayana[6]

*[1]Electronics and Communication Engineering Sri Indu Institute
of Engineering and Technology, Hyderabad, India*
*[2]Electronics and Communication Engineering,
CMR Technical Campus, Hyderabad, India*
*[3]Electrical and Electronics Engineering Dept., Sphoorthy Engineering College,
Hyderabad, India*
*[4]Electronics and Communication Engineering, Vasavi College of Engineering,
Hyderabad, India*
[5]ME Dept., SIIET, Sheriguda, Hyderabad, India
[6]ME Dept., SIIET, Sheriguda, Hyderabad, India

Abstract

In this article, a 24-GHz DCR for frequency-modulated continuous wave ranging radar based on short flicker noise mixer in 90-nm SOI CMOS technology is available. A low-noise and low-power LNA acquire SNIM method is discovered. Nullify tools and enhance inductor are found to extend production. The expanse result of discrete low-noise amplifier proves the peak gain is 17.2 dB at 23.8 GHz and the frequency range is approximately 2.2 GHz from 22.8 GHz to 25 GHz. The low-noise amplifier achieves standard 3 dB NF inside the 24-GHz band. A current-bleeding mixer is used for lower noise and the elements effect FN has been considered. Appropriate component values and local oscillator power has been selected to create the mixer lesser noise. Evaluation outcome demonstrate the Rx displays 20.3 dB peak gain, 7 dB SSB noise figure. FN of the mixer and the Rx is calculated correspondingly and the noise knee-point of Rx was noticed 60 kHz. The Rx absorbs only 16 mW with chip size of 0.65 mm^2

*Corresponding author: laxmanrecw@gmail.com

Budati Anil Kumar, S. B. Goyal and Sardar M.N. Islam. *Cognitive Computing Models in Communication Systems*, (165–180) © 2022 Scrivener Publishing LLC

with pads. The outcome express that the future Rx can be a good applicant for frequency-modulated continuous wave ranging radar.

Keywords: Rx (receiver) 24 GHz, SOI, flicker noise (FN), mixer, DCR, frequency-modulated continuous wave (FMCW)

11.1   Introduction

Since the Federal Communications Commission (FCC) established unlicensed 24 GHz band as ISM band, extreme examine activity near recognition of decidedly integrated solutions around 24 GHz band is currently underway [1]. Advances in integrated circuit and semiconductor device tools allow the expansion of low-cost radar objects for the automotive [2], industrial [3], and consumer electronics [4].

A basic block diagram of a DCR is illustrated in Figure 11.1. The echo signal is primary gathered up through an Rx antenna before being passed across a band select filter. The system was typically executed in a PCB. Afterwards, the function was scaled up by using LNA and is eventually frequency down-transformed via the mixer with an LO signal produced by the voltage-controlled oscillator (VCO). The LNA and mixer are key components to complete the down-conversion operation and their performance has an impact on next detection circuit block maximum. In this work, the designs mainly cover the implementation and optimization of the low noise amplification and next frequency down conversion. Then, they are integrated into a low-power radar receiver RF front-end.

Figure 11.1 shows that the FN is the largest obstacle in pursing the DCR layout. In mm-wave radars, the FMCW type has been tired the maximum concentration because of its thick area and toughness above climate conditions and mild situations [5–8]. But, when DCR radar is used to calculate the distance, the intermediate frequency (IF) calculated from FMCW may lie within the excessive flicker noise region. As shown in Figure 11.2, the functional baseband wave will be "buried" in noise, leading to bad measured result. A short FN Rx is attractive in DCR applications. Several publications mentioned low FN designs. Traditional current bleeding method was described in [9, 10] and in [11] a gm-boost

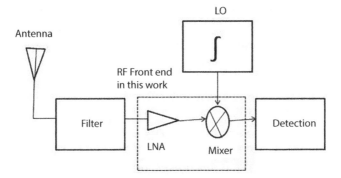

Figure11.1 Block diagram of direct conversion receiver (DCR).

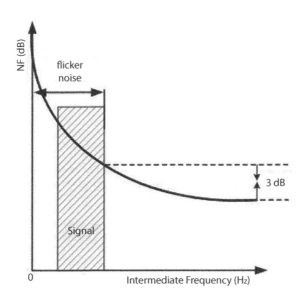

Figure 11.2 Baseband signal degraded by FN.

method was introduced with an additional circuitry connected to the switching pair transistor of the mixer to enhance gain. No measured results have been reported on 24 GHz low FN Rx. In this paper, an intuitive and comprehensible contemporary bleeding approach is introduced to get relatively low FN. FN of the mixer and the Rx are measured correspondingly for the primary time.

The Si Ge technology was once the first options due to its wonderful performance and excessive productivity [2]; however, the low integration level and high cost are unbearable. In the latest years, the burgeoning CMOS technology has become a hotspot for low-cost mm-wave radar chips [12] with its high integration and low cost. But, the lossy substrate and low-Q-factor passive components, such as inductors and capacitors, make it hard to reach a high-gain, low-noise and low-power-consumption Rx.

In this article, a low-noise Rx is proposed. This paper was prepared as follows: in segment two, the FMCW theory is granted. In Section 11.3, the low-noise receiver circuit implication is described in detail. A low-noise and low-power LNA is present. The factors affect flicker noise of mixer are examined and a low-flicker noise mixer is designed. Measurement outcomes and comparison with simulation results are shown in Section 11.4. Results imply that the proposed receiver promises for 24 GHz FMCW Ranging Radar.

11.2   FMCW Principle

The frequency of FMCW wave changes linearly with time. A simplified version of FMCW wave can be visible in Figure 11.3. By manipulating the frequency distinction, the delay joining the Tx function and the reflected function can be identified to conclude the location of the object. It can be expressed as

$$R = \frac{c\,T\,f_r}{2B}$$

where R = The distance between target and radar
c = The speed of light

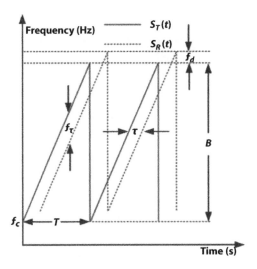

Figure 11.3 FMCW principle of a sawtooth wave.

T = Duration of the chip
fr = Beat frequency
B = Bandwidth of carrier frequency.

As mentioned above, the beat frequency fr moves linearly with distance R. If the goal is relatively close to the radar, the R is small; thus, the beat frequency fr is also small. For example, when the distance between radar and target is 3 m, B is 250 MHz and T = 0.5 ms is a regular resolution. Thus, the calculated 10 kHz beat frequency fr is lying within the excessive flicker noise area exactly. As an outcome, the short-range detecting capacity deteriorates.

The beat frequency containing facts of goal is calculated from acquired RF wave and LO wave and it's inappropriate to the received signal scope. In this way, receiver used for FMCW can loosen limit of linearity.

1. Circuit Implementations

Figure 11.4 indicates the proposed direct DCM with dimensions of the RF active devices. The passive element values of prefer circuit are appeared in Table 11.1. These section values are found on the outcome of EM simulation. The Rx is constructed through zero Intermediate Frequency structure with Radio Frequency and Local Oscillator waves employing in the range of 24 GHz band. Less noise, less power consumption and excessive consolidation within the major system specifications of the Rx.

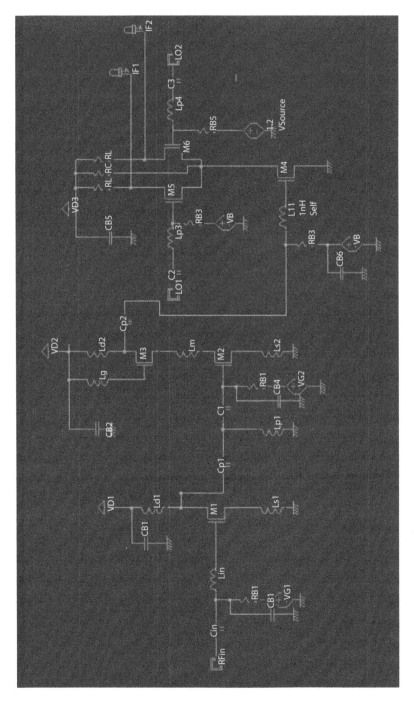

Figure 11.4 Schematic of proposed Rx.

Table 11.1 Values of the circuit elements of the proposed receiver.

C_{in}	C_{B1-6}	C_{p1}	C_{p2}	C_{1-3}	L_{in}	L_{s1}	L_{s2}	L_{d1}
1.25 pF	2pF	200fF	550fF	1pF	720pH	300pH	270pH	600pH
L_{d2}	Lm	Lg	Lp1	Lp2	Lp3–4	RB1–5	RL	RC
450pH	130pH	150pH	180pH	300pH	430pH	1.2kΩ	800Ω	60Ω

To turn away the lossy balun and reduce the power utilization of this circuit, single-end topology is used. Ld2 was the load of LNA and its inductance was suitable form the matching circuit with Cp2 and Lp2 between the output of LNA and input of mixer. The LO input ports of the mixer were matched to 50 Ω impedance by establishing the matching inductors Lp3 and Lp4.

According to the system noise cascading solution, to keep the whole system low noise, LNA as the first stage should have adequate gain and low noise [15]. The mixer used for down-converting RF signals should keep low flicker noise. Exhaustive design methods are described in following parts.

As represented in Figure 11.4, a two-stage single-end LNA is considered in our work. The first stage plays the key part in the noise figure of the system. To gather the essentials of NF, gain and common source amplifier is placed to be first stage to area of the circuit small-noise, observed by a cascade amplifier to improve gain. As shown in Figure 11.4, Ls1 and Ls2 worked as source degeneration inductors to simplify the LNA's input and noise matching.

To decrease the power utilization as much as possible, bias voltage of amplification transistors are involved to place of 0.55V as an adequate gain, appropriate noise figure and power utilization. In addition, dimensions of transistors M1, M2, and M3 were preferred through the procedure. Lm as an inductor is connecting the common source and CG transistors to the parasitic capacitance which will resonate to reduce the noise figure and amplify the gain [13–17]. A conventional single-balanced mixer is shown in Figure 11.5a, b shows a single-balanced mixer with current-bleeding mechanism. The transistor M1 acts as the driver-stage to transform the i/p radiofrequency voltage into current waves and transistors M2–3 are biased at nearby pinch-off region to take action as switches and steer the current depending on the LO signal.

From Figure 11.5a, the driver-stage current ID1 is equal to switch-stage current ID2 plus ID3. Rising in the ID1 forces the decreasing of load

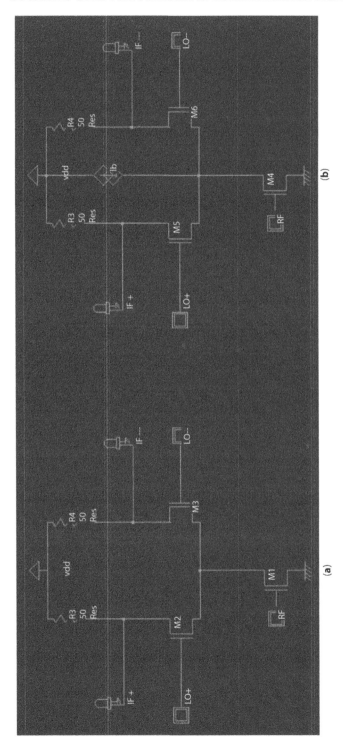

Figure 11.5. (a) balanced mixer; (b) balanced mixer with current-bleeding technology.

resistance RL to maintain the fixed DC operating state, degrading conversion gain of the mixer. Consequently, at that case, current- bleeding mechanism is established. In Figure 5b, the driver-stage current ID4 is equal to switch-stage current including ID2 and ID3 plus bleeding current Ib. By these means, ID4 is better than ID5 and ID6 and switch-stage current can be lowered to decrease the flicker noise of present mixer.

Considering the driver-stage current I_{D1} in Figure 11.5a is equal to the driver-stage current I_{D4} in Figure 11.5b. Based on Equation (11.2), the mixer flicker noise in Figure 11.5a,b can be expressed as:

$$V_{n,out}(f)a = \frac{4I_{D1fLO}}{S_{LO}} R_l V_{n,LO}(f) \tag{11.4}$$

$$V_{n,out}(f)b = \frac{4I_{D1fLO}}{S_{LO}} R_l V_{n,LO}(f) \tag{11.5}$$

Because of the bleeding current Ib, flicker noise in Equation (11.5) is miniature than that in Equation (11.4). In this way, the flicker noise with current-bleeding formation in Figure 11.5b promises portable than that with conventional formation in Figure 11.5a.

Mentioned in Figure 11.4, the present mixer followed a resistor R_C. Resistances of load resistor R_L and bleeding source resistor R_C are selected by involved simulation to maintain good performance. Within the layout, R_C was selected to be 60Ω and load resistor was 800Ω. The study on the mixer of fixed operating point shows that the bleeding current I_b takes 97% of whole DC current I_{D4}. The drain voltages of M_4 and M_5/M_6 are 0.5 V and 1.1 V. The voltage drop of load resistor R_L is 0.1 V, making sure the headroom of this plan under 1.2V supply voltage. Though, the tiny resistance R_C causes conversion gains loss to a positive level. The simulation outcomes how that signal power loss caused by R_C was about 70%, leading to 5 dBc on version gain loss.

Based on the bleeding-current mixer, the model was passed away on different LO power to locate a suitable one to each low flicker noise. Result is depicted in Figure 11.6, showing that flicker noise is declining with LO power growing. The result is in deal with Equation (11.3). From Figure 11.6, the LO power is rising from 15 dBm to 0 dBm. Bigger LO power was not adopted, because the 24GHz frequency source could only suggest moderate LO power in a system, for example, 10 dBm. Larger LO power needs

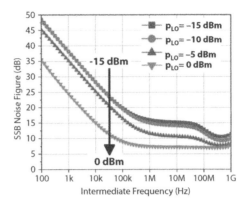

Figure 11.6 Simulated FN of mixer with different LO power.

extra amplifiers and power consumption, making system not cost-efficient. At last, a 0 dBm LO power was preferred.

11.3 Results

The 90 nm SOI CMOS tools are preferred in this work for the Rx recognition. The tool capabilities of 5 metal surfaces with two bulky radiofrequency metals on the top. The top 2 radiofrequency metal surfaces with 3.3 um width has been broadly used for the awareness of on-chip Tx lines and coils. The design benefited from the high resistivity of the SOI substrate; thus, the traditional attractive floor shields on the bottom of on-chip spiral inductors can be misplaced. High-Q inductors and capacitors can be realized.

Performance of the LNA has been presented in Figure 11.7. The measured and simulated small-signal S-parameters, NF, P_{1dB} and IIP_3 of LNA are depicted in Figure 11.7a–d, discretely. The precise S_{21} reached 17.2 dBm fits peak at 23.8 Giga Hz and the cut-off frequency is approximately 2.2 Giga Hz from 22.8 Giga Hz to 25 Giga Hz. Compared with simulation results, the deteriorated S_{11} and S_{22} worsen gain and band width. The S_{11} is lesser than 10 dB from 22.5 Giga Hz to 26.6 Giga Hz and S_{22} is under 10 dB from 23.2 GHz to 24.6 GHz. The parameters standing for isolation from output to input S_{12} is below 30 dB inside the whole working band. The results in Figure 11.7b show that the low-noise amplifier reaches an average of 3 dB noise figure within the 24 GHz band. The linearity performance is illustrated in Figure 11.7c,d. Figure 11.7c plots

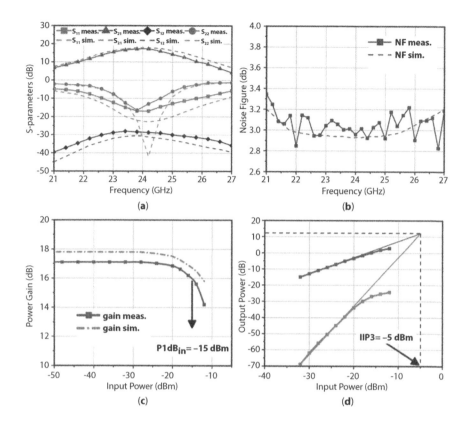

Figure 11.7 (a) S-parameters of LNA; (b) Noise figure of LNA; (c)P1 dB of LNA; (d) IIP₃ of LNA.

the power gain versus input power and the IP_{1dB} could be observed −15 dBm. The IP_3 is found to be −5 dBmin (Figure 11.7d).

A second set of assessment was approved out on the Rx including LNA and mixer. Another signal source has been introduced to feed the 0 dBm LO signal to mixer. The measurements were approved out by sweeping the RF and local oscillator frequency with fixed IF of 125 MHz. Figure 11.8 presents the calculated and output of the Rx chip. Figure 11.8a represents the conversion gain and NF performance of the Rx. Compared with the simulation results, with influence of parasitic part and test environment, the calculated transfer gain is 3.5 dB lower and the NF is 1 dB higher. The 3 dB bandwidth of receiver is controlled mainly by LNA synchronization between the radio frequency and local oscillator of the receiver is represented in Figure 11.8b.

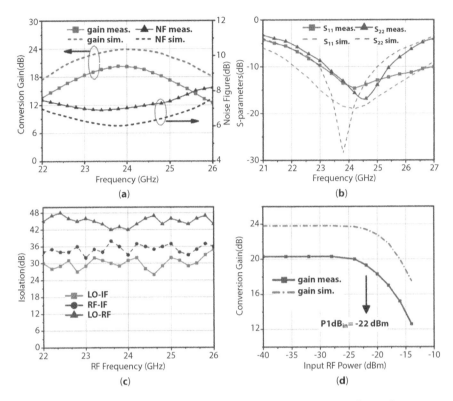

Figure 11.8 (a) Conversion gain and NF of receiver; (b) S-parameters of RF and LO ports; (c) Measured port isolation of receiver; (d) P1 dB of receiver.

Even if measured results are worse than simulated results, the S_{11} is below 10 dB from 23 GHz to 27 GHz and S_{22} is below 10 dB from 23.2 GHz to 25.4 GHz. It means that RF port and LO port input match well, correspondingly. Figure 11.9c represents the port-to-port separation of the Rx. All the separation levels are more than 30 dB in 24 GHz band. The LO-IF isolation is much lesser, because the LO signal is fed directly to the mixer with relatively higher amplitude. Figure 11.8d represents the input RF power with conversion gain of −22 dBm.

Considered flicker noise results of standalone mixer and receiver are shown in Figure 11.9. To prove influence of LO power on flicker noise, two local oscillator power are located to 10 dBm and 0 dBm. The IF is selected from 100 Hz to 10 MHz and logs cal is used to make results clear and intuitive. The results indicate that better LO power can decrease the flicker noise of receiver, same as the simulated results. From Figure 11.9a, the flicker noise of mixer is higher than over simulation result. The cause may

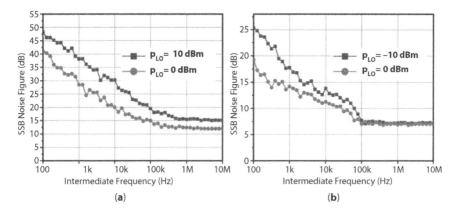

Figure 11.9 (a) FN results of mixer; (b) FN results of Rx.

be inaccurate noise model of transistor and loss introduced by determines equipment. The literature frequently uses the term "knee-point" for the frequency below which the flicker noise dominates above thermal noise.

In Figure 11.9b, because of the former-stage high-gain LNA, the involvement about NF of mixer part has been reduced. Then, a relatively low noise is achieved. Moreover, as shown in Figure 11.9, noise below two different LO power stays be almost the same when IF is better than 100 kHz; with parameters in Equation (11.1), 100 kHz. IF results from 30 m target distance. In an actual situation, when the target distance is larger than 30 m, a lower LO power can be used to save power utilization while introducing no additional noise.

In Table 11.2, differentiate the recognize Rx execution with the available development of the K-band Rx's. From this assessment, it can be visible that the recognized 24 GHz CMOS Rx contrasts the attainment with a balanced performance even in a non-superior process. The gain is not so high as [16] because high-gain variable-gain amplifier (VGA) can be integrated in afterward design simply. This design achieves a knee-point of 60 kHz. It's the first time to detail a low flicker noise measured result. In order to differentiate if the power consumption of bias circuit is incorporated or not, the P_{DC} part has been separated into two lines: P_{DC1} and P_{DC2}. The former stands for the power utilization including the bias circuit and the latter stands for the power consumption apart from the bias circuit. As talked above, the linearity control can be loosened in FMCW application, so the −22 dBm IP1 dB is tolerable.

Table 11.2 Performance comparison table.

	This work	[14]	[15]	[16]	[17][1]
Technology	90 nm SOI	0.13 μm CMOS	65 nm CMOS	65 nm CMOS	45nm SOI
Inclusion	LNA + Mixer	LNA + Mixer + VGA	LNA + Mixer	LNA + Mixer	LNA + Mixer
RF/IF (GHz)	24/0.125	24/0.1	24/0.002	21.5/0.1	24/NA
CG (dB)	20.3	36	28.3	14.5	26.2
NF (dB)	7	9.9	5	5.7	5.6
$1P_{1dB}$ (dBm)Kn	−22	−35	−28	−40	na
ee-point (kHz)	60	NA	NA	NA	na
P_{DC1} (mW)	21.1[1]	40.8	26	NA	na
P_{DC2} (mW)	16	NA	NA	0.683	na
Area[2] (mm[2])	0.65	0.8	0.66	0.4	na

[1]Simulation results.
[2]Including pads.

11.4   Conclusion

In this chapter, a low-noise 24 GHz DCR for FMCW ranging radar is considered and fabricated in 90 nm silicon-on-insulator CMOS technology. A low-noise and low-power low-noise amplifier was planned. To develop gain of the receiver and decrease NF, the SNIM method was used in the input. Neutralized method and boost coils are recommended to increase performance. A 24 GHz current-bleeding mixer was introduced. The measured results show the proposed Rx provides 20.3 dB peak gain and 7 dB SSB NF. A 22 dB IP1 dB and well-matched RF port S11 and LO port S22 have been calculated. More than 30 dB isolations between RF, LO, and IF ports are obtained within working frequency band FN of both mixer and Rx is calculated and the knee point of Rx is noticed 60 kHz. Combined with the FMCW principle, the receiver indicates when the target distance is larger than 30 m, a lower LO power can be used to save power consumption. The Rx absorbs only if

16 mW with chips is zero f0, 65 mm^2 including pads. It suggests the at the proposed silicon-on-insulator CMOS direct conversion Rx can be a capable applicant for FMCW ranging radar.

Applications

- It is used for wireless systems using RF and microwave.
- This circuit is designed with nanometer SOI CMOS with good gain and noise figure which is very useful in communication system.
- This circuit uses increasing the gain of the receiver.
- It is also used in wireless communications, antenna, and transmitter testing.
- It is also used in wireless LAN's and surveillance.
- It is used in base station monitoring and cable testing.

References

1. Mazzanti, A., A 24 GHz Subharmonic Direct Conversion Receiver in 65 nm CMOS. *IEEE Trans. Circuits Syst. IRegul .Pap.*, 58, 88–97, 2010.
2. Ragonese, E., A fully integrated 24GHz UWB radar sensor for automotive applications, in: *Proceedings of the 2009 IEEE International Solid-State Circuits Conference—Digest of Technical Papers*, SanFrancisco, CA, USA, pp. 306–307, 8–12 February 2009.
3. Subramanian, V., Low Noise 24 GHz CMOS Receiver for FMCW Based Wireless Local Positioning. *IEEE Microw. Wirel. Compon. Lett.*, 21, 553–555, 2011.
4. Evans, R.J., Technology and limitations, in: *Proceedings of the International Conference on Radar, Adelaide*, Australia, pp. 21–26, 9–12 September 2013.
5. Park, J., 76–81-GHz CMOS Transmitter With a Phase-Locked-Loop-Based Multichirp Modulator for Automotive Radar. *IEEE Trans. Microw. Theory Tech.*, 63, 1399–1408, 2015.
6. Luo, T.-N., A 77-GHz CMOS Automotive Radar Transceiver With Anti-Interference Function. *IEEE Trans. Circuits Syst. IRegul. Pap.*, 60, 3247–3255, 2013.
7. Ginsburg, B.P., A multimode 76-to-81GHz automotive radar transceiver with autonomous monitoring, in: *Proceedings of the 2018 IEEE International Solid-State Circuits Conference—(ISSCC)*, San Francisco, CA, USA, pp. 158–160, 11–15 February 2018.

8. Dudek, M., System Analysis of a Phased-Array Radar Applying Adaptive Beam-Control for Future Automotive Safety Applications. *IEEE Trans. Veh. Technol.*, 64, 34–47, 2015.

9. Wei, P., Diao, S., Huang, D., Fu, Z., Lin, F., A K-Band Down-Conversion mixer design with integrated baluns in 65nm CMOS, in: *Proceedings of the Proceedings of 2012 5th Global Symposium on Millimeter-Waves*, Harbin, China, pp. 282–285, 27–30 May 2012.

10. Ali, M.K., Low flicker noise high linearity direct conversion mixer for K-band applications in a 90 nm CMOS technology, in: *Proceedings of the 2014 20th International Conference on Microwaves, Radarand Wireless Communications (MIKON)*, Gdańsk, Poland, pp. 1–4, 16–18 June 2014.

11. Ahn, D., Kim, D.-W., Hong, S., A K-Band High-Gain Down-Conversion Mixer in 0.18 μm CMOS Technology. *IEEE Microw. Wirel. Compon. Lett.*, 19, 227–229, 2009.

12. Krishna swamy, H., A Fully Integrated 24GHz 4-Channel Phased-Array Transceiver in 0.13 μm CMOS Based on a Variable-Phase Ring Oscillator and PLL Architecture, in: *Proceedings of the IEEE International Solid-State Circuits Conference. Digest of Technical Papers*, San Francisco, CA, USA, pp. 124–591, 11–15 February 2007.

13. Huang, B.-J., Lin, K.-Y., Wang, H., Millimeter-Wave Low Power and Miniature CMOS Multi cascode Low-Noise Amplifiers with Noise Reduction Topology. *IEEE Trans. Microw. Theory Tech.*, 57, 3049–3059, 2009.

14. Wang, H. and Jiao, C., A low-power ESD-protected 24GHz receiver front-end with π-type input matching network, in: *Proceedings of the 2011 IEEE International Symposium of Circuits and Systems (ISCAS)*, Riode Janeiro, Brazil, pp. 2877–2880, 15–18 May 2011.

15. Cheng, J.A., 0.33V683uw K-Band Transformer-Based Receiver Front-End in 65nm CMOS Technology. *IEEE Microw. Wirel. Compon. Lett.*, 25, 184–186, 2015.

16. Ding, Y., A24GHzZero-IF IQ-receiver using low-noise quadrature signal generation, in: *Proceedings of the 2017 IEEE Asia Pacific Microwave Conference (APMC)*, Kuala Lumpur, Malaysia, pp. 1226–1229, 13–16 November 2017.

17. Wang, Y., Cui, J., Zhang, R., Sheng, W., Fully differential Ultra-wideband LNA-Mixer for K to Ka Band receiver in 45nm CMOSSOI technology, in: *Proceedings of the 2019 IEEE Asia-Pacific Microwave Conference (APMC)*, Singapore, pp. 16–18, 10–13 December 2019.

12

A Highly Integrated CMOS RF T_x Used for IEEE 802.15.4

Dayadi Lakshmaiah[1]*, Subbarao[2], C.H. Sunitha[3], Nookala Sairam[4] and S. Naresh[5]

[1]*Professor of Electronics and Communication Engineering Department, Sri Indu Institute of Engineering and Technology, Hyderabad, India*
[2]*Professor of Electronics and Communication Engineering Department, Siddartha Institute of Engineering and Technology, Hyderabad, India*
[3]*Professor of Electronics and Communication Engineering Department, Vignana Bharathi Institute of Technology, Hyderabad, India*
[4]*Professor of Electronics and Communication Engineering, KPRIET, Hyderabad, India*
[5]*Assoc. Professor of Electronics and Communication Engineering, SIIET, Hyderabad, India*

Abstract

IEEE 802.15.4 is a network maintained by the IEEE 802.15 work group. The CMOS radio frequency (RF) transmitter is widely used in the latest wireless communication systems. The CMOS RF transmitter will use both MOS technology and RF. RF CMOS circuits are widely used for transmitting and receiving wireless signals. RF CMOS technology is widely used for WLAN networks. RF CMOS technology is also used in radio transmitters and receivers such as GSM, WIFI, *etc.* CMOS devices have high noise immunity and low power consumption. Hence, they are widely used for integrated circuits. This work gives the objective solutions of a low-power radio frequency T_x for 2.4-GHz-band IEEE 802.15.4 standard in 0.18-μm CMOS. For an adaptive radio frequency T_x, more elements are admired. The important influential elements here are executions, energy utilization, product energy, and price. Radio frequency T_x has nonresistant mixers and a power amplifier. This aimed radio frequency T_x simply needs 10.8 mW under a force voltage of 1.8 V and delivery of 2 V.

Keywords: Complementary metal oxide semiconductor, power reduction, WSN, IEEE standard 802.15.4 T_x

**Corresponding author*: laxmanrecw@gmail.com

Budati Anil Kumar, S. B. Goyal and Sardar M.N. Islam. Cognitive Computing Models in Communication Systems, (181–188) © 2022 Scrivener Publishing LLC

12.1   Introduction

New increase of reduced power complementary metal oxide semiconductor transmitters and receivers of 2.4-GHz in furrowing drastically with the origin of IEEE 802.15.4 (1). IEEE 802.15.4 needs a good backup and low-price answers in favor of operations. This set indicates the high-level consumption of tiny, cheap, and high-backup scenting genius called, detector knot, by panel dispensation and wireless communication capacities which reach a complexion-arranged, infrastructure-less, and fault-tolerant detector network within a concerted manner. By connate system, three working frequency bands—868-MHz European, 915-MHz America, and 2.4-GHz— are available he widely. There are three possible data rates of this standard based upon the working bands: 20, 40, and 250 kbps. IEEE 802.15.4 is stationed for more days or a longer time in a broad variety of implicit operation screenplays like mechanization, refined home electronic products, patented personal care, and consanguineous miracles. In line with this, energy utilization is an elemental issue relative to achieving the duration demanded by the system, as the hourly battery change of the detector knots was insolvable [1–2].

This subsystem needs above 50% of power at the time of processing. This design of a radio frequency (RF) front unit in favor of wireless sensor networks (WSNs) results in the transmitter unit being one of the most high-power-consuming components. As a result of improving the power utilization, overall utilization, and power needs, our radio frequency components developed immensely. Thus, here we set a goal for the T_x plan to reduce the power expenditure. Here the intension and execution of a low-power CMOS radio frequency T_x for IEEE-802.15.4 have unique targets, namely, minimum power, lower distortion, and more uniqueness. In our method, a passive mixer operating in the present scenario is paired with a booster amplifier [2]. The remaining work is illustrated below.

12.2   Related Work

Recently, there have been several low-power and CMOS-based 2.4-GHz transmitters and receivers of IEEE 802.15.4 [3]. Unfortunately, these works do not serve IEEE 802.15.4 applications well in terms of energy efficiency. These search results, however, silently scatter more power rakishness. Accordingly, it is advantageous to reduce the power rakishness. The most common solution to address the above-mentioned concern is to use a currently reused method [4]. This method has a limited increase because of the queue of more transistors.

Figure 12.1 shows the power utilization using processing and transferring modes. There are two modes of operation, namely, active mode and sleeping mode. The Y-axis shows the power utilization in milliwatts. The sensing, meeting, and percentage are shown in Figure 12.1. The transmitter and receiver designs of WSN are of three types: (1) super heterodyne, (2) small transitional frequency, and (3) straight translation (5). Super heterodyne architectures require many combiners, resulting in greater power and complicating transceiver implementations. Low-intermediate-frequency (IF) architectures are divided as per large analog-to-digital converter sample speed, which leads to more power utilization [5–8]. The direct conversion type uses a minimum number of exterior devices, like infrared filter; it is unnecessary and an intermediate frequency. The band-pass filter is adjusted by the low-pass filter.

In this design, the direct conversion scheme is taken from a minimum price and minimum energy perspective. The minimum power utilization and minimum development prices of the direct conversion type, as well as its effortless assimilation in the design, make it attractive. With the low-IF receiver, the image signals are rejected in the transmitter chain. As the phase changer is an intrinsically thin band, this architecture uses a 90° phase changer in the gesture line which limits the signal bandwidth. The transmitter under consideration has a quad inactive mixer and a tiny noise power amplifier.

In this type, an o/p radio frequency signal from the up-switch mixer is then improved by a usual cascade technique through an extra condenser C1 as presented in Figure 12.3. Power amplifiers enable a signal to be transmitted with the necessary output power. It is necessary to add a capacitor to the input end of the i/p-transistor M1 in order to maintain a proper i/p

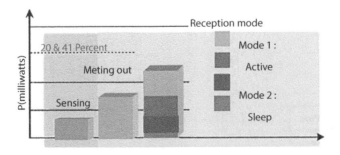

Figure 12.1 Sharing of power utilization using processing and transferring.

line straight, as C1 is basically a bias reliant and can give rise to small noise at soaring i/p booster levels (8). Here the i/p-transistor is influenced with a large gate-source voltage to run in group A method. This amplifier has a current utilization of 6 mA at 1.8 V.

The above-mentioned method is used because of the following advantages:

- High power boundary—linearity can be increased.
- The gain is restricted by changing the direct current of the P-type metal oxide semiconductor by altering the direct voltage to the cascode transistor input.

With these power amplifiers, the setup $L_1 - C_1$ removes the tough 2nd vocal of the transporter, while the setup L_2 and C_2 set at the transporter frequency. The Z_{in} of the planned power amplifier is as follows:

$$Z_{in} = \frac{1}{jLw(C_{gs} + C_1)}$$

Here C_{gs} is gate-source capacitance, L is inductance, and C_1 is capacitance. The setup $L_2–C_2$ is used to set the output impedance to 50 Ω.

Our standard utilities have a small duty factor because of this architecture. Thus, it is important to minimize their utilization both in action type and while sleeping. A 1-μA power supply is required for the latter mode. Consequently, a small silicon surface and small number of exterior mechanisms are essential to reduce the cost of such circuits.

Figure 12.2 shows the schematic diagram of a transmitter radio frequency amplifier. It uses low-pass filters. The outputs of two low-pass filters

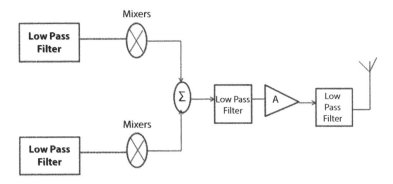

Figure 12.2 Schematic of the T_x radio frequency amplifier.

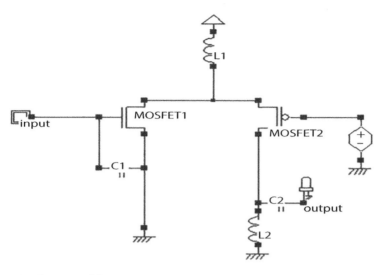

Figure 12.3 Power amplifier.

are connected to two mixers. Then, the output of the two mixers was added by an adder. The output of an adder is passed through the low-pass filter and then amplified by an operational amplifier. Finally, the amplified signal is filtered by a low-pass filter. Then, it is transmitted by an RF antenna.

Figure 12.3 shows the power amplifier. It uses two MOSFETs, namely, MOSFET1 and MOSFET2. It uses two capacitors, namely, C1 and C2. It uses two inductors which are named L1 and L2. Input is applied to MOSFET1, and the amplified output is collected from MOSFET2.

12.3   Simulation Results and Discussion

Advanced Design System simulation tools were used to simulate the circuit in a 0.18-μm complementary metal oxide semiconductor. The route has been planned for a 2.4-GHz system; 2.4–2.48 GHz b/w is used. Furthermore, 1.8 V gives 6 mA on the T_x. The S parameters of the power amplifier (PA) are given at Figure 12.4. The I/P and O/P combinations are efficient in the required IF = 6 MHz. From Figures 12.4a, b, it is clear that the i/p and o/p resistance of the planned power amplifier is finely achieved at 2.4 GHz. The output power signal is used to determine the transmission reliability as the sensor setup is utilized for a few serious sensing applications. The O/P shows that the designed plan extensively reduces the power utilization.

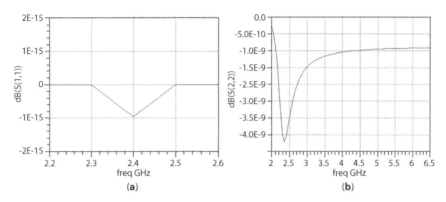

Figure 12.4 *S*-parameters: (a) I/P return loss (S_{11}) and (b) reverse isolation (S_{22}).

Table 12.1 Performance comparison.

Parameters	[7]	[8]	[9]	[10]	This work
CMOS technology (μm)	0.25	0.18	0.18	0.18	0.18
Output power (dBm)	0	0	-4	0	1.7
Power dissipation (mW)	12	18	17	25	10.8
Architecture	SHD	DCT	DCT	DCT	DCT

Here we offer a judgment of the O/P of this plan with the various studies in Table 12.1. In Table 12.1, this plan has tiny power dissipation but obtains a good performance compared to others.

12.4   Conclusion

A 2.4-GHz CMOS radio frequency transmitter for IEEE 802.15.4 with reduced power has been planned in this work. Then, the provisions for the sensitive unit, which is the power amplifier, were given. At a voltage of 1.8 V, the transceiver was manufactured in 0.18-μm technique. The PA showed an increased competence of 38.8% and rakishness of 9 mW. Here the entire T_x sequence, with 1.7 dBm of O/P power and 3.98 dBm of O/P 3rd-order cutoff point, is achieved. According to the planned T_x, it dispensed 10.8 mW.

References

1. Sasilathaa, T. and Raja, J., A 1 V, 2.4 GHz low power CMOS common source LNA for WSN applications. *Int. J. Electron. Commun.*, 64, 10, 940–946, 2010.
2. Vladimir, K., Nguyen, T.-K., Lee, S.-G., Choi, J.-C., A direct conversion CMOS front-end for 2.4 GHz band of IEEE 802.15.4 standard. *Proceedings of IEEE Asian Conference on Solid-State Circuits*, Hsinchu, 1-3 November 2005, pp. 449–451.
3. Byun, S., Park, C.-H., Song, Y., Wang, S., Conroy, C.S.G., Kim, B., A low power CMOS bluetooth RF transceiver with a digital offset canceling DLL-based GFSK demodulator. *IEEE J. Solid-State Circuits*, 39, 10, 1609–1618, 2004.
4. Zolfaghari, A. and Razavi, B., A low-power 2.4-GHz transmitter/receiver CMOS IC. *IEEE J. Solid-State Circuits*, 38, 2, 176–183, 2003.
5. Mirabbasi, S. and Martin, K., Classical and modern receiver architecture. *IEEE Commun. Mag.*, 38, 11, 132–139, 2000.
6. Le, V.H., Nguyen, T.-K., Han, S.H., Lee, S.-G., High linearity, 900 MHz RF transmitter front-end. *IEICE Trans. Electron.*, 90, 1, 201–203, 2007.
7. Christensen, K.T., *Low power RF filtering for CMOS transceiver*, Ph.D. Thesis, Technical University of Denmark, Copenhagen, 2001.
8. Ikeda, S. and Lee, S-y, A 0.5-V 5.8-GHz ultra-low-power RF transceiver for wireless sensor network in 65nm CMOS. *IJTIR*, 8, 78–29, 2014.
9. Vatti, R.A. and Kumar, K., *Design of low power RF CMOS power amplifier structure with an optimal linear gain controller for future wireless communication*, vol. 21, pp. 35–39, Springer, 2021.
10. Hejazi, A., Jang, B.G., Rad, R.E., A 2.4 GHz power receiver embedded with a low-power transmitter and PCE of 53.8%, for wireless charging of IoT/wearable devices. *IEEE Xplore*, 12, 62–68, 2021.

13

A Novel Feedforward Offset Cancellation Limiting Amplifier in Radio Frequencies

Dayadi Lakshmaiah[1]*, L. Koteswara Rao[2], I. Satya Narayana[3], B. Rajeshwari[4] and I. Venu[5]

[1]*Professor of Electronics and Communication Engineering Department, Sri Indu Institute of Engineering and Technology, Hyderabad, India*
[2]*Professor and Principal of Electronics and Communication Engineering Department, KL University, Hyderabad, India*
[3]*Professor of Mechanical Engineering Department, Sri Indu Institute of Engineering and Technology, Hyderabad, India*
[4]*Professor of Electronics and Communication Engineering Department, Vignana Bharathi Institute of Engineering and Technology, Hyderabad, India*
[5]*Assoc. Professor of Electronics and Communication Engineering, SIIET, Hyderabad, India*

Abstract

A communication system is used in radio frequency and microwave, local area networks, mobile phones, base station monitoring, surveillance, satellite communications, transmitter antenna, and receiver antenna testing. A multi-stage limiting amplifier and a frequency modulation or frequency shift keying demodulator is used in a 455-kHz signal processor. On-chip feedforward offset cancellation circuit uses a limiting amplifier. A quadrature detector is used in the frequency modulation or frequency shift keying demodulator, and a detector consists of a phase recognizer built into the chip and a tank phase shifter external to the chip. The image frequency signal processor consumes 2.3mW at 2-V power supply and has a sensitivity of about 72 dBm, with a demodulation constant of 20 mV/kHz and 10-kHz deviation. The active area is 0.2 mm^2, and it uses 0.3-μm digital complementary metal oxide semiconductor technology. A limiting amplifier is used in communication systems and wireless communications.

*Corresponding author: laxmanrecw@gmail.com

Budati Anil Kumar, S. B. Goyal and Sardar M.N. Islam. Cognitive Computing Models in Communication Systems, (189–198) © 2022 Scrivener Publishing LLC

Keywords: Complementary MOS IC, analog and digital demodulators, image frequency signal processing, quadrature detector and limiting amplifier

13.1   Introduction

The complementary metal oxide semiconductor (CMOS) 455-kHz signal processor designed for super-heterodyne communication system has two functions: they are for magnitude control and for frequency modulation or frequency shift keying demodulation. In frequency modulation or frequency shift keying applications, the limiting amplifier is selected as a magnitude control. In this case, the DC offset reduces the sensitivity, which consequently degrades the bit error rate recovery. At each gain stage, feedforward offset cancellation technology is implemented, which demonstrates instantaneous response and high-level integration compared to conventional external passive approaches [1–4].

Frequency shift keying (FSK) is a discrete frequency modulation (FM) signal that may be dealt with, as such frequency shift keying frequencies are spread out and arranged on a nominal service frequency. The FSK or 4-FSK bandwidth (BW) is lesser, and the frequency modulation/frequency shift keying demodulator has strong frequency discrimination. The quadrature detector has a FM/FSK demodulator. It consists of an external tank phase-shift network and an integrated phase detector for low-voltage operation [7–16].

13.2   Hardware Design

13.2.1   Limiting Amplifier

It has various stages of input magnitudes in an amplifier chain. The input active range should be in a pager application; this amplifier chain must produce a tiny signal gain which is not less than 70 dB. It must produce a high-pass function in order to compensate for the mean amplitude displacement from zero which is caused by a mismatch. To lessen the AM–PM conversion effect, the top BW is 10 times the intermediate frequency (IF) [3] of 10 kHz selected at the bottom. It has no effect at 455 kHz [4] of the data band. The suggested limiting amplifier has three levels of gain cells. Among the three cells, the first and the second cells are similar, while the third has a built-in auxiliary output driver. This architecture uses a feedforward offset cancellation technique rather than the traditional negative feedback method [5].

The amplifier's core is made up of cross-connected source-coupled pairs with differential input pairs. The previous stage is connected to all of these source-coupled pairs. In addition, the offset extraction circuit is implemented as an RC network at each pair's input. When $f_{in} > RC\, f_{cutoff}$, then the traditional source-coupled pair is equal to the circuit topology. When f_{in} is lower than the RC f_{cutoff}, on the other hand, the offset voltage is higher. As a result, the input common-mode voltages of the two source-coupled pairs diverge. The amplifier rejects the offset voltage equipped and supplied at input due to the move-connected mechanism and cross-connected mechanism. The offset generated within the cutting-edge level may be cancelled within the subsequent degree, and the offset generated in the current stage may be cancelled as well because each step's offset extractor circuit nearby wishes to cut the offset voltage caused through the prior degree and offers an immediate response. As a result, each gain cell uses lesser R and C. In conventional digital CMOS technology, triode-biased pMOS resistor and pMOS gate-to-bulk capacitor are used for getting the offset extractor's long-time constant RC network. While the pMOS is in accumulation mode, the gate-to-bulk capacitance is 2 to 3 pF.

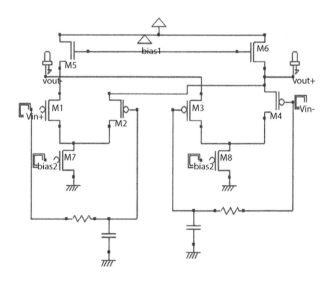

13.2.2   Offset Extractor

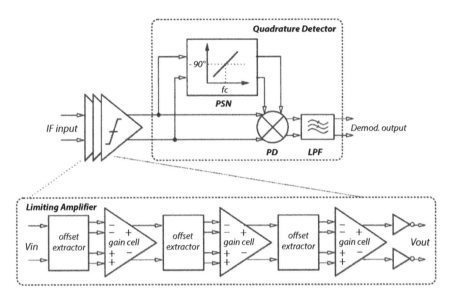

13.2.3   Architecture and Gain

The created high-pass function's 3-dB corner frequency is 10 kHz. The offset causing the CMOS process fluctuation covering the planned offset cancellation range is 230 mV. The source-coupled pair output impedance and accompanying parasitic capacitance govern the gain stage's high-frequency roll-off, as shown in Equation (13.1).

$$f_{-3\,dB} = \frac{1}{2\pi(r_{o1}//r_{o5}//r_{o3})\cdot(C_{gd5}+C_{gd1}+C_{gd3})}. \qquad (13.1)$$

A three-stage topology is chosen, taking into account the balance between BW, gain, and usage of power. The first two identical stages have a 4.6-MHz bandwidth and a 28-dB differential voltage gain. The last stage includes the addition of two supplementary output drivers.

13.2.4   Quadrature Detector

FM/FSK demodulation is used by the quadrature detector. Phase-shift network shifts the phase that is proportional to f_{inst}. The difference between the original FM and the phase-shifted signal is detected by a phase detector. Finally, low-pass filter is used to recover the demodulated output and remove the high-frequency noise. The frequency deviation is converted into phase shifting. The phase-shift network response is given by Equation (13.2), where the incoming FM signal is at an amount that is proportional to its instantaneous frequency. The phase difference between the original FM signal and the phase-shifted signal is then detected using a phase detector. Finally, the low pass filter is used to remove high frequency noise and recover the demodulated. The frequency deviation is converted into phase shifting. In the phase-shift network phase response of the carrier frequency a proportional constant. Thus, a good phase-shift value can help with frequency discrimination in demodulation.

$$\phi(f) = \frac{\pi}{2} + 2\pi K(f - f_o).$$

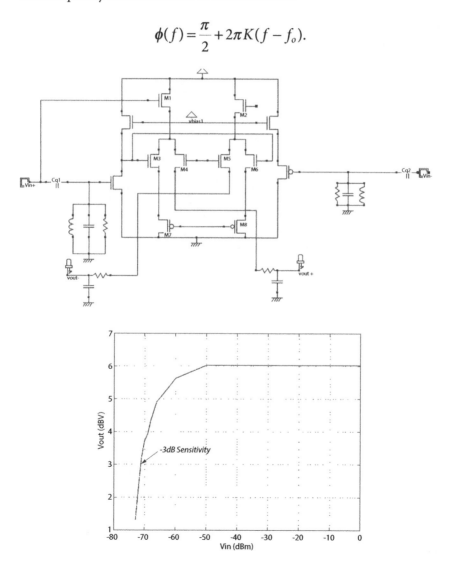

13.2.5   Sensitivity

A differentiative circuit structure was used for the quadrature detector. The phase-shifting network has external tank circuits with $Q = 20$, and the quadrature capacitors are assembled on the chip. At the IF signal band, a linear phase shift is given as output. A Gilbert-type phase detector is used to detect the difference between the output of the limiting amplifier and the output waveform of the phase-shift network. The upper and lower pMOS devices, which function as commuting switches, are connected to the output of the phase-shift network. For low supply voltage and good linearity, no tail current source is working in the phase detector [6]. First-order external low-pass filter was used to remove the high-frequency harmonics. The modulating signal's frequency variation is proportional to the demodulated signal amplitude at the filter output.

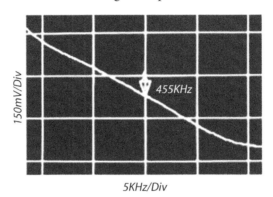

V_{out} *versus* input frequency deviation.

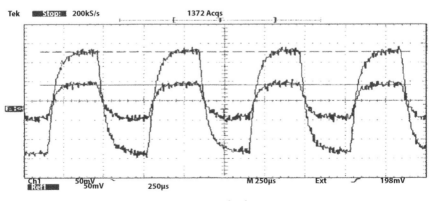

FSK output levels.

In spite of that, all the data are single-ended. The four levels are separated by more than 70 mV.

13.3   Experimental Results

Technology	0.6 μm CMOS
Limiting amplifier	
Single-stage gain	28 dB
Single-stage bandwidth	4.6 MHz
-3dB sensitivity	-72 dBm at 50 Ω
Quadrature detector	
Demodulation constant	20 mV/kHz
Maximum frequency deviation	±10 kHz
Output LSB for 4 FSK signal and supply voltage	70 mV and 2 V
Power consumption	2.3 mW

The 0.6-m, single-poly-double metal digital CMOS technology is used in IF 455-kHz signal processor. From a single 2-V power supply, the whole circuits draw 1.15 mA. The circuits can work with a low supply voltage of 1.8 V. Each stage has limiting amplifier's gain stages; each has a gain of 28 dB and a bandwidth of 4.6 MHz. When the input impedance matches 50, the 3-dB sensitivity input level is 72 dBm.

At IF 455 kHz, the quadrature detector's demodulation constant is 20 mV/kHz. The range of the FM deviation can extend well beyond 20 kHz. The four levels are separated by more than 70 mV despite the fact that all the data in this paper are single-ended.

13.4   Conclusion

Feedforward offset cancellation is used by the limiting amplifier. It consumes less than 0.5 mA at each of the three gain stages. This limiting amplifier's sensitivity is 72 dBm. Each gain cell's passive offset-extraction network is included on the same chip. The quadrature detector is made up of an external tank phase-shifting network, and an on-chip phase detector is utilized in the FM/FSK demodulator. The demodulator runs on less than 0.7 mA and processes a high demodulation constant of 20 mV/kHz.

References

1. Nakamura, M., Ishihara, N., Akazawa, Y., Kimura, H., An instantaneous response CMOS optical receiver IC with wide dynamic range and extremely high sensitivity using feedforward autobias adjustment. *IEEE J. Solid-State Circuits*, 30, 991–997, Sept. 1995.

2. Thomas, V., Fenk, J., Beyer, S., A one-chip 2 GHz single superheat receiver for 2-Mb/s FSK radio communication, in: *IEEE Int. Solid-State Circuits Conf.*, Feb. 1994, pp. 42–43.

3. Klumperink, E.A.M., Klein, C.T., Ruggeberg, B., Tuijl, A.J.M.V., AM suppression with low AM–PM conversion with the aid of a variable-gain amplifier. *IEEE J. Solid-State Circuits*, 31, 625–633, May 1996.

4. Abidi, A.A., Direct-conversion radio transceivers for digital communications. *IEEE J. Solid-State Circuits*, 30, 1399–1410, Dec. 1995.

5. Wilson, J.F., Youell, R., Richards, T.H., Luff, G., Pilaski, R., A single-chip VHF and UHF receiver for radio paging. *IEEE J. Solid- State Circuits*, 26, 1944–1950, Dec. 1991.

6. Rofougaran, A., Chang, J., Rofogaran, M., Abidi, A., A 1-GHz CMOS RF front-end IC for a direct-conversion wireless receiver. *IEEE J. Solid-State Circuits*, 31, 880–889, July 1996.

7. Hirose, T., Osaki, Y., Kuroki, N., Numa, M., A nano-ampere current reference circuit and its temperature dependence control by using temperature characteristics of carrier mobilities. *IEEE European Solid-State Circuits Conference*, pp. 114–117, 2010.

8. Chouhan, S.S. and Halonen, K., A 0.67-μW 177-ppm/oC All-MOS current reference circuit in a 0.18-μm CMOS technology. *IEEE Trans. Circuits Syst. II*, 63, 8, 723–727, Aug. 2016.

9. Yang, G. *et al.*, Low power and high performance circuit techniques for high fan-in dynamic gates, IEEE Computer Society, pp. 77–78, 2004.

10. Allam, M.W., Anis, M.H., Elmasry, M.I., High-speed dynamic logic styles for scaled-down CMOS and MTCMOS technologies. *2000 International Symposium on Low Power Electronics and Design*, pp. 155–160, 2000.

11. Thandri, B.K. and Silva-Martinez, J., A robust feedforward compensation scheme for multistage op. transconductance amplifiers with no Miller capacitors. *IEEE J. Solid-State Circuits*, 38, 32, 237–243, Feb. 2003.

12. Solis-Bustos, S., Silva-Martínez, J., Malloberti, F., Sánchez-Sinencio, E., A 60 dB dynamic range sixth order 2.4 Hz lowpass filter for medical applications. *IEEE Trans. Circuits Syst. Part II*, 47, 12, 1391–1398, December 2000.

13. Nakamura, M., Ishihara N., Akazawa, Y., Kimura, H., An instantaneous response CMOS optical receiver IC with wide dynamic range and extremely high sensitivity using feed-forward auto-bias adjustment. *IEEE J. Solid-State Circuits*, 30, 9, 991–997, Sep. 2008.

14. Steyaert, M.S. *et al.*, A CMOS rectifier-integrator for amplitude detection in hard disk servo loops. *IEEE J. Solid-State Circuits*, 30, 743–751, July 2015.
15. Klumperink, E., Klein, C., Rauuggeberg, B., Tuijl, E., AM suppression with low AM–PM conversion with aid of a variable-gain amplifier. *IEEE J. Solid-State Circuits*, 31, 625–633, May 2016.
16. Huang, P.-C., *Analog front-end architecture and circuit design techniques for high speed communication VLSIs*, Ph.D. dissertation, National Central University, Taiwan, 2017.

14

A Secured Node Authentication and Access Control Model for IoT Smart Home Using Double-Hashed Unique Labeled Key-Based Validation

Sulaima Lebbe Abdul Haleem

Department of Information & Communication Technology, Faculty of Technology, South Eastern University of Sri Lanka, Oluvil, Sri Lanka

Abstract

Internet of Things (IoT) is the global trend, which has been used everywhere and anywhere. When used in sensitive places, privacy becomes the concern. IoT security has to be taken seriously. When it comes to implementation, we have to think of restrictions in processing power and energy consumption which are the major obstacles that can give huge chances to intruder and third party access, compared with the normal system. Here we are discussing about considering resource scarcity and vulnerabilities for the IoT smart home, concerning the node to node throughout the wireless network communication and transmission of data via providing the uniquely labeled key generation model, double hashed unique labeled key-based validation, which was proposed for efficient and simplest authentication mechanism to the IoT smart home.

Keywords: Smart home, access control, node authentication, IoT, double hashed unique labeled key

Email: ahaleemsl@seu.ac.lk

Budati Anil Kumar, S. B. Goyal and Sardar M.N. Islam. Cognitive Computing Models in Communication Systems, (199–220) © 2022 Scrivener Publishing LLC

14.1   Introduction

Internet of Things (IoT) builds a global network of linked objects or items that will play an active part in Future Internet (FI). It is assumed that 50 billion devices will be connected to the internet by 2020, and there will be multiple applications and services. In order to create safety solutions, the heterogeneous nature of IoT communications, and the imbalance in resources between IoT devices, IoT presents new challenges to security and privacy, which render the provision of the necessary protected connections end-to-end. Most IoT devices have limited power, energy, and memory capacities, and have therefore limited the possible security solution choices because many of the security mechanisms developed cannot be supported by low-capacity devices. IoT needs comprehensive security solutions that meet the relevant safety and privacy criteria effectively and that have a small effect on system resources.

The IoT incorporates many current technologies, including wireless sensor networks (WSN) since the 1980s. It is an integral IoT component since it consists of a set of sensing nodes that are wirelessly linked to each other and afford real-world digital interfaces. However, while IoT infrastructure needs to be secured as a matter of urgency, the above resource limitations of underlying platforms and instruments confront such a need. The identity of the devices and techniques to verify is one of the main aspects of securing an IoT infrastructure. Many IoT devices have very poor passwords and many are still using the default passwords provided by the manufacturer, which makes them botnet prone and allowing hackers to hack the IoT networking kits. At the same time, hackers can use false or multifaceted identities to link malicious devices to IoT networks without being detected. The uses of IoT in several areas are depicted in Figure 14.1.

It is a fact that control devices, as well as resource-restricted devices, cannot sufficiently compute and store existing mechanisms which require overall complex calculations that present an enormous challenge in deploying robust authentication mechanisms. In this proposed model, a double hashed unique labeled key-based validation is proposed for an IoT smart home environment. The IoT node routing module redirects the instructions as per the user and node requests and the local authorization authority will authenticate the users and grant access to them based on their validity. The IoT nodes can be accessed only by the authorized nodes. Nodes can authenticate anonymously and log in to the local authorization authority with unlike dynamic identities and symmetric keys. The security policy implementation between nodes is further guaranteed by the proposed access control mechanism by the configuration of limitation of

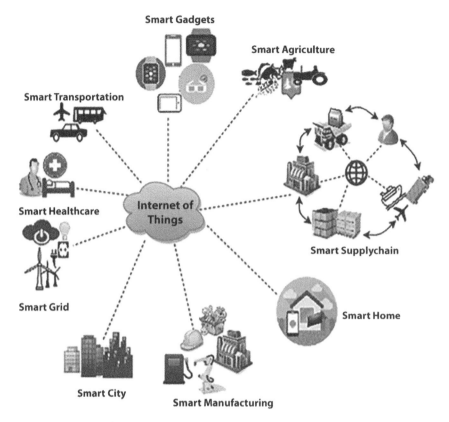

Figure 14.1 IoT applications.

nodes to send and receive instructions and controls to or from other nodes. The IoT network can be established by connecting to various devices that are indicated in Figure 14.2.

IoT transforms objects from classical to intelligent by manipulating the primary technology, such as computer technology, communication skills, protocols for the Internet, and applications. It makes things smarter and more available to us by combining them with sensors, and connectors, which lead to better human lives, more comfort, protection, and the efficient use of natural resources. In the past decade, IoT has been quietly and steadily addressing human lives, the developments in wireless communications, embedded systems, and energy-efficient radio technology are the most important steps in enabling smaller devices to respond to their environment and control it and form a new physical object networking paradigm. IoT vision makes it possible to connect all to any place and anytime and to develop more applications and services that will change the way of interaction with the health, economics, and social life.

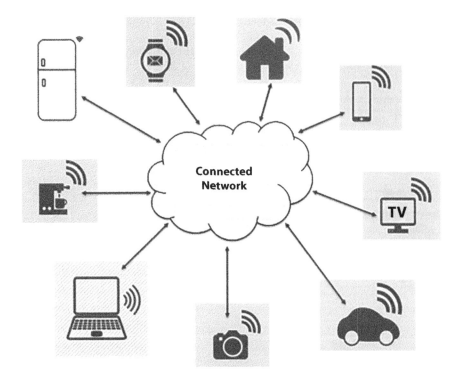

Figure 14.2 IoT network linked devices.

Traditional network solutions do not fit well with the development of IoT applications, so the risk of malicious attacks is increased, and confidentiality becomes vulnerable if any of the devices are compromised. Downloading cameras, breaching confidentiality, and accessing material are some of the security risks to IoT and could lead to dangerous results. The IoT world is becoming complicated and emerging technologies are complicating privacy concerns. The modern network structure, scene, terminal equipment, and other IoT factors are raising these concerns and cannot solve these problems via conventional IoT firewalls or key chain pairs, or authentication protocols. Unlicensed access, therefore, needs to be adequately assessed. As IoT is still an immature technology, and in particular its protection of access control of miniaturized items has now developed to the forefront in terms of safety and privacy, as access control technologies remain an important element for addressing security and privacy risks in the computer grid.

Although IoT's futures prospects are better, the implementation of IoT does create little known safety challenges. In this proposed work, problems relating to access control and authentication are taken into account. The recent creation of IoT results in an increasingly difficult situation in which data protection issues are being maintained, tracked, and managed across the network of items, such as data related to healthcare and personal and official records, for example.

Information technology is a new paradigm that concentrates on how objects or devices interconnect with one another and with users. The majority of IoT interactions move from 'human to stuff.' This technology is expected to become a key milestone in the creation of intelligent homes to make our lives and homes more comfortable and efficient. By taking this IoT smart home technology, the safety of these systems would have significant consequences. Connecting any intelligent entity inside the house with and without the Internet leads to privacy and security issues, such as confidentiality, validity, and integrity of data. These technologies are highly vulnerable to various security attacks which make an IoT-based intelligent home insecure for people to live in, and so safety risks need to be assessed to measure the smart house situation. For any technology to succeed and become commonly used, proper security and privacy guarantees must win the confidence of users. As in every industry, protection is a vital task. As homes are computerized and supplied with computers, it is essential to examine the possible computer protection and impacts on residents.

14.2   Challenges in IoT Security and Privacy

The challenges due to the specific characteristics of IoT are indicated here.

14.2.1   Heterogeneous Communication and Devices

The IoT network is an integration between the physical world and the cyber world means it is a diverse range of devices from small sensors to bigger devices like servers. It is heterogeneous since devices are manufactured by different producers with different software and hardware specifications. The IoT network includes various platforms. For example, IP-based security solutions like IPsec, SSL, and SSH cannot be applied directly to restricted devices such as sensors which leave an unsecured class of devices that threaten the overall network, making this heterogeneity difficult to use traditional security mechanisms.

14.2.2   Physical Equipment Integration

The attacker can interfere even more than before to surrounding gadgets in a smart home where the owner can have remote control access and if an attacker violates the protocol services in-home safety, and gain access to the lighting system that can be controlled, the TV channels are deleted and can lock the doors, etc. The presence of physical devices in contact raises the risk of violation of safety. A recent study has shown that 32% of the total botnet is triggered by smart appliances such as smart television and monitors using physical devices by attackers. For example, the lights of a smart house might be jeopardized by an intruder or for the whole city, which would endanger the lives of the people.

14.2.3   Resource Handling Limitations

Manufacturers of IoT devices aim to reduce production costs and improvements, which means that the majority of IoT devices have a limited resource capacity, limited memory space, limited resources, and bandwidth. These strict characteristics have considerably limited the security solutions' potential choices and made conventional safety strategies unenforceable for such a setting. Nevertheless, some IoT units have only minimal battery capacity to perform planned functions and severe security guidelines on cryptographic algorithms that can drain the batteries of the equipment in outdoor or aggressive environments where constant power is not available for charging.

14.2.4   Wide Scale

The number of computers connecting to the Internet is now higher than the number of people on the planet. This is already substantially increasing and is predictable to range up to 55 billion by 2022. Moreover, the management of this number of devices is difficult with this large number of intelligent devices inevitably leading to increased safety risks.

14.2.5   Database

The ubiquitous IoT computing concept makes it possible for IoT physical devices to communicate seamlessly with Internet infrastructure via different wireless communication technologies. IoT allows the idea of anywhere contact that creates an enormous amount of data produced by IoT devices, and a wide range of applications that challenges IoT confidentiality.

Thousands of heterogeneous devices in open-ended and complex spaces would certainly increase the risk of privacy. Sensitive and private information is shared in applications such as smart homes or smart healthcare that exploit attackers to use such information to breach privacy. In addition, information related to the position of certain sensitive network nodes like the source node and sink node location, which can be used by eavesdroppers to develop further attacks aimed at these nodes or events.

IoT devices are usually lightweight, low-cost, and have resource constraints. The challenges and problems of IoT are growing. In IoT applications such as intelligent buildings, security and privacy problems in smart homes are among the major issues. Remote cybersecurity attacks are attacks that do not include physical IoT network access, in which an attacker can access and communicate with IoT devices remotely via a wireless channel. Remote attacks on cyber security are also a major challenge. Emerging technologies in intelligent environments like smart buildings require both users and resource remote access. As the user/constructor communication channel is vulnerable the authentication protocol must be light and stable. In the proposed model, a secure user authentication protocol for smart homes with restricted access control is proposed. The protocol makes it possible to anonymously, unlikely, and untraceably authenticate only legitimate users using smart controllers.

The wide range of IoT applications reveals that emerging technologies have personal, social, and cultural consequences. IoT is also used to improve the productivity of households and employment. The sensors can interact and function, such as ordering food in the refrigerator when the refrigerator is empty. They can alert smartphones when the washing machine is finished. However, the consequences of these device failures may be too expensive because they rely heavily on IoT. The failure will generate incorrect data and lead to dangerous results if this information is used in automated households or production for decision-making purposes.

IoT has been proposed for a variety of authentication systems; it is aware that none of the contributions considered the authentication and access control anonymous of IoT sensor nodes. The proposed protocol allows shared authentication and anonymity and the ability to unlink information transmitted. In addition, the possibility of insider threats was mitigated by establishing the virtual domain segregation within IoT standalone networks, limiting the ability of IoT nodes, and implementing a cumulative double hashed unique labeled key validation model for user authentication and restricting access control. The main feature of IoT nodes is that the approved user can collect environmental information and can gain access to the network. These sensor nodes are accurate, mobile, affordable, and easy to fit. These innovations serve the automotive, health, logistics, environmental monitoring, and many other building blocks. In a centralized approach, the application platform collects information from network entities and supports other entities.

Home automation transforms ordinary home appliances into intelligent and smart devices that enable system remote control and administration through the internet. In smart home appliances such as refrigerators, lights, air conditioning, door locks, camera surveillance, etc. can be operated remotely, simplifying and comfortably making life easier. Security violations could be dangerous, imagine a robber hacks the door lock system and successfully open the door or the perpetrator monitors the lighting system to make your life miserable. These systems continue to record conduct and actions that could pose a direct threat to personal privacy. To minimize the risk of such attacks, however, protection and privacy should be maintained by strong authentication and access control mechanisms.

In this proposed work, an IoT environment Access Control Management Model is introduced including automatic settings to reduce the burden of users. The proposed model is necessary when IoT devices first bind to the access control server, exchanging application and authentication information for authentication information to the device. The access destination often requests the management system to authorize the access source. Control source can therefore access like an IoT system without taking the scope of access into account. Without the preconfiguring and reconfiguring of IoT devices, the proposed approach enables effective and unified access management for IoT settings.

Access control in the IoT environment is necessary to ensure that software updates, access sensor data, and the sensors cannot be controlled by trusted users alone. Access control addresses problems in data ownership and allows new services, including Sensors As a Service, where customer information is supplied by sensors. Access controls enable IoT device data to be shared with approved users so that sensitive data can be predictively maintained as well as protected. The development of the Internet has led to new types of services with particular reference to the use of sensors and actuators. The Internet of Things is known for these services. A secure and simple access control system for the data handled in these facilities is a major challenge currently.

By modeling IoT communication elements as tools, the incorporation of IoT devices into an access control framework is proposed. This would enable us to achieve a unified system of access control between heterogeneous devices. To that end, we examined the most important communication protocols for such environments and then proposed a methodology that enables communication behavior to be modeled as tools. Then, through access control mechanisms, we can secure these services.

The key elements in dealing with protection and privacy problems on the Internet of Things are authentication and access control technologies. Every successful access control system should meet the core security characteristics of confidentiality, trust, and availability. Information on models, policies, and mechanisms for access control is available. The following functions are covered by a comprehensive access control system. They are authentication and accountability.

A smart environment uses rich combinations of small computer nodes to define and provide users with customized services when interacting and exchanging information with the environment. To offer intelligence and enhance the quality of life, IoT is used to build smart homes. "Internet of things technology" can be described as a "smart home" that is automated and can respond to people's needs to offer them comfort, security, and entertainment. The IoT is expected to develop in the future important applications for home and industry, enhancing the quality of life and the world economy. With IoT, electrical and electronic devices mounted in the smart home can be accessed and controlled from anywhere in the world remotely. Intelligent houses, for example, allow their people to open their garage automatically when they reach home, make coffee, monitor air-conditioning systems, intelligent TVs, and other home appliances. Smart Homes are composed of smart devices and automation systems. It's all related to Internet assistance.

Smart homes (SH) are fitted essentially with sophisticated automated systems for different pre-programmed operations like controlling temperature, lighting, multimedia, operations of the windows, doors, etc. The intelligent home environment is also known as environmental intelligence, responsive, and adaptive to modern social and human needs. SH has various advantages, such as increased comfort, improved safety, and protection, more efficient use of energy and other resources, leading to considerable savings. This proposed model will expand over time as it provides strong ways to serve the special needs of seniors and disabled people, for environmental monitoring and regulation. This research application field is extremely important. The main aims of a smart home are to improve domestic automation, facilitate control of electricity, and reduce environmental emissions. Smart home environments are key in terms of energy usage and comfort for the inhabitants. The figure indicates the operations applied to smart homes. Figure 14.3 indicates the smart home controlling models.

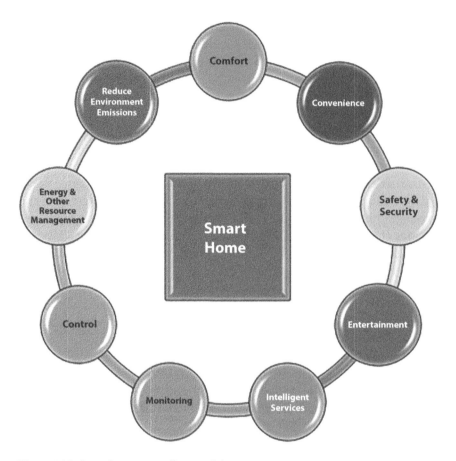

Figure 14.3 Smart home controlling models.

Bringing IoT technology to smart homes will lead to new security problems and, as IoT-based intelligent homes contain significant and private information, they need a high degree of safety. Modern technologies provide both benefits and threats. A Smart Home based IoT is highly vulnerable to internet attacks if an attacker has compromised a clever home or smart computer, which can inhibit consumer privacy, steal and track personal information inside the home, thus taking appropriate action.

The intelligent home has security and confidentiality problems as sensitive data collected by intelligent devices are interchanged through wireless networks. If an opponent obtains the data, the opponent abuses it for his ends. Security and privacy are also key requirements to safe home services. The data shared should furthermore follow the requirements of confidentiality, completeness, and availability. Safe and easy authentication protocols are therefore required in IoT-based smart homes to ensure security and privacy. The proposed model has to implement a strong authentication mechanism and allows only authorized users to gain access control on the system. The proposed model uses a cryptography-based hashing technique for improving the security levels of the IoT network.

14.3   Background

Kumar *et al.* [1] launched a lightweight and stable IoT smart home session key set-up scheme. They have taken advantage of a short token to create a session key between and an intelligent computer. The stable key agreement for smart home systems is proposed by Han *et al.* [2]. The proposed arrangement is appropriate for smart home consumer electronics products. Li [3] proposed a small, essential setup protocol, and a session key between nodes and control was created. There is no reciprocal authentication among users in their scheme.

Santos *et al.* [4] implemented a smart home remote user authentication system that uses Elliptical Curve Cryptography (ECC). Two main safety features called anonymity and traceability were not achieved by the authors. In addition, the regime is vulnerable to smart card attacks by privileged insiders and theft. Shuai *et al.* [5] proposed a smart home authentication system using ECC. For authentication purposes, the authors do not need to store the test table. The writers have however not performed satisfactorily.

XACML has been developed to provide standardized descriptions of the access control policies, based on the extensible markup language (XML). OAuth is a tool for providing web services and applications with a system of access control that is used in this model. It is currently the most widely used application of this kind, which has led to considerable efforts to provide IoT-based OAuth solutions. Dahshan *et al.* [6] suggested a distributed IoT key management system in which Secret sharing is used by the Protocol. The cloud certificate authority and the relevant CA Public Key will be shared by each entity during offline development. After network implementation, companies can run a distributed protocol to create a private/public session key for each network entity. These keys are used to ensure communication among IoT network entities.

Das *et al.* [7] introduced a new hierarchical WSN authentication management model that supports the dynamic node function of adding a system that is called lightweight as it uses lightweight primitive cryptography. Yeh *et al.* [8] proposed an ECC-based user authentication program that is vulnerable to high calculation and security drawbacks. The user authentication with access control system for IoT is proposed by Liu *et al.* [9]. RBAC access control is included in the scheme.

Chu *et al.* [10] suggested a scheme for authentication based on elliptic curve cryptography (ECC) for a public and a private key pair. During the initialization process, the elliptical curve public parameters are initialized and calculated. Next, during authentication, these criteria are used. Lee *et al.* [11] implemented a lightweight shared authentication protocol based on RFID-based XOR encryption. The authors have eliminated complex encryption systems such as a single-way hash function, asymmetric encryption.

The two-factor one-time password (OTP) technique proposed by Shivraj *et al.* [12], based on an easy ECC system based on identity. Compared with current approaches, this approach was better in performance and safety for two reasons. First, there are no key storage requirements for the key distribution center (KDC). Secondly, it does not store other devices' private and public keys. A limited number of resources were used in this protocol, which negatively affected security. The two problems with this approach are that a device wants to manage another device in another gateway and that the device wants to manage the instance in which it wishes to monitor using a different security system. This method has no protection for the instance in which a device wants to manage the other device.

Hernández *et al.* [13] introduced a range of Slim Extensible Authentication Protocol over LAN (SEAPOL), an improved version of the Extensible Authentication Protocol on LAN, lightweight authentication, and authorization mechanisms (EAPOL). Authentication and permission features have also been integrated with restricted devices through the proposed frameworks. In addition to data graph transport layer protection, EAPOL weights down the restricted strategies by helping them to implement and execute EAPOL. However, not only can these proposed mechanisms optimize interoperability among IoT devices, they also address safety and privacy issues in the IoT environment.

14.4   Proposed Model

IoT is a system in which computers are networked through Unique Identifiers by using Node Identities (NID) as a unique recognition model and can transmit data without any contact between humans. In 1975, the first home automation technology is introduced using X10, a network technology. Electrical cables are used to signal and monitor different electronic devices. To monitor a digital electronic system installed in a building, radiofrequency signals were used as a piece of digital information.

User authentication is established on the last accessed applications classification scoring before and continuously with an access request for home appliances. This model categorizes the unwanted access for each event obtained from the user's computer and enhances the classifier output by tuning the parameters during the training stage. User Access Request (UAR) is taken on the basis of the last node accessed. The next request will be approved if the last event accessed is classified to the current user and completed without any loss. An authentication procedure will decline the user's access or user demands when the registration authority identifies a duplicate entity or wring information and report it to the local authorization authority and then update a new event model for attaining access to the network.

The authenticity of the information source must first be checked by the registration authority in order to ensure the reliability of the device control. While some authentication frameworks were already proposed by academic fields, they are not fully compliant with IoT environment authentication models. The control system terminal devices generally have increased processing and storage power, which offers new factors for authentication mechanisms of the IoT control system. The features of terminals need to be combined in the control system, balance resources, performance, and protection need to be assessed and considered, and an authentication method that best suits the IoT control system must be introduced.

A specific unique label is allotted to the registered users by the registered authority and the data are updated to the local authorization authority to grant access to the networks. The mechanism for User Access Control (UAC) specifying admission to certain resources or facilities provides safety, security, and privacy for IoT devices. UAC is the process that determines who is allowed to have what communications rights that object in respect of certain security models and policies as a fundamental mechanism for ensuring security in computer systems that is completely monitored by the local authorization authority. An efficient UAC system is designed in this model to meet the most important safety criteria, such as privacy, honesty, and availability. The proposed model framework is depicted in Figure 14.4.

Here Ti is the Time Instance, NID is the Node Identity and RC is the Request Code. The IoT nodes will register with the registration authority by providing the details. The users who want to access the devices have to initially get authenticated by the local authorization authority of the IoT network. The authenticated users only will get access rights so that they can access the required IoT nodes to complete the operation. The double hash key generator will generate and distribute keys using the double hashing

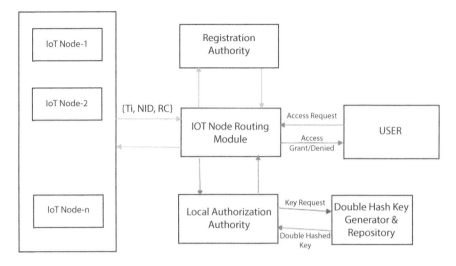

Figure 14.4 Proposed model framework.

technique and these keys are used for the user authentication process and granting access rights to them.

The node registration process by the Registration Authority (RA) is performed as:

For each I in N(ID)ε NS

$$\{RM \leftarrow N\{Ti, NID, RC\}$$

$$RA \leftarrow RM\{ Ti, NID, RC\}$$

$$RA \rightarrow Ti \oplus Th \; \&\& \; NID \; || \; Rid$$

$$RM \leftarrow RA\{UL\}$$

$$N(ID) \leftarrow RM(N(UL))\}$$

Unique Label UL is calculated as:

$$P1 = N_i \begin{pmatrix} M \\ N \end{pmatrix} \oplus Ti * Th$$

$$P2 = P1 <<M \oplus N + NID \; (i)$$

$$P3 = N << P2 >> M \| P1 \oplus P2 >> M + N$$

$$P4 = leftcirshif(P2 \oplus P3) + M \&\& N \oplus mod(M,N) \oplus rightcirshif(P1 \oplus P3)$$

$$N(UL) \leftarrow P4 \oplus P2$$

Here NS is the Nodes Set, N(ID) is the current node identity, Ti is the time instance, RC is the request code, NID is the node id, Th is the threshold value considered, and UL is the unique label generated and allotted.

The user authentication process is as follows:

Initially User U provide the basic information to the Local Authorization Authority (LAA) via Node Routing Module (NRM)

$$U \to UID_i : \operatorname{Re} s_i \to NRM$$

$$\operatorname{Re} s \to U(L) : \operatorname{Re} s_i, \operatorname{Re} s_j \to NRM$$

$$L \to R : M_i (ID \| \operatorname{Re} q_t \| \operatorname{Re} q_D), \operatorname{Re} s_n$$

$$NRM \leftarrow N_i \leftarrow R : M_i (L)$$

$$\forall (U_i, \operatorname{Re} s_i) \in Rs_n, (M_i (ID \| \operatorname{Re} q_t \| \operatorname{Re} q_D), H_L (\operatorname{Re} s_i)), (M_i (ID \| \operatorname{Re} q_t \| \operatorname{Re} q_D) \cong M_i))$$

$$LAA (U(ID)) \leftarrow NRM \{U, \operatorname{Re} s_i, \operatorname{Re} s_j, M_i, \operatorname{Re} qt, \operatorname{Re} q_{iD}, Rs\}$$

Here U is the user, UID is the user ID, Res is the resource need to request, L is the limit of resources, Res_i and Res_j are the neighbor resources to request, M is the total resources allotted, Req_t and Req_D are the requests for resource and neighbor resource. The user will be registered with the local authorization authority as

$$LAA (U(i)) = \sum_{i \in U, \operatorname{Re} s, Req, L}^{N} U(ID)^n + \min(Mi)$$

The process of Double hash key generation and access control is performed as

1. LAA chooses a random number N_r and calculates $NID_n = h (U (ID)_n \| Ti_n)$. Then NRM sends $\{UID_n, \operatorname{Re} s_i\}$ to LAA using a private channel.

2. LAA generates a unique label UL and computes Initial Hash Key $IHK_{N(i)} = h\ (U\ (ID)_i || \text{Re } s_i || Mi \oplus Th)$. Where Res is the resource, M is the limit, and T_h is the threshold.

3. The IHK will be updated using a double hash model that finally generates the Double hash key that is used for the user authorization and grants access to the network. The process of double hashing is done as

$$DH_{N(i)} = IHK_{N(i)} \oplus h\ (U\ (ID)_i || Ti_n) || \text{Re } s\ (U\ (ID)_n \ || \ M_n \oplus \text{Re } q\ (ID))$$

After calculating the DH value, the Double Hash Key (DHK) is calculated as:

$$DHK(UID)(i) = \sum_{I=1} \sum_{j=i-1} M_j^I * Res_i^N + \sum_{i,j \in N} DH_{i,j}(Req_N(i))$$

After calculating the double hash key, the user authentication process will be performed and then the access will be granted based on the status of authentication. The access grant is scheduled as:

$$AG(U(iD)_n = \begin{cases} if\ (U(ID_i) \in US_i, N\ permit\ access \\ otherwise\ (U(ID_i) \notin US_i, N\ deny\ access \end{cases}$$

14.4.1 Communication Flow

14.4.1.1 IoT Node and Registration Authority

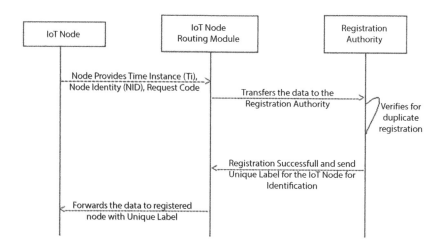

14.4.1.2 User and Local Authorization Authority

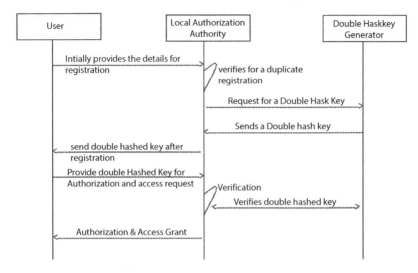

14.5 Results

The proposed double hashed unique labeled key-based validation model exhibits better performance in providing strong authentication and access control mechanisms. The parameters exhibited are User Authentication Time Levels, Unauthorized User Detection Time Levels, Unique Labeled Key Generation Time Levels, Smart Home Security Levels during Instruction Transmission, and Access Control Restriction Level for Unauthorized Users as shown in Figures 14.5–14.9.

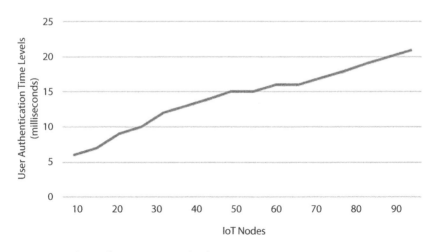

Figure 14.5 User authentication time levels.

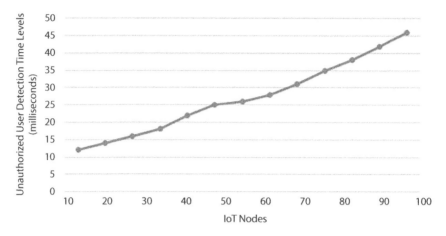

Figure 14.6 Unauthorized user detection time levels.

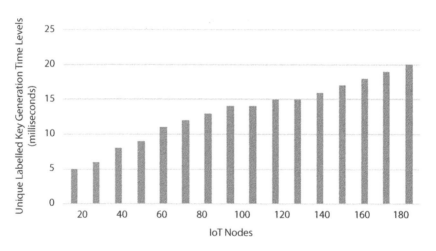

Figure 14.7 Unique labeled key generation time levels.

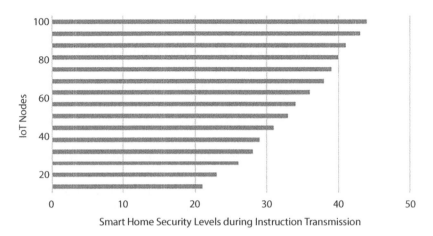

Figure 14.8 Smart home security levels during instruction transmission.

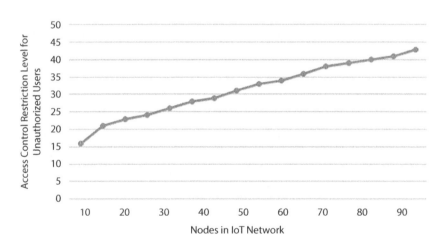

Figure 14.9 Access control restriction level for unauthorized users.

14.6   Conclusion

Protection of IoT control is one of the world's leading research areas. The authenticity of the information source must first be checked in order to ensure the reliability of the device control. The proposed model aims to include a suitable IoT control system authentication method with restricted access control. The proposed model suggested an improved system of shared authentication, discussed in depth the mechanism including the steps for enhancement, the authentication, and the access control model. The results of the analysis show that the concept is a reasonably viable model of IoT-control security authentication. The proposed model demonstrates a methodology and presents an application for user authentication model using double hashed unique labeled key and allows access control for authorized users only. The main focus of this model is user authentication with restricted access control. The proposed model generates a unique labeled key that is generated using double hashing. The generated key is used among the IoT devices to authenticate with the central node verification mode for gaining access control on the network. The proposed model security levels are high and the user authentication accuracy levels are better than the traditional models.

14.7   Claims

1. In the proposed model, a Secured Node Authentication and Access Control Model for IoT Smart Home using Double Hashed Unique Labeled Key-based Validation is proposed that is used for enhancing the security models in the wireless networks.
2. We claim a secured node authentication model that authorizes the nodes involved in the network for communication.
3. We claim an efficient access control model in the proposed work that is used to grant or restrict access to the nodes in the IoT for completing the data transmission.
4. We claim the double hashing model in the proposed work to generate a key that is used for the authorization of the nodes in the network.
5. We claim the unique label generation process that is used for node authentication in the sensor networks to improve security levels.

References

1. Kumar, P., Gurtov, A., Iinatti, J., Ylianttila, M., Sain, M., Lightweight and secure session-key establishment scheme in smart home environments. *IEEE Sens. J.*, 16, 1, 254–264, 2016.

2. Han, K., Kim, J., Shon, T., Ko, D., A novel secure key paring protocol for RF4CE ubiquitous smart home systems. *Pers. Ubiquit. Comput.*, 17, 5, 945–949, 2012.

3. Li, Y., Design of a key establishment protocol for smart home energy management system, in: *2013 Fifth Int. Conf. on Computational Intelligence, Communication Systems and Networks*, Madrid, Spain, pp. 88–93, 2013.

4. Santoso, F.K. and Vun, N.C.H., Securing IoT for smart home system, in: *Int. Symp. on Consumer Electronics*, Madrid, Spain, pp. 1–2, 2015.

5. Shuai, M., Yu, N., Wang, H., Xiong, L., Anonymous authentication scheme for smart home environment with provable security. *Comput. Secur.*, 86, 2, 132–146, 2019.

6. Dahshan, H., An elliptic curve key management scheme for internet of things. *Int. J. Appl. Eng. Res.*, 11, 20, 10241–10246, 2016.

7. Das, A.K. *et al.*, A dynamic password-based user authentication scheme for hierarchical wireless sensor networks. *J. Netw. Comput. Appl.*, 35, 5, 1646–1656, 2012.

8. Yeh, H.-L., Chen, T.-H., Liu, P.-C., Kim, T.-H., Wei, H.-W., A secured authentication protocol for wireless sensor networks using elliptic curves cryptography. *Sensors*, 11, 5, 4767–4779, 2011.

9. Liu, J., Xiao, Y., Chen, C.L.P., Authentication and access control in the internet of things. *2012 32nd International Conference on Distributed Computing Systems Workshops (ICDCSW)*, IEEE, 2012.

10. Chu, F., Zhang, R., Ni, R., Dai, W., An improved identity authentication scheme for internet of things in heterogeneous networking environments, in: *Proceedings of the 2013 16th International Conference on Network-Based Information Systems (NBIS)*, IEEE, pp. 589–93, 2013.

11. Lee, J.Y., Lin, W.C., Huang, Y.H., A lightweight authentication protocol for internet of things, in: *Proceedings of the 2014 International Symposium on Next-Generation Electronics (ISNE)*, IEEE, pp. 1–2, 2014.

12. Shivraj, V.L., Rajan, M.A., Singh, M., Balamuralidhar, P., One time password authentication scheme based on elliptic curves for internet of things (IoT), in: *Proceedings of the 2015 5th National Symposium on Information Technology: Towards New Smart World (NSITNSW)*, IEEE, pp. 1–6, 2015.

13. Hernandez-Ramos, J.L., Pawlowski, M.P., Jara, A.J., Skarmeta, A.F., Ladid, L., Toward a lightweight authentication and authorization framework for smart objects. *IEEE J. Sel. Areas Commun.*, 33, 4, 690–702, 2015.

Index

Printed and bound by CPI Group (UK) Ltd, Croydon, CR0 4YY

27/10/2024

14580174-0001